Oracle APEX 4.0 Cookbook

Over 80 great recipes to develop and deploy fast, secure, and modern web applications with Oracle Application Express 4.0

Marcel van der Plas

Michel van Zoest

[PACKT] enterprise
PUBLISHING   professional expertise distilled

BIRMINGHAM - MUMBAI

Oracle APEX 4.0 Cookbook

First published: December 2010

Production Reference: 1081210

Published by Packt Publishing Ltd.
32 Lincoln Road
Olton
Birmingham, B27 6PA, UK.

ISBN 978-1-849681-34-6

www.packtpub.com

Cover Image by Dan Anderson (Dan@CAndersonAssociates.com)

Credits

About the Authors

Marcel van der Plas has been an Oracle Consultant for over 15 years. And from the beginning, he learned to work with Oracle Forms, Oracle Reports, and Oracle Designer. Marcel has worked on many projects with these tools. Later on, he became interested in APEX and did some projects with APEX.

Marcel currently works for Ciber. Other companies he worked for are Atos Origin and Whitehorses. For Whitehorses, he wrote some articles ("Whitebooks") about Oracle.

I would like to thank Michel van Zoest, my co-author for helping and working together. I also want to thank the reviewers Maarten van Luijtelaar, Dimitri Gielis, and Surachart Opun. Their comments were so valuable and helpful. I would like to thank Douwe Pieter van den Bos for introducing us to Packt and I would like to thank Packt for giving me this opportunity to write this book. I would like to thank my employer, Ciber, for giving me the freedom to write this book.

Last but not least, I would like to thank my wife Yvonne and my children Vera, Laura, and Joey for inspiring and supporting me. At the same time, I would like to apologize to them for not having time to play on the weekends during the months that I wrote this book.

Michel van Zoest is a consultant with more than 10 years of experience in building (web) applications using Oracle technology such as Oracle (web) Forms, Oracle Designer, MOD_PLSQL, ADF, SOA Suite and of course, APEX.

He is one of the first Oracle Application Express Developer Certified Experts in the world.

He has used his APEX knowledge in projects for companies ranging in size from a single employee to large multinationals. His experience in these projects has been used in the realization of this book.

Michel currently works at Whitehorses in the Netherlands and runs his own blog at `http://www.aboutapex.com`. Next to that, he blogs at the company website on `http://blog.whitehorses.nl` and he regularly writes Whitebook articles (in Dutch) for Whitehorses.

First of all, I would like to thank my co-author Marcel van der Plas. Thanks to the easy way that we could work together, the writing of this book has gone as smooth as possible.

I would like to thank the people at Packt Publishing for offering me the chance to write this book. It has been a long process with a lot of hard work, but I'm very happy with the result. I also would like to thank Douwe Pieter van den Bos for introducing me and Marcel to Packt and his invaluable help in the early stages of the book.

Furthermore, I would like to thank Maarten van Luijtelaar, Dimitri Gielis, and Surachart Opun for their hard work in reviewing our drafts. This book has become so much better thanks to you guys.

I also would like to thank my employer Whitehorses for the support I have been given.

And last but not least, I would like to thank my family for their love and support. Without the help of my wife Jamila and the "dikke kroelen" from my daughters Naomi and Aniek, this result would not have been possible.

About the Reviewers

Dimitri Gielis was born in 1978. Together with his family he lives in Leuven, Belgium.

At an early age, Dimitri started working with computers (Apple II, IBM XT) and he quickly knew he would like to work with computers and especially with databases all his life.

In 2000, Dimitri began his career working as a consultant for Oracle, Belgium where he got in touch with almost every Oracle product. His main expertise was in the database area, but at that time he was also exposed to HTMLDB, which was renamed Oracle Application Express later on. From the very start he liked the Oracle database and APEX so much that he never stopped working with it. Dimitri then switched to another company to create an Oracle team and do pre-sales, to later create and manage an Oracle Business Unit.

In 2007, Dimitri co-founded APEX Evangelists (http://www.apex-evangelists.com), together with John Scott. APEX Evangelists is a company which specializes in providing training, development, and consulting specifically for the Oracle Application Express product.

On his blog (http://dgielis.blogspot.com) he shares his thoughts and experience about Oracle and especially Oracle Application Express.

Dimitri is a frequent presenter at OBUG Connect, IOUG Collaborate, ODTUG Kaleidoscope, UKOUG conference, and Oracle Open World. He likes to share his experience and meet other people. He's also President of the OBUG (Oracle Benelux User Group) APEX SIG.

In 2008, Dimitri became an Oracle ACE Director. Oracle ACE Directors are known for their strong credentials as Oracle community enthusiasts and advocates.

In 2009, Dimitri received the "APEX Developer of the year" award by Oracle Magazine.

You can contact Dimitri at dimitri.gielis@apex-evangelists.com.

Surachart Opun has been working with Oracle products for over six years. Surachart is co-founder for Oracle User Group in Thailand. He is Oracle ACE, OCE RAC, and OCP 10g/11g. He implemented, migrated, and operated about Oracle Products including Oracle Database, Application Express and so on. He contributes more about Oracle Products.

Blog: http://surachartopun.com

www.PacktPub.com

Support files, eBooks, discount offers and more

You might want to visit www.PacktPub.com for support files and downloads related to your book.

Did you know that Packt offers eBook versions of every book published, with PDF and ePub files available? You can upgrade to the eBook version at www.PacktPub.com and as a print book customer, you are entitled to a discount on the eBook copy. Get in touch with us at service@packtpub.com for more details.

At www.PacktPub.com, you can also read a collection of free technical articles, sign up for a range of free newsletters and receive exclusive discounts and offers on Packt books and eBooks.

http://PacktLib.PacktPub.com

Do you need instant solutions to your IT questions? PacktLib is Packt's online digital book library. Here, you can access, read and search across Packt's entire library of books.

Why Subscribe?

- ▸ Fully searchable across every book published by Packt
- ▸ Copy and paste, print and bookmark content
- ▸ On demand and accessible via web browser

Free Access for Packt account holders

If you have an account with Packt at www.PacktPub.com, you can use this to access PacktLib today and view nine entirely free books. Simply use your login credentials for immediate access.

Table of Contents

Preface

Oracle Application Express 4.0 is a rapid web application development tool that works with the Oracle database. Using features like Plug-ins and Dynamic Actions, APEX helps you build applications with the latest techniques in AJAX and JavaScript.

The Oracle Application Express 4.0 Cookbook shows you recipes to develop and deploy reliable, modern web applications using only a web browser and limited programming experience.

With recipes covering many different topics, it will show you how to use the many features of APEX 4.0.

You will learn how to create simple form and report pages and how to enhance the look of your applications by using stylesheets. You will see how you can integrate things such as Tag Clouds, Google Maps, web services, and much more in your applications. Using Plug-ins, Dynamic Actions, BI Publisher, Translations, and Websheets, you will be able to enhance your applications to a new level in APEX.

This book will show you how to be agile in the development of your web applications by using Team Development, debugging, and third-party tools.

After reading this book, you will be able to create feature-rich web applications in Application Express 4.0 with ease and confidence.

What this book covers

Chapter 1, Creating a basic APEX application, describes the basic steps to create an APEX application. We will learn to make an intranet application where employees can get information.

Chapter 2, Themes and Templates, presents some recipes which will make your application look better using themes and templates by creating your own theme, including images in it and so on.

Chapter 3, Extending APEX, shows us how to we will extend our application with some nice features like visual effects, a tag cloud, and a Google map.

Chapter 4, Creating Websheet Applications, teaches us how to create a websheet application, create a page in the application, add a navigation page to the websheet, and allow multiple users to access the websheet.

Chapter 5, APEX Plug-ins, describes the four types of plug-ins: Item type, Region type, Dynamic action, and Process type plug-ins.

Chapter 6, Creating Multilingual APEX Applications, shows us how we can fully translate an application using built-in functionality to translate applications, without having to rebuild the application completely and adding something of ourselves to easily switch between languages.

Chapter 7, APEX APIs, shows us how to use APIs as they offer a lot of flexibility and speed in developing web applications.

Chapter 8, Using Webservices, teaches us how to use webservices in APEX.

Chapter 9, Publishing From APEX, shows you how to export reports and get the output in some kind of digital format and how to interact with BI Publisher.

Chapter 10, APEX Environment, contains recipes that will show how to set up and use a development environment, how to use version control and how to deploy Application Express on a web container with the APEX Listener.

Chapter 11, APEX Administration, shows you how to create a workspace, how to create users on the workspace and how to manage the workspaces.

Chapter 12, Team Development, we will see how we can take advantage of the features in Team Development in our project. Each recipe will show how a part of Team Development can be put to use in a specific part of the project cycle.

What you need for this book

APEX 4.0 or higher.

Oracle RDBMS database 10.2.0.3 or higher.

Either one of the following Internet browsers:

- ▶ Microsoft Internet Explorer 7 or later
- ▶ Mozilla Firefox 3.5 or later
- ▶ Google Chrome 4.0 or later
- ▶ Apple Safari 4.0 or later

Who this book is for

This book is aimed both at developers new to the APEX environment and at intermediate developers. More advanced developers will also gain from the information at hand.

If you are new to APEX you will find recipes to start development. If you are an experienced user you will find ways to work smarter and more easily with APEX and enhance your applications.

A little knowledge of PL/SQL, HTML and JavaScript is assumed.

Conventions

In this book, you will find a number of styles of text that distinguish between different kinds of information. Here are some examples of these styles, and an explanation of their meaning.

Code words in text are shown as follows: "We can include other contexts through the use of the include directive."

A block of code is set as follows:

```
select rv_meaning display_value
     , rv_low_value return_value
  from app_ref_codes
 where rv_domain = 'ADDRESSES'
```

When we wish to draw your attention to a particular part of a code block, the relevant lines or items are set in bold:

```
select rv_meaning display_value
     , rv_low_value return_value
  from app_ref_codes
 where rv_domain = 'ADDRESSES'
```

In this book, code snippets are followed by a small note, for example, *[1346_01_01.txt]* which points to that particular code file in the code bundle available on the Packt website.

Any command-line input or output is written as follows:

```
# cp /usr/src/asterisk-addons/configs/cdr_mysql.conf.sample
    /etc/asterisk/cdr_mysql.conf
```

New terms and **important words** are shown in bold. Words that you see on the screen, in menus or dialog boxes for example, appear in the text like this: "clicking the **Next** button moves you to the next screen".

Warnings or important notes appear in a box like this.

Tips and tricks appear like this.

Reader feedback

Feedback from our readers is always welcome. Let us know what you think about this book—what you liked or may have disliked. Reader feedback is important for us to develop titles that you really get the most out of.

To send us general feedback, simply send an e-mail to feedback@packtpub.com, and mention the book title via the subject of your message.

If there is a book that you need and would like to see us publish, please send us a note in the **SUGGEST A TITLE** form on www.packtpub.com or e-mail suggest@packtpub.com.

If there is a topic that you have expertise in and you are interested in either writing or contributing to a book, see our author guide on www.packtpub.com/authors.

Customer support

Now that you are the proud owner of a Packt book, we have a number of things to help you to get the most from your purchase.

Downloading the example code for this book

You can download the example code files for all Packt books you have purchased from your account at http://www.PacktPub.com. If you purchased this book elsewhere, you can visit http://www.PacktPub.com/support and register to have the files e-mailed directly to you.

Errata

Although we have taken every care to ensure the accuracy of our content, mistakes do happen. If you find a mistake in one of our books—maybe a mistake in the text or the code—we would be grateful if you would report this to us. By doing so, you can save other readers from frustration and help us improve subsequent versions of this book. If you find any errata, please report them by visiting http://www.packtpub.com/support, selecting your book, clicking on the **errata submission form** link, and entering the details of your errata. Once your errata are verified, your submission will be accepted and the errata will be uploaded on our website, or added to any list of existing errata, under the Errata section of that title. Any existing errata can be viewed by selecting your title from http://www.packtpub.com/support.

Piracy

Piracy of copyright material on the Internet is an ongoing problem across all media. At Packt, we take the protection of our copyright and licenses very seriously. If you come across any illegal copies of our works, in any form, on the Internet, please provide us with the location address or website name immediately so that we can pursue a remedy.

Please contact us at copyright@packtpub.com with a link to the suspected pirated material.

We appreciate your help in protecting our authors, and our ability to bring you valuable content.

Questions

You can contact us at questions@packtpub.com if you are having a problem with any aspect of the book, and we will do our best to address it.

1

Creating a Basic
APEX Application

In this chapter, we will cover:

- ▶ Creating an APEX 4.0 application
- ▶ Creating a simple form page
- ▶ Creating a simple report page
- ▶ Implementing an interactive report
- ▶ Creating a chart
- ▶ Creating a map chart
- ▶ Creating a navigation bar
- ▶ Creating a list of values
- ▶ Including different item types
- ▶ Protecting a page using an authorization scheme
- ▶ Securing an application with authentication
- ▶ Controlling the display of regions and items with dynamic actions
- ▶ Creating a computation
- ▶ Creating an automated row fetch via page process
- ▶ Putting some validation in a form
- ▶ Creating a report with PL/SQL dynamic content

Introduction

This chapter describes the basic steps to create an APEX application. Using APEX, it is really simple to create a basic application. The user interface is web-based and very intuitive. A lot of objects can be created using wizards which will guide you through the creation process.

Our aim is to make an intranet application where employees can get information. When starting the application, it shows a homepage with information such as weather, traffic company information, latest news, blogs, and so on. Employees can see their colleagues' profiles, just like in Facebook. Employees also have access to documents like timesheets and project plans.

Creating an APEX 4.0 application

This recipe describes the tasks needed to create an APEX 4.0 application. You should have APEX 4.0 installed or have an account on Oracle's online APEX environment at `http://apex.oracle.com` and your web browser should be a modern browser like Microsoft Internet Explorer 7 or higher or Mozilla Firefox 1.0 or later. The starting point is the **Oracle Application Express** home page:

How to do it...

1. Click on the Application Builder icon on the left side of the screen.

    You will see a page where you can choose between database applications or websheet applications. Furthermore, you see already created applications.

2. Click on the **Create** button on the right side of the screen. Two options are shown. You can now choose between a database application and a websheet application. We select the database application.

    In APEX you have two ways of selecting and proceeding to the next step most of the time. Usually, there is an icon accompanied by a radio button. When you check the radio button, you must click the **Next** button after that to proceed. When you click the icon, you automatically go to the next step. In this book, when there is the situation that you have to select one of the shown options, we will only tell which one of the options you should select. You can decide yourself which way to select and proceed.

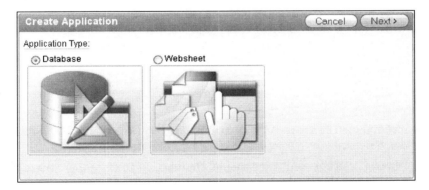

3. Select **Database**.

4. In the next step we can now choose between **From Scratch**, **From Spreadsheet** and **Demonstration Application**. When you choose **Demonstration Application**, Oracle APEX creates an application which shows the possibilities of APEX. However, we want to create an application by ourselves, and we can install this demonstration application at a later time. For now, we select "From Scratch".

5. Enter a name and an application ID . Preferably choose a name which covers the goal of the application. In our case, we call the application "Intranet".

6. Application ID is a generated and unique identification number, but you can also use some other number for your convenience.

7. At the create application radio group, leave this option to "from scratch".

8. Finally, select the schema where the tables that you want to use for your application reside and click **Next**.

    The next step in the wizard is the pages. You can start with a blank page and, from that starting point, extend your APEX application. You can also choose to add reports and forms beforehand. At this point you don't actually define the contents of the pages, you just create the 'skeleton' of them.

9. We choose to add one blank page and proceed to the next step.

10. Now you can choose to include tabs in your application. Tabs are components that help you navigate through the application. For now, we are not going to use tabs, so select "No Tabs".

The next step is the option to copy shared components from another application. Shared components are objects that can be used throughout the application, for example a list of values or images. Since we create a simple application from scratch, we don't want to copy shared components from another application. Select **No**.

An authentication scheme is a means of allowing users access to our application. APEX offers different methods for this. More will be explained in another recipe. The scheme for this application will be selected in the next step.

1. Select the standard Application Express authentication scheme.

2. You can select the language used in your application, as well as where the user language should be derived from.

3. The last option in this step is the date format mask. Click on the **LOV** button next to the text item to get a list with possible date format masks and select one.

4. The last step in the wizard is the theme. Theme 1 and Theme 2 are basic themes. If you don't like all those colors, just select something like Theme 18. That is quite a simple theme.

5. We select Theme 1 and that completes the create page wizard.

Now that we have completed the wizard, we can click on the create button to confirm. The application will be created and we will see a number of pages, depending on how many pages we already created in step 6.

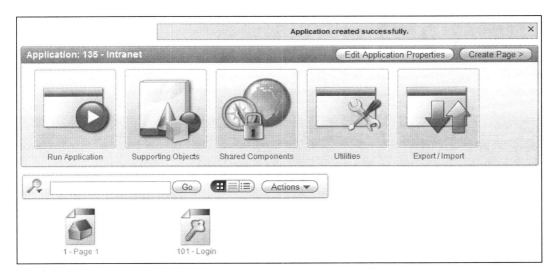

Depending on the type of authentication, we will also see page 101—**Login**. This is the default page APEX navigates to when you run an application using authentication. It is generated automatically with all functionality to allow users to log in to our application.

Click the large **Run Application** button to go to the login page.

We can log in on this page with the same credentials we use to gain access to the APEX development environment. So enter this username and password and click the **Login** button.

Well, that's it! We've created and run our first Oracle APEX 4.0 application. We can now click on the pages to define them, or we can add new pages to extend our application. We can also click the run application icon to see what has actually been created. Since we only included an empty page, we will see something like this—an empty application except for a single, also empty page:

How it works...

We have just created our first application. Even though it's just an empty shell, this is the starting point for all APEX applications. Creating content for our application is a whole different story and will be explained in the following recipes.

Creating a simple form page

After you have created the application it is time to create one or more forms and reports. First let's get started with a simple form. We will build a tabular form with insert, update, and delete possibilities.

Getting ready

Make sure that the table our form is based on contains a primary key and a sequence to update the primary key. In this case, we will be using the EMP table, so we have to make sure it is available in our database schema.

Also we have to make sure the application that we created in the previous recipe is available.

How to do it...

The starting point for this recipe is the overview of the Intranet application we created in the previous recipe.

1. Click on the **Create Page** button.

2. You will get an overview of page types. Select **Form**.

3. Now you get an overview of types of Forms pages such as form based on a procedure, forms based on a table or view, or form on a query. Select tabular form.

4. The next step is the table owner and the allowed operations. Here you can decide what your form should do: update only, update and insert, update and delete or all operations (update, insert, delete). Select all operations.

5. Select the table or view your form should be based on. If you know the table name you can type it in the text field. Otherwise, click on the button next to the field and select a table from the pop-up list. We choose the employees table, EMP.

6. Now you can select the columns, which should be visible in the form. You can select columns by clicking on the column while holding the control key. To select all columns you can click on the first column and drag your mouse to the last column.

7. If a primary key constraint is defined on the table we use, then it will automatically be selected. Otherwise, select the primary key by hand. APEX needs to know this to be able to update the changed rows.

8. Next, you can choose which way the primary key is automatically filled. Maybe you created a trigger which updates the primary key in case it is empty. However, we choose to update the primary key via an existing sequence. Select this option and in the following listbox, select the appropriate sequence and proceed to the next step.

9. Next, you can select which columns in the form should be updatable. Select the desired columns and click next.

10. In this step, you can give the page a name and a page ID. Furthermore, you can fill in the region title, the region template, the report template and if your forms page should contain breadcrumbs. A breadcrumb is a navigation component that shows the path to the current page. Leave the options as they are and click next.

11. We are not going to use tabs, so leave this option on its default selection and click next.

12. Next, fill in the names that should appear on the buttons in the form and click next.

13. In this step, you must define the branches. Branches are links to other pages. It is important to know which ID a page had, in order to fill in the branches at this point. Usually, the cancel button branches to the main page of the application. But it's also possible to find the page to branch to by using the LOV button. For the page submit branch, select the page ID assigned to the page we want to branch to. Click **Next**.

14. The last step in the wizard is the confirmation page. Check the data. If something is wrong you can go back using the **Previous** button. Otherwise click the finish button.

The form will be created and here you can choose to run the form to see how it looks or you can edit the form to define things. When running the form, it should look like the following:

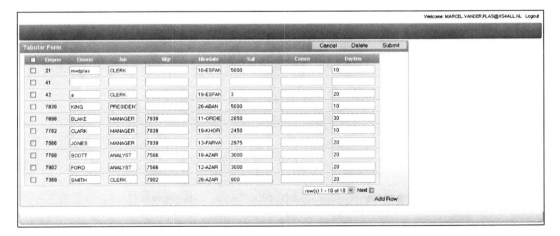

How it works...

A tabular form is actually an updateable report. In the region section you can find the query which populates the data to show on the screen. By default, every row of the table is shown. We can restrict the result set by adding a where-clause to this query.

When we edit the page we can see that the wizard created the four buttons and the processes for the DML (data manipulation language). The tree view shows an overview of the components the page is built up of. On the left we can see the components used for the rendering of the page (Regions, Items and such). It is built up in such a way that we can see the order of the components that are rendered when the page is loaded.

The middle section shows the components used for the processes on the page; in this case, these are validations, data manipulation, and branching. The right section shows an overview of all shared components used on this page, if any are available.

We can right-click on any component in the tree view to see the possible actions for that component.

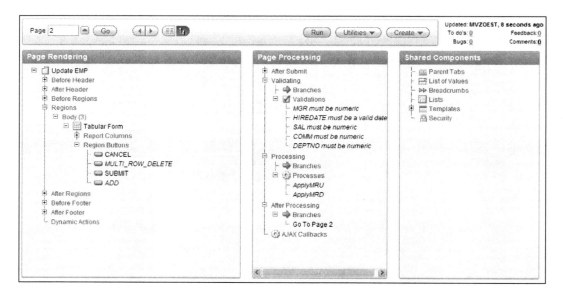

You can see that there are two multi-row update processes. The first one is triggered by the submit button and updates the changed rows. The add rows button initiates two processes: the second multi-row update process and the add rows process. So, actually the add rows button submits the changes the user made so far and after that it creates an empty row.

The delete button initiates a JavaScript process that asks the user for confirmation. And this confirmation starts the delete process. This JavaScript function can be found in the HTML header section of the page properties.

There's more...

You can also make a simple single record form. Here's how to do it.

In the application builder, click on the created application.

1. Click **create page**.
2. Click on the **form** icon.
3. Click on **form on table** or **view**.
4. Select the schema where the employees table resides and click **Next**.
5. Enter the table name. In this case it is EMP. Click **Next**.
6. In the page number/page name dialog, just leave the settings as they are and click **Next**.
7. Select **do not use tabs** and click **Next**.
8. Select the primary key and click **Next**.
9. Select **Existing** and select the desired sequence name in the listbox. Click **Next.**
10. Select all columns and click **Next**.
11. Change the button labels or leave them as they are and click **Next**.
12. Enter the page numbers APEX should call when submitting or cancelling and click **next**.
13. In the confirmation dialog, click **Finish**.
14. In the success message dialog, click **Edit**.

Creating a simple report

In our application we would also like to have an overview of all employees in the company. We can get this overview by creating a report. There are several types of reports and we just start with a simple report based on a query.

Getting ready

The starting point is our created application. You need an existing table, like EMP.

How to do it...

1. In the application builder, go to the application we just created and click on the **Create Page** button.

2. In the page type dialog, select **Report**.

3. A page is shown where we can choose between the different types of reports. Options are: interactive report, classic report, report based on a web service result, and wizard report. We will choose classic report so select classic report.

   Some of the other types of reports will be covered in other recipes in this book. The next recipe is on Interactive Reports. In *Chapter 8, Webservices*, some examples of building reports on Webservices are explained. The option wizard report is not explained separately, because it just offers an easier, step-by-step way of building a report.

4. In the next step you can assign a page number and a page name to the report. Furthermore you can indicate whether you would like to have breadcrumbs on your report page. Leave the breadcrumb option to "do not use breadcrumbs on page" and click **Next**.

5. In this step you can choose to include tabs in your report page. We leave it to "do not use tabs". Click **Next**.

6. In this step you must enter a query in the textarea. You can use the query builder to help you build your query, but you can also enter it manually. We use the following query:

```
select *
  from emp
```

7. After you have entered the query, click **Next**.

8. In the next step you can define a number of settings such as the report template, the region name, the number of rows displayed per page, and whether the user should be able to print the report on paper or spool it to a comma separated file. Leave the options as they are and click **Next**.

9. In the last step, you see the confirmation page. If the choices made are not satisfactory, click the previous button to go back and modify the options. Otherwise, click the **finish** button.

The report is ready now. You can edit the report to define the settings or you can run the report to see how it looks. The result should be something like this:

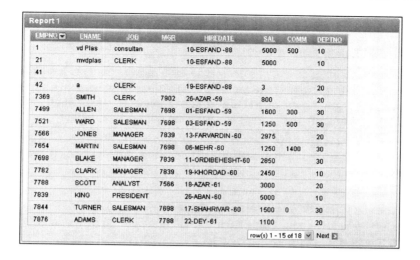

How it works...

When you look at the page in the Application Builder, you will see that APEX created a reports region.

1. Right-click on the region name of the report and click **Edit** to see the details of the report.

2. In the region source you can see the query you just entered. If you want to see the column details, click on the **Report Attributes** tab.

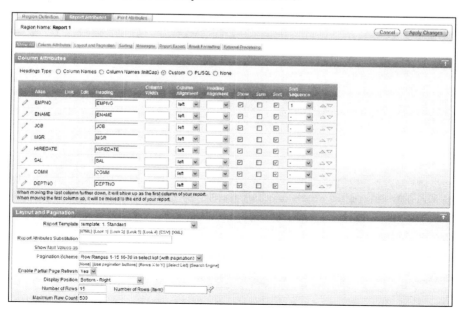

3. Here you can modify the column heading, the heading alignment, or the names of the columns. To go more into detail about the column you can click on the pencil icon next to the column name.

   Sometimes in a project, the business case for a report changes. Instead of a classic report, the customer would like an Interactive Report. In case there are two options, remove the current report region and create a new one based on an Interactive Report or just migrate the current report using built-in functionality.

   When we are looking at the Region Definition tab of the Edit region page, we can see a Tasks list on the right side of the screen. One of the options is **Migrate to Interactive Report**. This migration is not a Holy Grail, but can save a lot of time in the migration process.

4. Click the link to **Migrate to Interactive Report**.
5. In the following page, enter **EMPNO** in the Unique Column field and click the **Migrate** button to see what happens.

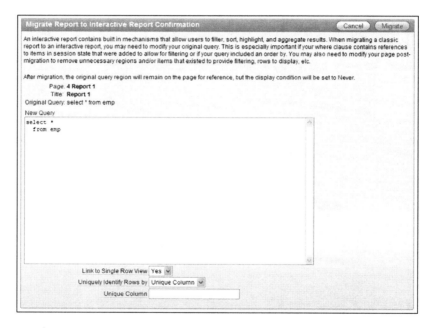

In the tree view of the page we can see that the old report region still exists but it's labeled **Disabled**. The new interactive report is added as we can see.

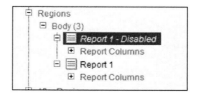

More on Interactive Reports is explained in the following recipe.

See also

Chapter 8 explains (among many other things) how to create a report on Webservice references.

The next recipe "Implement an interactive report" explains how to build a page with an interactive report and what options there are when using them.

Implementing an interactive report

In this recipe, we are going to create an interactive report and show you how to use it. An interactive report is a special kind of report, which offers a lot of options to the user for filtering, sorting, publishing, and much more.

Getting ready

It's always a good idea to start by creating a view that already selects all columns you want to show in your report. This simplifies the query required for your report region and separates the logic from presentation in your application architecture.

In this recipe, we are going to base the interactive report on the APP_VW_CONTACTS view that joins the tables for contacts, addresses, and communications. The query for this view is:

```
select  ctt.firstname
     ,  ctt.lastname
     ,  ctt.contact_type
     ,  ads.address_type
     ,  ads.address_line1
     ,  ads.address_line2
     ,  ads.postcode
     ,  ads.city
     ,  ads.state
     ,  ads.country
     ,  aac.default_yn
     ,  ctt.id
     ,  ads.id
  from app_contacts ctt
     , app_addresses ads
     , app_ads_ctt aac
 where aac.ctt_id = ctt.id
   and aac.ads_id = ads.id
```
[1346_01_01.txt]

We will also need a named LOV later on in the recipe. To create it, follow the next steps:

1. Go to **Shared Components** and then to **Lists of Values**.
2. Click **Create** to make a new LOV.
3. Create it from scratch and call it ADDRESS_TYPE, it should be a dynamic LOV.
4. The query that it's based on is:

```
select rv_meaning display_value
     , rv_low_value return_value
  from app_ref_codes
 where rv_domain = 'ADDRESSES'
[1346_01_02.txt]
```

How to do it...

The starting point for this recipe is an empty page, so the first thing that we're going to do is create a new region to contain the interactive report.

1. Create a new region by right-clicking on the **Regions** label and select **Create**.

2. Select **Report** as the type of region.
3. Then select **Interactive Report** as the Report Implementation.
4. Give the Region a title "**Contacts**".
5. Select Region Template **APEX 4.0 – Reports Region**. Keep the other fields on the default.
6. As the source for the Region, enter the SQL Query:

```
SELECT *
  FROM app_vw_contacts
[1346_01_03.txt]
```

7. Leave the other options on default.
8. Click **Create Region** to finish this part of the recipe.

As you can see in the tree view, we now have a new **Region** with all columns from the view.

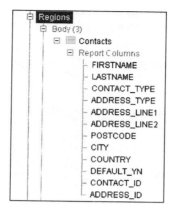

When we run the page now, we can already see some data. APEX also generated a toolbar above the report that we can use to filter data or change the way it is presented.

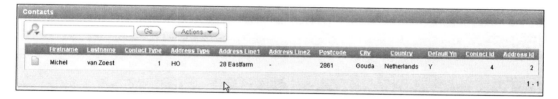

The next step is to alter the report, so we can customize the column labels and change the way some of the data is presented.

9. In the Page Definition's tree view, right-click on the **Contacts Region** and select **Report Attributes** from the pull-down menu.

10. Change the heading for some of the columns:

    ❑ Firstname -> First Name

    ❑ Lastname -> Last Name

    ❑ Default Yn -> Default Address?

11. Click **Apply Changes** to confirm the changes.

    This changes the labels for some of the columns in the report. Next, we will change the presentation of the data inside one of the columns.

12. Expand the tree view to show the contents of Report Columns of the Contacts Region.

13. Right-click on ADDRESS_TYPE and click **Edit**.

14. Change the item Display Text As to Display as Text (Based on LOV, escape special characters).

15. Under **List of Values**, select Use Named List of Values to Filter Exact Match from the pull-down Column Filter List of Values.

16. Select ADDRESS_TYPE as the Named List of Values.

17. Click **Apply Changes.**

When we take a look at the page by clicking Run we can see the changes to the column names and the **Address Type** no longer shows the abbreviation, but the full text.

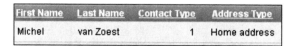

First Name	Last Name	Contact Type	Address Type
Michel	van Zoest	1	Home address

There's more...

After the developer is done with creating an interactive report, the user will have a host of possibilities in the action menu to change the way the information is presented and filtered. These possibilities can be granted or revoked by the developer to an extent.

To see these options, right-click on the region and click the option named **Edit region attributes**. When scrolling down this screen, there are two sections for Search Bar and Download.

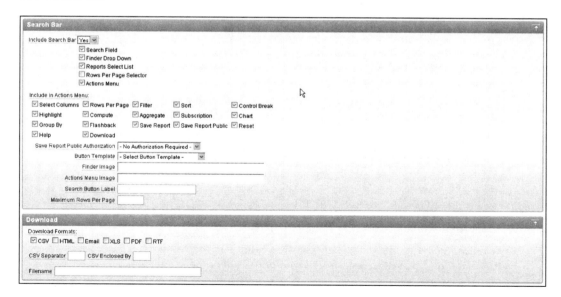

The first section holds the options that can be used in the Search Bar. When a user clicks the **Action** button in the **Search Bar**, a menu will unfold revealing all the possible options. Data can be filtered, sorted, highlighted, and aggregated for instance. It's also possible for the user to generate a chart.

When a user wants to save the changes he made to the report, this is also possible. He can save it for personal or public use, so other users can benefit as well.

The second section holds the file types that can be used to download the information in the interactive report. These include well-known formats such as CSV, PDF, and XLS.

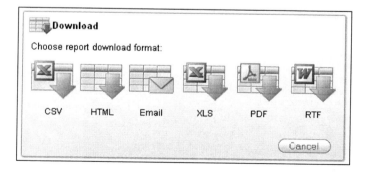

Creating a chart

In many reports it's required to show some (or all) of the figures in charts. This will give users the opportunity to quickly see the data and possibly take actions accordingly.

This recipe will show how to create a chart and some possibilities to configure them.

Getting ready

In the earlier recipes, we created the regions while building a new page. Of course it's also possible to add regions on existing pages. To do so in this example, first prepare an empty page which will hold the region with the chart.

How to do it...

1. Create a new region by right-clicking on the **Regions** label and choose **Create**.
2. Select **Chart** and click **Next**.
3. Choose **Flash chart** and click **Next**.
4. Select **Pie & Doughnut** and click **Next**.
5. Select **3D Pie** and click **Next**.
6. Enter **Employees in a department** in the title, leave the other fields on the default and click **Next**.
7. Enter **Employees in a department** in the **Chart** title, leave the other fields on the default and click **Next**.

   We are going to select all employees per department, so we will enter a query that will get us that data into the chart.

8. Enter the following query into the SQL Query field:

```
select null link
     , dept.name label
     , COUNT(emp.ID) value1
  from APP_EMPLOYEES emp
     , APP_DEPARTMENTS dept
 where emp.dept_id = dept.id
 group by dept.name
```
   [1346_01_04.txt]

9. Click **Create Region**.
10. Run the page.

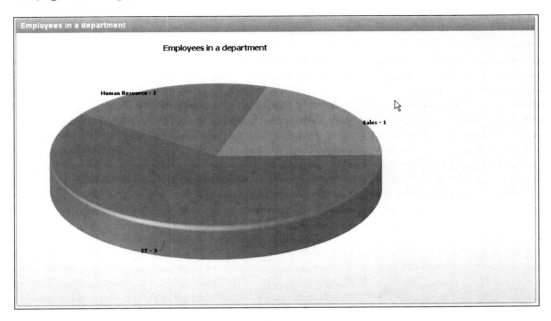

There's more...

There are a number of possibilities to change and enhance this chart. Besides the 3D pie we have created here, there are dozens of other chart types. But there is a catch. Once a chart is created, the number of types it can be changed to is limited. When we would like to use a completely different chart type, the chart region has to be re-created.

This recipe can be easily expanded with a link to another page which can be clicked inside the chart.

To do this, first navigate to the Chart Series by expanding the tree view under the chart region or by clicking the edit link in the chart properties page. Edit the query on which the chart is based and change the first column. If we, for example, would have a page with ID 888, a query with a link to that page would look like this:

```
select 'f?p=&APP_ID.:888:&APP_SESSION.::NO::P888_DEPT_ID:'||dept.id link
     , dept.name label
     , COUNT(emp.ID) value1
  from APP_EMPLOYEES emp
     , APP_DEPARTMENTS dept
 where emp.dept_id = dept.id
 group by dept.name, dept.id
[1346_01_05.txt]
```

We have chosen to show a dynamically generated link here. A few of the parameters need an explanation:

- APP_ID is the ID for this application.
- APP_SESSION is the ID for the current session.
- P888_DEPT_ID is the fictitious item on page 888 that holds the dept_id.

It is also possible to create a link by altering the action link region on the Chart Series page. The same items will be filled by this process, but it is easier to use when it is a relatively simple application.

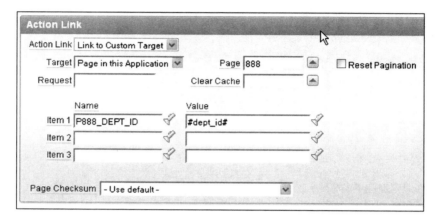

Creating a map chart

A new type of chart available in Application Express 4.0 is the map chart. This allows users to present data on a geographical map. APEX 4.0 offers many maps from a world overview to maps of single countries.

Map charts allow applications a new way to visualize location-related data without much programming.

In this recipe, we will show you how to create a map that lists all contacts in the United States by state.

Getting ready

First we need to have a structure ready in our database tables that holds at least one geographical related column (for example, country, state, or province names). This will be the pointer for our chart to which it can relate its map.

For this recipe, we will reuse the APP_VW_CONTACTS view. This view holds a column called STATE that we can use in our chart.

How to do it...

Our starting point is again an empty page. The first thing to do is to add a new region.

1. Right-click on **Regions** and select **Create**.
2. Select **Map** as the **Region Type**.

    This will bring up a window with a couple of main categories of maps. Selecting one of these categories will bring up a list of sub-categories that can be drilled-down even further.

3. Select **United States of America** and click **Next**.

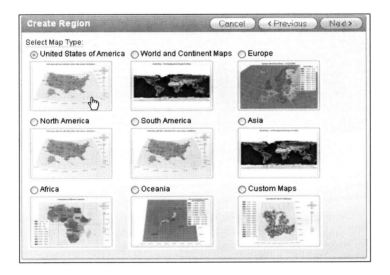

4. In the following list select **States**:

5. Enter **Contacts by State** for the title and leave the rest on default and click **Next**.

6. Enter the same text as the **Map Title**.

7. Enter the following query in the appropriate SQL Query area:

```
select null link
     , STATE label
     , COUNT(CONTACT_ID) value
  from   APP_VW_CONTACTS
 group by STATE
```
[1346_01_06.txt]

8. Click **Create Region**.

9. Run the page to see the result.

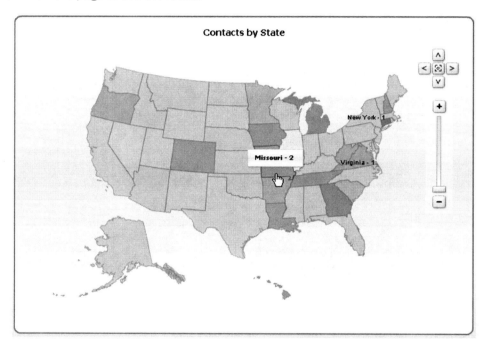

As we can see, each state that contains one or more contacts is highlighted. APEX also generates labels containing the state name and number of contacts if there is room for it. The other labels can be viewed by hovering over the state with the mouse pointer.

How it works...

Application Express uses AnyChart 5 for displaying its charts. This is different from earlier versions of APEX, so migrating applications that make use of charts from version 3.x to 4.0 is a little more complicated than migrating other functionality.

When using a Map chart it is important that a column for the label is used that contains the name of the geographical region that you want highlighted on the map. For the standard maps provided by APEX, it's not allowed to use abbreviations, but it has to be the full name (for example, New York instead of NY and Virginia instead of VA).

There's more...

Just like any other chart type it is possible to create links to other pages. This can be used to create, for instance, a drill down type of structure. We could create a series of pages from a world map, to a continent map, to a country map, and so forth.

How such a link can be created is explained in the chart recipe before this one.

Creating a navigation bar

The navigation bar is the area of an APEX application that is normally placed into the header of each page (unless the template is changed of course). As a standard, the Logout link is provided here, so users can quickly log out of the application from any page.

This recipe will show how a navigation bar can be customized. This will allow users to quickly reach certain pages in the application.

Getting ready

In this recipe we are going to see how you can create a quick link to a contact page. Before we can do that, we first need to have this page ready.

- Create a new blank page. Name it **Contact** and assign page ID **999** to it.
- Create a new HTML region on this page and enter the following text into it:

  "For more information send an e-mail to info@packtpublishing.com"

For the second part of the recipe, we need an icon available. This can be any available icon as long as it measures 32 x 32 pixels. The **Images** directory of APEX offers some examples like "fndtip11.gif".

- Go to **Shared Components**.
- Click on **Images**.
- Click on **Create**.
- Select your application.
- Select the image "fndtip11.gif" on your file system by using the Browse button.
- Click on **Upload**.

How to do it...

The navigation bar can be found in Shared Components. To reach it navigate to **Shared Components | Navigation Bar Entries**.

As a default there is already a Logout entry available. Our new entry will be added here:

- ▶ Click the button **Create**.
- ▶ Select **From Scratch** and click **Next**.
- ▶ Select **Navigation to URL** and click **Next**.
- ▶ In the **Entry Label**, enter "**Contact**" and leave the rest on default. Click **Next**.
- ▶ Enter 999 into Page and default the other fields. Click **Next**.
- ▶ Click **Create**.

As you can see, a new entry is created next to the Logout entry. This means we are done and can now test it by running the application.

Instead of a link text it is also possible to use images. This can be helpful when developing, for example, a multi language application with a short list of languages. Instead of writing the full language name, we can use small icons depicting the available language.

In this example, we will only show you how to create a navigation bar icon and reuse our Contact page for this. Later on in the book, we will show you the details of how to create a language switch.

- ▶ Go to **Shared Components | Navigation Bar Entries** and click the button **Create**.
- ▶ Select **From Scratch** and click **Next**.
- ▶ Select **Navigation to URL** and click **Next**.

    This time we need to enter some more information on this screen.

- ► Alter the **Sequence** to **15**.
- ► In the **Entry Label** enter nothing.
- ► In **Icon Image Name**, click the button to the right of the field and select the icon "fndtip11.gif."
    - ❑ Alternatively, you can enter "#APP_IMAGES#fndtip11.gif" into the field.
- ► Enter **Contact** into **Image ALT**.
- ► Enter **32** for both **Image Height** and **Width**.

- ► Click **Next**.
- ► Enter **999** into **Page** and default the other fields. Click **Next**.
- ► Click **Create**.

You will notice a new entry in the list of the Navigation Bar. When running the application, this will be shown with the selected icon.

There's more...

New in Application Express 4.0 is the possibility to add a feedback link to the navigation bar. This will allow visitors of the application to quickly send feedback to the application developers or administrators.

- ► Create a new navigation bar entry From Scratch.
- ► Select **Feedback** and click **Next**.
- ► In the next screen, find the Tasks section to the far right and click **Create Feedback Page**.

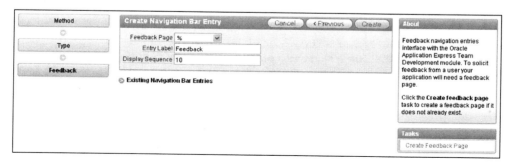

 ▶ Set the page number to 102, leave everything else at default, and click **Create**.

 ▶ The focus will be returned to the navigation bar overview, so we have to repeat the first two steps.

 ▶ Now select page 102 from the Feedback Page pull down list, enter 20 into the **Display Sequence**, and click **Create**.

If you were to run the application now, no feedback link would be visible, because we have to allow the feedback option first.

So click **Edit Application Properties** and find the option **Allow Feedback**. Set the pull down to **Yes** and click **Apply Changes**. Now the application is ready to receive some feedback from its visitors.

See also

Chapter 6, Creating multilingual APEX applications, will cover translating your application and offering quick language switching to the visitors.

Chapter 12, Team Development, will show how feedback can be used to the advantage of the development team.

Creating a list of values

When you use forms with items that are foreign keys to other tables, it would be handy to derive the primary key from the lookup table instead of having to enter this ID manually in the text field. Or, when dealing with lots of similar, predefined data, you don't want to enter the same values over and over again. In those cases, you would want to use items like listboxes, quick picks, or lists of values which display the data of the lookup items where the user can easily pick the right value.

In this recipe, we'll create a list of values. A list of values can be a list of predefined static values but it can also be a dynamic list with data retrieved from a table. We will create a static list of values. A list of values is a shared component so it can be used in more pages.

Getting ready

Starting point is an existing application like the one we created. To define a list of values you don't need to have a page. However, to make use of a list of values, you must define an item with a reference to the list of values. We will make a list of values on the JOB column.

How to do it...

There are two ways to start the Create List of Values wizard. The first one is in the edit page.

On the right side of the screen, under shared components, click on the **Add** icon under list of values.

The second one is via the shared components:

> ▶ In the application builder, go to the shared components and then list of values. On the list of values page, click the **Create** button.

> ▶ You can create a list of values from scratch or you can copy an existing list of values and make some modifications to the newly created list of values. In our case, we will create a list of values from scratch. Click **Next**.

> ▶ Enter a name for the list of values, Jobs for example, and select dynamic or static. Choose static and click **Next**.

In the next step, you can enter the desired values. There are two types of values: the display value and the return value. The display value indicates how it is displayed and the return value is the value which will be returned into the text item the list of values is called from.

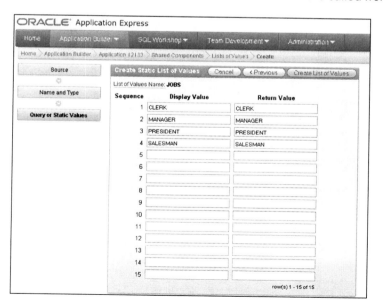

After you have entered the values, click on the **Create List of Values** button.

The list of values is created and can now be used by items. To assign an existing item to the list of values, go to the page where you want to include your list of values. In this case, we go to the tabular form based on the EMP table, that we created in the recipe called "Create a simple form page" in Chapter 1.

  ▶   Click in the regions section on the report link. Click on the pencil icon near the
       Job column.

  ▶   In the tabular form element section, select "select list (named lov)" at the
       "display as" field.

  ▶   Next, in the list of values section, at the named lov field, select the list of values you
       just created.

  ▶   Click on the apply changes button.

  ▶   Run the form to see the result. It should look like the following:

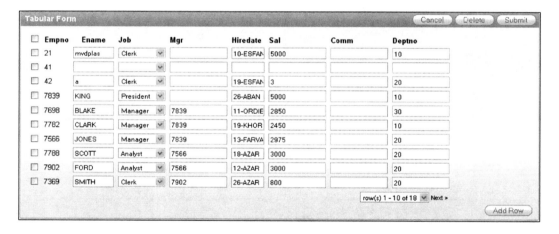

How it works...

The list of values serves as a source for items types like a list box or pop-up list of values. A list of values contains two columns: a display column and a column with the return value. This return value will be the actual data which will be stored in the item which is assigned to the list of values.

A list item can also be created directly upon a report column or item, but then is not reusable.

There's more...

Another possibility is to use a previously defined List of Values as a basis when creating a new item. This is useful in situations where you want to reuse a List of Values on more than one occasion. A question that requires the answer Yes or No for example, can return on many pages in an application.

1. Go to the page where you want to have the item.

2. Right-click on the **Items** section of the region where the item should go and select **Create Page Item**.

3. In the **Select Item Type** dialog, click on the **Select List**.

4. In the next step, enter a name for the item. You may also enter a sequence number and the region where the item should appear. Click **Next**.

5. In this step, provide some additional information such as the label, the height, and the alignment. Click **Next**.

6. Next, define what APEX should do when you select some value from the list. You can redirect the user to another page or you can submit the page. Another option in this step is the indication whether APEX should allow multi selection. Leave this option to **No** and click **Next**.

7. In the next step, enter the name of the existing List of Values that you want to use in the **Named LOV** field. Leave the other options and click **Next**.

8. In the last step, define the source of the item. Leave the options and click on the **Create Item** button.

Including different item types

In APEX it is possible to use many different item types. Some of these we've already seen in other recipes. In this recipe we're going to talk about some of the advanced item types like shuttles and HTML editors and how to interact with them.

Getting ready

To start with this recipe, create an empty page with ID 15 and put an HTML region with the name **IT Employees** on it.

How to do it...

The first example of an advanced item type is the shuttle list. We will use this list to add employees to the IT department. The shuttle will show a list of available employees on the left side and a list of employees already in the IT department on the right side.

1. Create a new item on your page by right-clicking on the IT Employees region and selecting **Create Page Item**.

2. Select **Shuttle** and click **Next**.

3. Name the item `P15_IT_SHUTTLE` and click **Next** until you reach the List of Values page in the wizard.

4. Enter the following query to populate the left side of the shuttle:

```
select username display_value
     , id return_value
  from app_employees
 where dept_id <> 3
```
[1346_01_07.txt]

5. After clicking **Next**, you will be asked to enter the Source Value. This will populate the right side of the shuttle. For this, we will use a PL/SQL Function Body as the Source Type that will return a list of usernames delimited by colons.

```
declare
   v_list apex_application_global.vc_arr2;
begin

   select username return_value
     bulk collect
     into v_list
     from app_employees
    where dept_id = 3;

   return(apex_util.table_to_string(v_list));
end;
```
[1346_01_08.txt]

6. Click **Create Item** to finish the wizard.

Now the item will be populated with the employees.

The right side of the Shuttle Item can also be populated by the Default value that can be defined on the item's properties.

Another type of item we want to discuss here is the Cascading Select Item. Let's say we want to make a list of all employees. This is potentially a very long list, so before showing the employees, we first want to select the department we are working with.

First, we create the item that shows all departments for our company:

1. Create a new page item.

2. Use item type **Select List**.

3. Name it **P15_DEPARTMENTS**.

4. Give it a label and click **Next** until you reach the LOV query, and enter the following SQL:

```
select name display_value
     , id return_value
   from app_departments
```
    [1346_01_09.txt]

5. Now create the item.

The next part is to create the select list for the employees in the department. Again, we create a select list like before and name it P15_EMPLOYEES.

Now when we reach the LOV wizard screen, we enter the following SQL:

```
select firstname||' '||lastname display_value
     , id return_value
   from app_employees
  where dept_id = :P15_DEPARTMENTS
```
[1346_01_10.txt]

Also on this screen change the value of Cascading LOV Parent Item(s) to P15_DEPARTMENTS. Click **Next** and **Create Item**.

When we now run the page and select a **Department**, we can see that the Employees list changes immediately.

 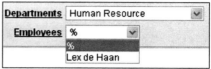

Protecting a page using an authorization scheme

In some cases, you might want to restrict access to certain parts of your application to certain users. For example not everyone should have access to the Form Page where you can alter the salaries. In such a case you can protect your page using an authorization scheme.

Getting ready

Before starting with the recipe you should have a table created in the database with usernames and roles. Let's say you have the following table APP_USERS:

```
ID         NUMBER(5)
USERNAME   VARCHAR2(50)
PASSWORD   VARCHAR2(50)
ROLE       VARCHAR2(10)
```

The table contains two rows. One is a user with admin privileges (role is ADMIN). The other one is a user with the no extra privileges (role is DEFAULT).

How to do it...

1. Go to the **Shared Components**.

2. Click on the link Authorization Schemes. You can find it in the Security section.

3. Next, you might see the authorization schemes that have already been created. If no authorization schemes have been created in the past, you see an empty page. Click on the **Create** button.

4. Next, select **From Scratch** and click **Next**.

5. Next, enter a name for this authorization scheme and enter the conditions in the authorization scheme section.

In our case, we name the scheme `AUTH_ADMIN`. The scheme type could be a PL/SQL function returning Boolean or an EXISTS SQL query. You have to create this function or query by yourself. The code could be included in the "Expression 1" textarea but you can also make a call to a function stored in the database. In our case, we put the code in here and we choose for the `EXISTS SQL` query. You see the query as follows:

```
select 1
from    app_users
where   username = :APP_USER
and     role = 'ADMIN'
```

[1346_01_11.txt]

The query returns 1 if the username is the current user (`:APP_USER`) and the user has admin privileges.

6. Also, enter the error message APEX should display if the query returns no rows. Click the **Create** button.

7. In the **Evaluation Point** section, select **Once per page view** to validate the authorization scheme. This will make APEX check the authorization for every call that is made to pages (or other components) using this scheme.

8. The other option is **Once per session**. This is much more efficient, because the check is only done once (at the start of the session). But when it's possible that the session state changes or there is anything else that is not consistent during the session, this option is not reliable.

9. The authorization scheme is now ready. Now, page access must be restricted by this authorization scheme.

10. Go to the page that requires authorization and click on the **Edit** icon (the pencil) in the page section.

11. Go to the **Security** section and select the **Authorization Scheme** we just created (`AUTH_ADMIN`) in the Authorization Scheme list element.

That's it. The page now requires authorization to be accessed. Run the page to see how it works. Also see what happens if you do an update on the `APP_USERS` table:

```
update app_users
set     role    = 'DEFAULT'
where   username = ...;
```

Or

```
update app_users
set     role    = 'ADMIN'
where   username = ...;
```

[1346_01_12.txt]

Don't forget the commit.

How it works...

Every time you navigate to this page, APEX executes the query in the Authorization Scheme. If the query returns one row, everything is fine and the user is authorized to view this page. If the query returns no rows, the user is not authorized to view the page and the error message is displayed.

There's more...

You don't have to go to the shared components to create an Authorization Scheme. It can also be done when you are on a page. In the Security section on the right side of the screen, click on the Add icon. The **Create Authorization Scheme** wizard will be started.

Securing an application with Authentication

Application Express comes with three standard ways to authenticate users on applications. We can use the credentials of Database users, we can use the credentials of users defined within APEX itself, or we can use the credentials defined in the Database Access Descriptor. In this recipe, we will show how to add our own Authentication Scheme to this list.

An Authentication Scheme controls access to an entire application as opposed to an Authorization Scheme that controls access to individual components inside the application.

Simply put, an Authentication Scheme is what is called when a user clicks the **Login** button.

Getting ready

First, we need a table to store the data for our users. In our application, this table will be APP_USERS. It contains columns for username and password, so we can create a very basic authentication scheme. Make sure this table is ready before continuing in this recipe.

Enter at least one row of data into the table that we can use to login at the end of the recipe.

Also we need two functions in place. APP_HASH is a function that will use a hashing algorithm and a salt to mask the real password. To make it more secure, the current date can be used in the algorithm, but this is enough for our example.

In a production environment, it is probably a good idea to wrap this code, because it can help intruders gain access to the application.

```
create or replace function app_hash (p_username in varchar2, p_
password in varchar2)
return varchar2
is
  l_password varchar2(4000);
```

```
  l_salt varchar2(4000) := 'DFS2J3DF4S5HG666IO7S8DJGSDF8JH';

begin

  l_password := utl_raw.cast_to_raw(dbms_obfuscation_toolkit.md5
  (input_string => p_password || substr(l_salt,10,13) || p_username ||
    substr(l_salt, 4,10)));
  return l_password;
end;
```
[1346_01_13.txt]

APP_AUTH is a function that will check if the user is valid and if the password is entered correctly.

```
create or replace function app_auth (p_username in VARCHAR2, p_
password in VARCHAR2)
return BOOLEAN
is
  l_password varchar2(4000);
  l_stored_password varchar2(4000);
  l_expires_on date;
  l_count number;
begin
  select count(*)
    into l_count
    from app_users
   where upper(username) = upper(p_username);

  if l_count > 0
  then
    select password
      into l_stored_password
      from app_users
      where upper(username) = upper(p_username);

    l_password := app_hash(p_username, p_password);

    if l_password = l_stored_password
    then
      return true;
    else
      return false;
    end if;
  else
    return false;
  end if;

end;
```
[1346_01_14.txt]

How to do it...

The first thing we have to do is add the new authentication scheme to the list of existing schemes.

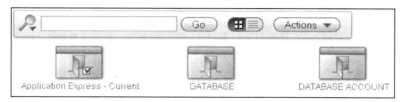

1. Click the **Create** button.
2. Choose From Scratch and click **Next**.
3. Name it **Application Authentication** and click **Next.**
4. Click **Next** on the following two screens as well.
5. Select **Page in This Application** and page 101 on the Invalid Session Target and click **Next** until you reach **Credentials verification method**.
6. Select **Use my custom function to authenticate** and enter **return app_auth** in the Authentication Function.
7. Click **Next** until you reach **Logout URL**.
8. The Logout URL is `wwv_flow_custom_auth_std.logout?p_this_flow=&APP_ID.&amp;p_next_flow_page_sess=&APP_ID.:1`
9. Click **Next** and Create Scheme.

The last step is to make the new Authentication Scheme the current for the application. To do this, navigate to the tab Change Current on the schemes overview screen. Select the new scheme from the list and click the **Make Current** button.

You can now log in to the application using a username and password from the `APP_USERS` table.

Control the display of regions and items with Dynamic Actions

Dynamic Actions are control items that dynamically can affect the display of regions or items on a page. There are several situations when you want to show or hide items. For example, a text item asking for a maiden name should only be displayed when the person is female and married. In other cases, it is irrelevant to ask for a maiden name (on the other hand, with homosexual marriages it's possible for a man to have a 'maiden' name, and in some cases a man can adopt the family name of his wife, but let's not make this example more difficult than necessary).

The same applies to the commission field in the employees table. This item should only be enterable when the employee's job is a salesman. Let's build the functionality for this last situation.

Getting ready

You should already have an application and a simple single record form on the employees table.

How to do it...

1. Right-click on the **Dynamic Actions** link in the leftmost section and click **Create**.
2. Select **Standard** and proceed to the next step.
3. Enter a name for this Dynamic Action. For example, **D_JOB_COMM_SHOW**. Click **Next**.
4. In the next screen the Selection Type is "Item(s)" and in the Item(s) field, enter the name of the item holding Job. You can use the **List of Values** button to select the right Page Item.
5. In the **Condition list** box, select **equal to**.
6. In the **Value** textarea, enter **SALESMAN**. Click **Next**.
7. Select **Show** as the **True Action** and go to the next step.
8. In the next screen select **Item(s)** in the **Selection Type**. In the Shuttle item that now appears, move the name of the commission field to the right.
9. Click the **Create** button.

You have now created a Dynamic Action which shows the commission field when the job is **SALESMAN** and hides the commission field when the job is not **'SALESMAN**.

How it works...

The Dynamic Actions are actually event handlers in HTML. There are several event handlers.

Because these events are HTML (or rather JavaScript) they are handled client side. This has the advantage that the page doesn't have to be reloaded completely when an action is triggered to show or hide items.

Event	Meaning
After refresh	Item has been refreshed (that is, by page refresh)
Before refresh	Fires before item has been refreshed (that is, by page refresh)
Blur	User navigates to another item
Change	User navigates to another item and the value of the item has changed

Event	Meaning
Click	User clicks on the item with a pointing device (like a mouse)
Dblclick	User double-clicks on the item with a pointing device
Focus	User navigates to the item via the tab key or a pointing device
keydown	User clicks a key on the keyboard
keypress	User "clicks" a key on the keyboard (=onkeyDown followed by onkeyUp)
keyup	User releases the key after having pressed it
load	The browser loads all content
mousedown	User clicks the mouse button when the mouse pointer is over the item
mouseenter	User clicks on the item with the pointing device
mouseleave	User moves away the mouse from the item
mousemove	User moves the mouse while the mouse pointer is over the item
mouseover	User moves the mouse pointer over the item
mouseout	User moves away the mouse pointer from the item
nmouseup	User releases the mouse button after having it pressed
submit	Form is submitted
Resize	Document view is resized
Scroll	Document view is scrolled
Select	User selects some text in a text field
Submit	Form is submitted
Unload	Page is unloaded

In our example, we use the onchange event handler. So, when the user changes the value in JOB, the onchange is triggered and it calls the action to show or hide the **COMMISSION** field, depending on the value in JOB. If it is **SALESMAN** then show commission, else hide commission.

There's more...

You can control the display of more than one item at a time. Simply separate the items by a comma in the items field.

You can also control the display of regions. So, you can show or hide a complete report. Instead of item, select region and the name of the region in the affected element section when defining an action.

Creating a computation

Computations are events that will prepare items with data. As the name implies, computations can 'compute' how data is to be shown on screen or how data is handled after submitting. Computations can be triggered during Page Rendering, but they can also be used in the **After Submit** process.

This example will show an implementation of a computation, but there are many more possible uses for computations.

How to do it...

Start by creating a normal text item on the form that was created in the second recipe of the first chapter. This is a normal form based on the EMP table. Normally, a user would have to manually enter the commission. What we are going to do is to create a computation that will automatically enter an amount into this field, based on a percentage of the salary and a bonus for people that work in the Sales department.

First, identify the item that holds the commission column.

The next step is to find the moment when we want to execute the computation. In this case, before the page is submitted but after the **Save** button is pressed. So in this case we will create the computation **After Submit**.

1. Right-click on the **Computations** under **After Submit** in the **Page Processing** component and click **Create**.

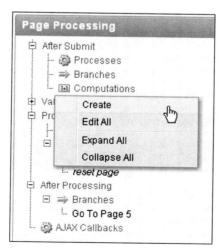

2. Choose **Item on this page** and press **Next**.

3. Select **P5_COMM** from the **Compute Item** select list, select **PL/SQL Function Body** from the **Computation Type** select list and click **Next**.

4. The next step is to enter the **PL/SQL** code for this computation:

```
declare
  l_comm number;
begin
  if :P5_DEPTNO = 30
  then
    l_comm := :P5_SAL * 1.10;
  else
    l_comm := :P5_SAL * 1.05;
  end if;
  return l_comm;
end;
```

[1346_01_15.txt]

5. Press **Create**.

The computation is now done. It can be tested by selecting an existing record from the list of employees and altering its salary and then saving the data. Another option is to create a completely new employee. You will see that an employee under the Sales department with dept no. 30 will receive a 10 percent commission whilst employees from all other departments will receive 5 percent.

There's more...

Computations can be used for far more situations than preparing an item before saving it to the database.

An example of another implementation can be an item that will show the current date when the page loads, or an item that will show a total amount when certain other amount items are entered. Used with dynamic actions, computations can be very powerful.

Creating an automated row fetch with a page process

When you create a Single Record Form you probably would like to see that the form automatically retrieves data on startup. You can do that with an automated row fetch. In this section, we will create a page process with an automated row fetch. We're going to make a form where users can update their data.

Getting ready

We will use the EMP table so make sure it exists, together with the primary key. Create a simple form page:

1. In the Application Builder, click the **Create Page** button.
2. Select the Blank page and click **Next**.
3. Assign a number and enter a name in the **Page Alias** field. The page number is automatically filled by APEX.
4. In the next step, enter a name for this page and click **Next**.
5. In the tabs dialog, select **No** and click **Next**.
6. In the page confirmation dialog, click **Finish**.

The page is now ready and we can start creating a region with items.

1. Click on the icon of the new page.
2. Create a region by right-clicking on the regions link and clicking **Create**.
3. Select HTML and click **Next**.
4. In the type of HTML dialog, select **HTML** and click **Next**.
5. In the next step, enter a title for the region and click Nxt.
6. In the **HTML text region source** step, leave all options and click **Create Region**.

    A region is created and now we will add some items to this region. We will start with the primary key of the table.

7. Right-click on the name of the region and select **Create Page Item**.
8. Select **Text Item** and click **Next.**
9. In the next step, select **Text Field** and click **Next.**
10. Next, enter a name for this item. Since this item will display the primary key we give it the same name as the primary key column, empno. So, the item will be named P11_EMPNO (11 is the page number, this can be different depending on your situation). Enter this name in the text field and click **Next**.
11. In the next step, you can enter a label for this text item. Enter **empno** and click **Next**.
12. In the source dialog, in the **Source Type** listbox, select **Database Column** and enter **EMPNO** in the **Item Source Value** textarea. Mind the capitals, otherwise it will not work.
13. Click the **Create Item** button.

The item has now been created.

Next, create another item. Let's say Ename.

1. Right-click on the name of the region and select **Create Page Item**.

2. Select **Text Item** and click **Next**.

3. In the next step select **Text Field** and click **Next**.

4. Next, enter a name for this item. Enter **P11_ENAME** (again, change 11 to the page number in your situation) in the text field and click **Next**.

5. In the next step you can enter a label for this text item. Enter **ename** and click **Next**.

6. In the source dialog, in the Source Type listbox, select **Database Column** and enter **ENAME** in the item **Source Value** textarea. Mind the capitals, otherwise it will not work.

7. Click the **Create Item** button.

The item has now been created.

How to do it...

1. In the page you just created, expand the **After Header** section and right-click the **Processes** link. Now click **Create**.

2. Select **Data Manipulation** and click **Next**.

3. Select **Automated Row Fetch** and click **Next**.

4. Enter a name for this process. In the Point listbox, select **On Load – After Header**. Click **Next**.

5. In the next step, enter the table name, the item containing the primary key column value, and the primary key column. In our case, the table name is EMP and the item containing the primary key column value is **P11_EMPNO**. The primary key column is the column in the table that is part of the primary key. In our case it is EMPNO. Again, mind the capitals, otherwise it won't work.

6. Click the **Create Process** button. The automated row fetch has been created and you can run the page to see what happens.

How it works...

The automated row fetch is executed when the page is run but after the page header section has been generated by APEX. A row is fetched by using the primary key value stored in the page item P11_EMPNO. If this item is empty in the session state, no row will be fetched at all.

When a row is fetched, the column values are put in internal arrays (memory cache), but will not be committed into session state itself. The session state is only populated when the page is submitted (using the values stored in the page items). This has to do with performance (insert/delete session state) for example, clicking a "cancel" link.

In this case, running the page without P11_EMPNO having a value will produce a page with empty items.

Putting some validation in a form

When you fill in a form, the entered data must be validated, just to make sure that it is correct. Date fields, number fields where the number should not exceed some defined limit, items with a certain format like a telephone number or an email address, all this data has to be validated. In APEX you can use Validations to check the user input.

Getting ready

For this recipe we will use a user profiles form where the user can enter some personal information. Make sure you have access to the **app_user_profiles** table and the **app_ups_seq** sequence. You can create a user profiles form using these steps:

1. Go to your application.
2. Click **create page**.
3. Select **Form**.
4. Select **Form on a table or view**.
5. Select the table/view owner and click **next**.
6. In the table/view name field, enter **app_user_profiles**. Click **Next**.
7. Click **Next**.
8. Select **do not use tabs** and click **Next**.
9. In the primary key column 1, select **ID**. Click **Next**.
10. Select **Existing sequence**. In the sequence list box, select app_ups_seq. Click Next.
11. Select all columns and click **Next**.
12. Click **Next**.
13. Enter the page numbers APEX should navigate to if the form is submitted or cancelled. You can use the page number of the home page, mostly 1, for both. But you can also use the same page number as this page. Click **Next**.
14. Click **Finish**.

Let's put some validation on the items. We are going to put validation on birthday, e-mail, and Twitter account. For the check of the Twitter account you must first create the following procedure:

```
create or replace procedure app_search_user (p_search   in  varchar2
                                            ,p_result   out varchar2)
is
  l_request      utl_http.req;
  l_response     utl_http.resp;
  l_tweet_url    varchar2(255) := 'http://api.twitter.com/1/users/
lookup.xml';
  l_content      varchar2(255) := 'screen_name='||p_search;
  l_line         varchar2(1024);
  l_result       varchar2(100) := 'no user';
  l_user         varchar2(100) := 'your user name';
  l_password     varchar2(100) := 'your password';
begin
  -- build the request statement
  l_request   := utl_http.begin_request(url    => l_tweet_url
                                        ,method => 'POST');
  -- set header
  utl_http.set_header(r      => l_request
                     ,name   => 'Content-Length'
                     ,value  => length(l_content));
  -- authenticate the user
  utl_http.set_authentication(r        => l_request
                             ,username => l_user
                             ,password => l_password);
  -- write the content
  utl_http.write_text(r     => l_request
                     ,data  => l_content);
  -- get the response
  l_response := utl_http.get_response(r => l_request);
  begin
    loop
      utl_http.read_line(r           => l_response
                        ,data        => l_line
                        ,remove_crlf => true);
      if instr(l_line,'<screen_name>') > 0
      then
        l_result := 'user found';
      end if;
    end loop;
  exception
    when utl_http.end_of_body
```

```
    then
       null;
    end;
    utl_http.end_response(r => l_response);
    p_result := l_result;
exception
    when others then
       utl_http.end_response(r => l_response);
       p_result := 'request failed';
       raise;
end app_search_user;
/
```

[1346_01_16.txt]

This procedure makes a call to the Twitter API and searches for the twitter username which was passed through. The request sent looks like the following URL:

```
http://api.twitter.com/1/users/lookup.xml?screen_name=<twittername>
```

Here, `<twittername>` is the twitter username you are checking. The result is an XML or JSONresponse. In this case, if the Twitter username exists, the procedure gets an XML response with a tag `<screen_name>`, which holds the username. If the Twitter username does not exist, the procedure gets an XML response with an error tag. The procedure makes use of the `utl_http` package so the database user must be granted execute rights to this package. Also, it is important to define the Access Control List (ACL) if your database version is 11*g*. To grant access, log in as SYS user and execute the following procedure:

```
begin
  dbms_network_acl_admin.create_acl (
    acl           => 'utl_http.xml',
    description => 'HTTP Access',
    principal   => '<oracle username>',
    is_grant    => TRUE,
    privilege   => 'connect',
    start_date  => null,
    end_date    => null
  );

  dbms_network_acl_admin.add_privilege (
    acl           => 'utl_http.xml',
    principal   => '<oracle username>',
    is_grant    => TRUE,
    privilege   => 'resolve',
    start_date => null,
    end_date    => null
```

```
   );

dbms_network_acl_admin.assign_acl (
   acl         => 'utl_http.xml'
   host        => 'api.twitter.com'
   lower_port => 80
   upper_port => 80   );
commit;
end;
/
```

[1346_01_17.txt]

How to do it...

1. In the **Page** view, go to the **Page Processing** section and right-click on **Validating**. Select **Create Validation**.

2. Select the **Validation Level**. In our case, we choose **Item Level**.

3. Select the Birthday item.

4. In the **select a validation method** dialog, select the PL/SQL validation method.

5. In the type of **PL/SQL** validation dialog, select **PL/SQL** error.

6. The sequence number has already been issued but you can change it to your own comfort. You can also enter a name for the validation. These two fields are mandatory. In the third field, the display location, you can select where the error message should appear. Click **Next**.

7. In the **Validation Text** area, enter the following code:

```
if :Pxx_BIRTHDAY > (sysdate - numtoyminterval(13,'YEAR'))
then
    raise_application_error (-20001,'You must be at least 13 years
old to register.');
end if;
```

[1346_01_18.txt]

xx is the page number. This code checks if the entered date is greater than the current system date minus 13 years. If so, the person is younger than 13 years and is not allowed to register. In that case an error message should be issued. You can enter the error message in the error message text area. In the next step, optionally you can specify the conditions when the validation should take place.

The first validation is ready now. The next validation is the e-mail.

1. Right-click on **Validating**. Select **Create Validation**.
2. Select item level validation and click **Next**.
3. Select the e-mail item.
4. In the next step, select regular expression.
5. Check the sequence number and the name of the validation. Click **Next**.
6. In the regular expression field, enter the following:

```
([[:alnum:]]+\.?){2}@([[:alnum:]]+\.?){3,4}/?
```

With regular expressions you can force a user to conform to a certain format when entering data. You can for example check on the format of telephone numbers, URLs, dates and, in this case, correct e-mail addresses. E-mail addresses should at least have the at sign (@) and a dot (.) , like abcd@abcd.com. But an e-mail address can have more dots, and numbers are also allowed. [[:alnum:]] indicates that characters and numbers are accepted. The + sign means that it can match 1 or more times. The dot followed by the question mark indicates that a dot can match 0 or more times. The {2} indicates that it must match at least two times. Behind the at sign again, numbers, characters, and dots are allowed.

1. In the error message text area, enter the error message: **The email address is not valid**.
2. Skip the condition and click the **Create** button.

The second validation has now been created. Now let's go to the validation of the Twitter account.

1. Right-click on **Validating**. Select **'Create Validation'**.
2. Select the item level validation.
3. Select the twitter item.
4. Select the **PL/SQL** validation method.
5. Select function returning error text.
6. Enter the sequence number and a name for the validation and select where the error message should appear. Make sure that the sequence number is higher than the sequence from the previous validations. Validations are processed in the order of these sequence numbers; lowest sequence numbers are processed first.
7. In the next step, in the validation text area, enter the following code:

```
declare
  l_result varchar2(100);
begin
  app_search_user(:P15_TWITTER,l_result);
  if l_result = 'user found'
```

```
    then
      return null;
    else
      return 'no valid user';
    end if;
  end;
  [1346_01_19.txt]
```

This PL/SQL code calls the stored procedure with the twitter username as a parameter and gets a result back. If the twitter username exists, 'user found' is returned, otherwise 'no valid user' is returned. In the latter case, an error message should be issued. You can enter the error message in the error message text area.

In the conditions dialog, leave the options as they are and click the **Create** button.

How it works...

On submitting the form, APEX validates the items. In the case of the birthday, it executes the PL/SQL code where the entered birthday is checked. In the case of the e-mail address, the item containing the e-mail address is checked against the regular expression.

There's more...

You can also validate multiple rows of an item in a tabular form. If one or more rows fail validation, APEX indicates this by showing the concerned items in red with an error message in the notification area. Also, you can validate at page level.

There are different validation methods. See the following table:

Validation method	Meaning
SQL	Enter a where exists SQL query, a not exists SQL query or a SQL expression SQL query
PL/SQL	Enter a PL/SQL expression, PL/SQL error (raise application_error) a function returning Boolean or a function returning error text
Item not null	Item should not be empty
Item string comparison	Compare the value of the item with a predefined string
Regular expression	Item value should meet a certain format, like a date format (dd/mm/yyyy) or an ip address (xxx.xxx.xxx.xxx)

See also

For more information on regular expressions, go to `http://psoug.org/reference/regexp.html`

Creating a report with PL/SQL Dynamic Content

APEX offers many item types and templates to use when designing an application. Sometimes this isn't enough, for example, when you have an existing web application built with mod PL/SQL that you want to reuse.

It's possible by using built-in packages like HTP or HTF, or by using some native APEX code to create these types of pages directly in PL/SQL.

How to do it...

In this example, we are going to build a report without using any items, but only PL/SQL code.

On an empty page, create a new region:

1. Choose a PL/SQL Dynamic Content region type.
2. Name it Employees.

The PL/SQL Source is the most important part of this region. With this we will be building up the report. To show how this works, we will first create the region without any layout.

Enter the following as the PL/SQL and click **Next**, create **Region**:

```
declare
  cursor c_emp
      is
          select apex_item.hidden(1,emp.id) id
              , apex_item.display_and_save(2,emp.firstname) firstname
              , apex_item.display_and_save(2,emp.lastname) lastname
              , apex_item.display_and_save(2,emp.username) username
              , apex_item.display_and_save(2,dept.name) department
              , apex_item.display_and_save(2,job.abbreviation) job
              , apex_item.display_and_save(2,job.description) job_desc
           from app_employees emp
              , app_departments dept
              , app_jobs job
          where emp.dept_id = dept.id
            and emp.job_id  = job.id;
begin
  for r_emp in c_emp
  loop
    htp.p(r_emp.id);
    htp.p(r_emp.firstname);
```

```
        htp.p(r_emp.lastname);
        htp.p(r_emp.username);
        htp.p(r_emp.department);
        htp.p(r_emp.job);
        htp.p(r_emp.job_desc);
    end loop;
end;
```
[1346_01_20.txt]

When the page is run, all data from each employee is placed on one continuous line. To change this and make it look more like a report, we will add some HTML encoding, using the `htp` package.

Change the code inside the begin-end to the following:

```
htp.tableopen;

for r_emp in c_emp
loop
    htp.tablerowopen;
      htp.tabledata(r_emp.id);
      htp.tabledata(r_emp.firstname);
      htp.tabledata(r_emp.lastname);
      htp.tabledata(r_emp.username);
      htp.tabledata(r_emp.department);
      htp.tabledata(r_emp.job);
      htp.tabledata(r_emp.job_desc);
    htp.tablerowclose;
end loop;

htp.tableclose;
```
[1346_01_21.txt]

This looks a lot better and gives us a starting point to apply a better layout.

Dynamic content				
Steven King	sking	Sales	CEO	Chief Executive Officer
Neena Kochhar	nkochhar	IT	MGR	Manager
Lex de Haan	ldehaan	Human Resource	CLERK	Clerk
Marcel van der Plas	mvdplas	IT	CONS	Consultant
Michel van Zoest	mvzoest	IT	CONS	Consultant

Applying layout can now be done on multiple levels. For starters, the APEX_ITEM package can be used to select different item types in the cursor query. We have now used APEX_ITEM. DISPLAY_AND_SAVE to show the data as text only, but we could also use item type TEXT to make it a text field.

On a second level, we can start using classes from the CSS that is used by the application. These can be applied to the items, tables, tablerows, and so forth. How this can be done is explained in *Chapter 2 ,Themes and Templates*.

2
Themes and Templates

In this chapter, we will cover the following topics:

- ► Creating your own theme
- ► Importing a theme
- ► Creating a custom template
- ► Including images in your application
- ► Referencing CSS classes in your application
- ► Controlling the layout

Introduction

Now that we have an application we would like to give it more looks. Maybe the application has to adhere to certain corporate layout standards. Or maybe you just want to add some more colors. Using themes and templates it is possible to give your application some cosmetic changes. A theme is a collection of templates and a template is a collection of components ranging from pages and reports to controls like calendars. A template consists of a header template, a body template, and a footer template. A template also contains some sub-templates, for example, for the success message.

In this chapter, we will present some recipes which will make your application look better.

Creating your own theme

When working with themes, there are some important things to know. First of all, there is the theme export SQL file in which all templates of the theme are included. Second there are the images that belong to your theme. And third, there are the `.css` files. CSS is an abbreviation of Cascading Style Sheet and describes the style of the elements in a web page. For example, the font of the text or the color of the background. In the stylesheet there are also references to images. It is important that the references in these files are correct, otherwise you will see no style at all, just plain text.

When you want to create your own theme you can do two things: start from scratch or copy an existing theme and adapt it. Starting from scratch is more work as you have to create all the templates as well. Copying and modifying an existing theme costs less time but if you have to change a lot in order to get the desired layout, you might as well start from scratch.

Getting ready

If you use the embedded PL/SQL gateway to run APEX, you must have FTP access to the host where APEX resides. You can enable FTP by specifying the FTP port. Log in to SQLplus as sys or system and execute the following query:

```
Select dbms_xdb.getftpport() from dual;
getftpport.sql
```

The result should be a number, like 2100. In that case, that is the port to which you can connect with your FTP client. You need the database system account with the system password to connect to FTP. If the result is 0, there is no port open and you have to set the port number. You can do that with the following command:

```
Exec Dbms_xdb.setftpport(2100);
setftpport.sql
```

In this example, you set the FTP port number to 2100. You can choose the port number by yourself but be aware that if you choose the standard port 21, you might encounter problems if another FTP service is running on the host.

By the way, you can also get and set the HTTP port number. The HTTP port number is used to access APEX. Instead of `getftpport()` and `setftpport()`, you use `gethttpport()` and `sethttpport()`.

To access the FTP, use an FTP client like FileZilla. Use the following parameters:

Parameter	Value
Host	Name of the database host
Port	2100
Server type	FTP
Login type	Normal
User	System
Password	<your system password>

When you log in to the FTP, go to the images directory. It is possible that you see other directories starting with images and a number which obviously looks like a date and a sequence number. Those are the image directories from previous releases from APEX and it means that your current APEX version has been upgraded.

In the images directory, you can see the themes directories. There you can make your own new theme by adding a directory in which you can upload your images and .css stylesheets.

In this recipe, we will use an existing theme and adapt it to our own standards. For this recipe make sure Theme 18 is installed. Theme 18 is a simple theme which you can find in the repository. If you haven't installed it, do it now:

1. In the application builder, go to the application you are working on. In the application go to the **Shared Components**.

2. In the shared components, go to the **Themes**. You can find the themes in the user interface section.

3. In the themes page, click the **Create** button.

4. Select **From the repository** and click **Next**.

5. Select theme 18 and proceed to the next step.

6. In the last step, confirm by clicking the **Create** button.

How to do it...

1. First we have to make an export of the theme you want to copy. So go to **Application | Shared components | Themes** and click **Export theme**. You can find export theme on the right side of the screen, under tasks.

2. In the next step, in the **Export theme** list box, select theme 18. In the file format list box, you can enter UNIX or DOS. If you are using Microsoft Windows as your computer's operating system, select DOS and click on the export theme button. If you use Linux or UNIX as your operating system, select UNIX. Click on the **Export theme** button.

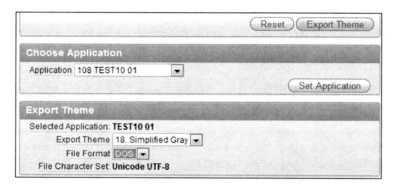

The theme will now be downloaded as an SQL file and you will be asked to enter a directory where the file will be stored.

3. Next, create a directory on your local filesystem. We will call the new theme `theme_115` so create a directory with that name.

4. Open your FTP client and log on to the localhost.

5. Go to the `directory /images/themes/theme_18` and transfer (download) the contents to your local directory called **theme_115**.

6. In the CSS files, replace all occurrences of **t18** with **t115** and save the files. Don't forget to check if the references in the stylesheets are pointing to the newly created theme directory.

7. Locate the exported theme (it is an SQL file) and open it. Replace `theme_18` with `theme_115`, replace `t18` with `t115` and save the file under the name `theme_115.sql`.

8. Transfer (upload) the entire directory `theme_115` to the FTP server under the `directory /images/themes`. So after the upload you should see a directory theme_115 on the host, like in the following screenshot:

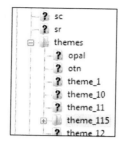

9. In the application builder, go to your application and click **Export/Import**.

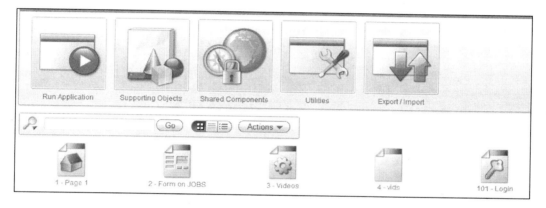

10. Select **Import** and proceed to the next step.

11. In the import file item, enter the filename of the theme (SQL file) you just modified. In our case it is `theme_115.sql`. You can also use the search button to locate and select the file.

12. At the file type list box, select **Theme Export**. Click **Next**. The theme will be imported.

13. After the import has been successful, the new theme has to be installed to use it. So, click **Next**.

14. In the last step, you will be asked to enter the application where the new theme has to be installed. Furthermore, you can opt between **Replace existing theme** and **Create new theme**. Select **Create new theme** and click the **Install theme** button.

15. Now, the new theme has been created but it probably does not have the ID 115. In that case you can modify the theme ID. In the theme page, click **Change Identification Number** on the right side of the screen, under **Tasks**. You can then select the theme and the new ID you would like to assign. In this case, that would be 115. Click **Next**.

16. To confirm, click the **Change theme ID** button in the last step.

Your theme is now ready to use and as a last step, you must switch to the new theme:

1. Go to the **Themes** page.
2. Click the **Switch theme** button.
3. In the **Switch to theme** list box, select the new theme and click **Next**.
4. If everything is OK (the status column shows **OK** checks) you can click **Next** and switch theme to confirm. If there is something wrong, for example missing templates (this can happen if an existing application has a reference to a template class which doesn't exist in the newly applied theme), the status will show error for the type of template which is missing. In that case, check if everything is complete or select another theme.

Your newly created theme is now active. Run the application to see what it looks like. Actually, you should see no change compared to the theme 18, as you just made a copy of theme 18.

How it works...

We made an export of a theme and imported it under another name into APEX. We also created a new directory with the images and the CSS files in it. So far nothing special, it is actually a copy of the other theme. But now we can adapt this new theme and add our own style to it, leaving the original theme intact.

Importing a theme

The themes that come with APEX offer enough different styles and layouts to give your application a unique and satisfying look. However, if your application must conform to a specific corporate layout or your application must look the same as another APEX application you can import a theme. APEX offers an easy way to import and use a theme. You can find several themes (free or commercial) on the Internet.

Getting ready

Make sure you have already downloaded the theme and put it on your filesystem.

How to do it...

1. In the application builder, go to the application you are working on.
2. Click the **Export/Import** button.

   Select **Import**. In the next step, enter the name and path of the theme. You can also use the find button to locate the file. An APEX import or export theme file is just a `.sql` file. You can even view the contents of the file. It should begin with something like this:

```
set define off
set verify off
set serveroutput on size 1000000
set feedback off
WHENEVER SQLERROR EXIT SQL.SQLCODE ROLLBACK
begin wwv_flow.g_import_in_progress := true; end;
/

--        AAAA      PPPPP    EEEEE  XX      XX
--       AA  AA     PP  PP   EE      XX    XX
--      AA    AA    PP  PP   EE       XX  XX
--     AAAAAAAAAA   PPPPP    EEEE      XXXX
--     AA      AA   PP       EE       XX  XX
--    AA        AA  PP       EE      XX    XX
--    AA        AA  PP       EEEEE   XX      XX
prompt   Set Credentials...

begin

   -- Assumes you are running the script connected to SQL*Plus as the Oracle use
   wwv_flow_api.set_security_group_id(p_security_group_id=>990412166842593);

end;
/

begin wwv_flow.g_import_in_progress := true; end;
/
begin

select value into wwv_flow_api.g_nls_numeric_chars from nls_session_parameters

end;

/
begin execute immediate 'alter session set nls_numeric_characters='',.''';

end;
```

3. In the file type radio group, select **Theme Export**. Optionally, you can select the file character set but most of the time Unicode UTF-8 is sufficient. Click **Next**. The file will be imported.

4. If the file has been successfully imported, you get a successful message. This does not mean that you can use it already. The theme has to be installed first. Click **Next** to install now.

5. In the next step, you can click on the **Install into application** list box to select the application where it has to be installed. Click on the **Install theme** button.

6. After successfully installing the theme, you will see the other installed themes. The active theme is marked with an asterisk (*). If you want to make the newly installed theme the current one, click on the **Switch theme** button in the upper-right corner.

7. In the switch to theme list box, select the desired theme. Click **Next**.

8. In the next step you get an overview of the templates and the status of the templates. If there is any problem check the templates and the classes. If everything is ok, click the **Next** button.

9. In the last step, click **Switch theme** to confirm. You can now run your application to see what it looks like.

How it works...

A theme consists of templates. There are nine different types of templates:

1. Breadcrumb
2. Button
3. Calendar
4. Label
5. List
6. Page
7. Popup lov
8. Region
9. Report

In the template you can edit the contents. You can make more templates of a certain type. For example, you can make two templates of type label. However, only one can be set as default for use in an application. Up till APEX 3.2, APEX makes use of an HTML table with the `<td>`, `</td>`, `<tr>` and the `</tr>` tags. As from version 4.0, APEX also uses div-based templates. It will load pages faster with better accessibility.

In a template you see substitution strings, keywords between pound signs (#), which Oracle replaces on rendering. Examples of substitution strings are title, user, and error message. The substitution strings appear in the form of:

`#SUBSTITUTION STRING#`

So with the pound signs at the beginning and the end of the string and in uppercase. For example the substitution string `#TITLE#` will be replaced with the title of the page, and `#REGION_POSITION_02#` will be replaced by the contents of the region where the display point (you can find it under the user interface section on the region definition) is set to region position 2.

Creating a custom template

When you create a theme from scratch, you also have to link the templates to the theme. You can copy templates from another theme to your newly created theme. But you can also create new templates from scratch. We will create a new template in this recipe.

Getting ready

We can go on with theme 115 that we made in the first recipe, so make sure you already created this theme.

How to do it...

1. In the application builder, go to the application you are working on. After that, go to the **Shared components**.

2. In the shared components page, click **Templates**.

3. Click the **Create** button to start the wizard.

4. In the next step you see nine types of templates. Select the **Region template**.

5. Click **From scratch** and click the **Next** button.

6. Enter a name for this new template, that is, **cust_rep_reg**. You can also select the theme this new template should be part of. And finally, select the template class. In our case, we select the **Reports** region. Click the **Create** button to finish the wizard.

Region				
	Borderless Region	0	-	-
	Borderless Region	0	35 hours ago	admin
	Bracketed Region	0	-	-
	Bracketed Region	0	35 hours ago	admin
	Breadcrumb Region	1	-	-
	Breadcrumb Region	0	35 hours ago	admin
	Button Region with Title	0	-	-
	Button Region with Title	0	35 hours ago	admin
	Button Region without Title	0	-	-
	Button Region without Title	0	35 hours ago	admin
	Chart List	0	-	-
	Chart Region	0	-	-
	Chart Region	0	35 hours ago	admin
	cust_rep_reg	0	2 minutes ago	admin
	Form Region	2	-	-

7. The new template has now been created and you can see it in the list. Edit the new template by clicking on the template name (**cust_rep_reg**).

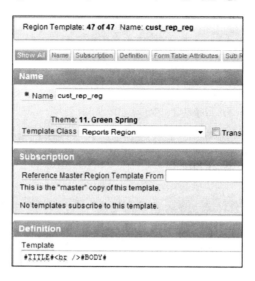

8. You can use HTML in combination with the substitution strings to create a layout. Oracle replaces the substitution strings with the component values. You can find the substitution string at the bottom of the page:

9. You can use the following example to enter in the definition section:

```
<table class="t115Region" id="#REGION_STATIC_ID#" #REGION_
ATTRIBUTES# border="0" cellpadding="0" cellspacing="0" summary=""
width="97%" style="border:none;">
<tbody class="ReportsRegion">
<tr>
<th class="t115RegionHeader">#TITLE#</th>
<th class="t115ButtonHolderHeader" width="100%">#CLOSE#  
;#PREVIOUS##NEXT# #DELETE##EDIT##CHANGE##CREATE##CREATE2##EXP
AND##COPY##HELP#</th>
</tr>
<tr>
<td class="t115RegionBody" colspan="2" bgcolor="lightgrey">#BODY#<
/td>
</tr>
</tbody>
</table>
```

[T115region.txt]

This template code is a copy of the original code from theme 18, but with the background color set to light grey.

Substitution strings should be written in uppercase and should begin and end with a #-sign. As from APEX 4.0, new templates use the `<div>` tag. The older templates from APEX 3.2 and before used the `<table>` - `<tr>` - `<td>` tags.

10. Click the **Apply changes** button.

11. If you want to use the new template, you have to change the pages/regions which will use this new template. Suppose you have a page with a tabular form. Click on the page you want to edit.

12. Click on the region you want to edit.

13. In the template list box, select the new template, **cust_rep_reg**. You can find the template list box in the user interface section.

14. Click the **Apply changes** button. The region will now use this new template.

There's more...

You can make your newly created template the default template for that specific component type. Just go to the **Shared components** page, go to the themes, and select the theme you want to edit. On the right side of the screen, under **Tasks**, click **Edit theme**. You will see the component defaults. In the region list box, select the new template. Click the **Apply changes** button. The new template is now the default for the region component type.

Including images in your application

A web application will look better when you use images. Of course, APEX 4.0 supports the use of images in web pages. You can easily upload images to the APEX host with your FTP client. To connect to the APEX host, see the description at the beginning of this chapter. You should copy your images to the images directory. APEX uses a shortcut or prefix for this path. Mostly it is /i/ but you can change that. Go to shared components and click on the edit definition link on the right side of the screen, under **Application**. In the name section you can find this image prefix text item where you can modify the prefix. It is advised to always use the substitution string #IMAGE_PREFIX# instead of /i/ when referring to images in templates or button images to safeguard the URI to the images when modifying the virtual directory on the HTTP server (EPG or Apache).

There is another way to upload images to the APEX environment. In the application builder, go to the application you are working on. Click on the **Shared components** icon. In the **Files** section, click on the **Images** link. You have workspace and application images.

Getting ready

1. First you have to import the images into the APEX environment.
2. There are two ways to import images. We will discuss the images upload via APEX.
3. Go to the application builder and select an application.
4. Click on the **Shared components** icon.
5. Click on the **Images** link in the files section at the bottom of the screen.
6. Click on the **Create** button.
7. In the next step, you can choose whether the image should be available just for one application or for the entire workspace. If you want your image to be available throughout the entire workspace, leave the application list box to no application associated. Otherwise, select an application. We want the image to be available to the entire workspace, so select **No application associated** in the **Application** list box. Click the **File** button to locate and select the image to be uploaded from your file system.
8. Click the **Upload** button to upload the image. The image will be uploaded and after that you see the icon of the image to indicate that the image file has been successfully uploaded.
9. If you want more images to be uploaded, repeat these steps.

How to do it...

First, let's include an image of the company's logo. To include a logo in the top-left corner, follow these steps:

1. In the application builder, go to the shared components by clicking the **Shared components** icon.

2. Click the **Edit definition** link on the right side of the screen, under application.

3. Go to the **Logo** section and select **Image** as the **Logo Type**.

4. In the logo text field, enter the name of the image. It can be any image file type like a Bitmap (.bmp), a JPEG (.jpg), a PNG (.png) or a GIF (.gif) file. The image filename should be prefixed #IMAGE_PREFIX# when the image resides as an external resource, #APP_IMAGES# when uploaded as application image and #WORKSPACE_ IMAGES# when uploaded as workspace image. We uploaded a workspace image so prefix the image filename with #WORKSPACE_IMAGES#.

5. In the **Logo Attributes** text field, you can define the width and height of the image. The logo area in the top-left corner is a fixed height area so if your image is too large, you might set the width and height. In this case, we set it to the following:

```
Width="200" height="30"
```
[Img_size.txt]

6. Run the page. You should see a logo, something like this:

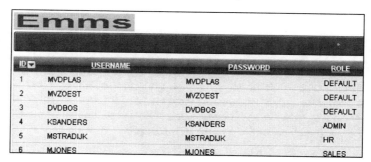

Now we will include an image in a region, just for the illustration.

Suppose you have an HTML region, you can use the following to show an image:

```
<img src="#WORKSPACE_IMAGES#emms.GIF">
```
[Img_wsi_emms.txt]

How it works...

If you uploaded the image with an application specified, you can use #APP_IMAGES# as well:

```
<img src="#APP_IMAGES#emms.GIF">
```

[Img_ai_emms.txt]

However, if you uploaded the image for the workspace, so with no application specified, you can only use #WORKSPACE_IMAGES#.

If you uploaded the images to the images directory using FTP, you can use #IMAGE_PREFIX#. This is a substitution string for the images directory or /i/ if you specified the image prefix.

There's more...

You can also include images by specifying the complete URL from another website. Create a HTML region and include the following in the region source:

```
<img src="http://www.example.com/frontpageimage.jpg">
```

[Img_ex.txt]

Where http://www.example.com/frontpageimage.jpg is the reference to an image on a host. Be careful though, as some website owners don't like it when images on their webpages are used on another webpage. Loading images can be very bandwidth consuming, which in the end can lead to extra costs for the website owners.

When you upload images to APEX, the images are stored in the database. When you use images copied via FTP or copied to the webserver, the files are actually physically there. However, the images that are stored on the webserver load faster and can be cached by the browser.

Referencing CSS classes in your application

Cascading Stylesheets offer an easy way to quickly change the look and feel of a web application. They hold information about colors, sizes, borders, and fonts. Working with stylesheets is a good way to separate the style and the actual content of a webpage. The HTML document should only contain text and HTML tags.

In this recipe, we will make a simple stylesheet, upload it to the APEX environment, and use it in our application. We will change the buttons and the background of the region. All this is done by referencing classes in the stylesheet.

Getting ready

We will use the user profiles page we made in Chapter 1, so make sure this page is ready. For the buttons we will use other background images. You can make them yourself or you can copy some from the Internet (mind the copyrights). You can find them anywhere. Make sure these buttons have the same size as the original buttons. Once you have made the images you have to upload them using the FTP client. Copy the images to the /images/ directory.

For this example, we will use theme 1. If you haven't installed theme 1 yet, follow these steps:

1. Go to the **shared components**.

2. In the user interface section, click the **themes** link.

3. Click the **Create** button.

4. Select **From the repository** and click **Next**.

5. Select **theme 1**.

6. Click the **Create** button. The theme will now be created but it still isn't the active theme, so click the **Switch theme** button.

7. In the **Switch to theme** list box, select **theme 1** and click **Next**.

8. In the next dialog you see the templates and the status. If the status is OK for all templates, click **Next**.

9. In the last step, click the **Switch theme** button. Theme 1 is now the active theme and this is indicated by an asterisk (*) near the theme.

How to do it...

1. Create a new text file and put the following in it:

```
.bgregion {
border: 1px solid;
background-color:lightblue;
}

button {
border: 0;
cursor: pointer;
font-weight: normal;
padding: 0 10px 0 0;
text-align: center;
}

button span {
position: relative;
```

```
display: block;
white-space: nowrap;
font-size: 13px;
padding: 0 4px 0 15px;
}

button.button_custom {
background: transparent url('../images/rb_a.GIF') no-repeat scroll
top right;
color: black;
display: block;
float: left;
font: normal 12px arial, sans-serif;
font-face:bold;
height: 24px;
margin-right: 6px;
padding-right: 18px; /* sliding doors padding */
text-decoration: none;
}

button.button_custom span {
background: transparent url('../images/rb_span.GIF') no-repeat;
display: block;
line-height: 14px;
padding: 5px 0 5px 18px;
}
```
[buttons.css]

2. Save the file and give it a name, that is, `custom_theme.css`.

3. In the application builder, go to the application you are working on.

4. Click on the **Shared components** icon.

5. In the **Files** section, click on the **Cascading style sheets** link.

6. Click the **Create** button.

7. In the next step, click on the **File** button.

8. A file dialog appears. Locate your created custom theme stylesheet and select this file.

9. You can also enter some comments in the notes text area. After that, click the **Upload** button.

10. The stylesheet will be uploaded and if you have succeeded, you will see an icon with the name **custom_theme.css**.

11. Go to the application and click on the **Userprofiles** page.

12. In the page section, click on the **Edit** icon (the pencil on the upper right corner).

13. Click **Show all**.

14. In the HTML header and body attribute section, enter the following in the HTML header text area:

```
<link href="#WORKSPACE_IMAGES#custom_theme.css" rel="stylesheet"
type="text/css">
```
[Link_css.txt]

15. This tag will be included in the webpage so that we can reference the styles from the stylesheet. Click the **Apply changes** button.

16. In the **Templates** section, click on the region template.

17. Replace **rc-content-main** with **bgregion**. You can find **rc-content-main** in the div just before the #BODY# substitution string.

18. Click the **apply changes** button.

19. Click on the button template.

20. In the definition section, replace **button-gray** with **button_custom** in the template text area.

21. Click the **Apply changes** button.

22. Run the page. You should see other buttons and a light blue background.

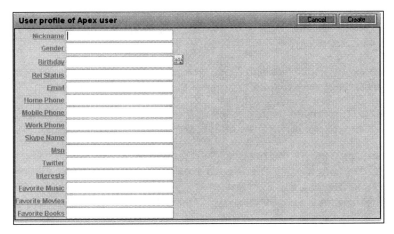

How it works...

In the HTML tags, you can reference to the stylesheet. This can be done in three ways:

1. Declare tags in the stylesheet, such as :

```
H1{font-family: verdana, arial; font-size: 200%; color: darkblue}
```
[Font_verdana.css]

2. This causes every <H1> tag in the HTML document to be formatted with an Arial-like font, a font-size of 200%, and in the color dark blue.

3. Name the objects in the HTML document and give it the same name as declared in the stylesheet:

   ```
   #reportarea {background-color:lightyellow}
   ```
   [Bg_ly.css]

4. Include a `div` in your HTML document and name it `reportarea`:

   ```
   <div id="reportarea">some text</div>
   ```
   [Div_reportarea.txt]

5. This causes to display a `div` with a light yellow background.

6. Reference by using classes

7. Declare a class in the stylesheet:

   ```
   .divbackground{border: 1px solid;
   background-image:url(background.gif);
   background-position:left top;}
   ```
   [div_bkg.css]

8. Include a `div` in your HTML document and use the class attribute to reference to `divbackground`:

   ```
   <div class="divbackground">some text</div>
   ```
   [Div_class_bkg.txt]

This displays a div with a solid line and a background image with the name `background.gif`. The image starts at the upper-left corner of the div.

In our webpage, we referenced using classes in the stylesheet. First, we referenced to the `bgregion` class and for the buttons we referenced the `button_custom` class.

There are two images used for the buttons. The first image, `bg_span.gif` is the actual background with the button label. The second image, `bg_a.gif` will be put on the right side of the first image. In this way, you will see two images that together look like one button. In this way, the button width is variable and dependent on the length of the label.

Be careful when you switch to another theme. You will possibly lose your template settings. You can avoid this by exporting the theme.

Controlling the layout

One of the most difficult tasks of web programming is the control of the layout. In previous versions of APEX, tables were used to place the items on the desired positions. You can use an HTML editor to see a preview of the layout. As from APEX 4.0, new themes are introduced that use divs to position the different components. Divs are almost necessary to be able to use dynamic actions layout. The biggest advantage from div-based layout over table-based layout is that you can precisely position components of the webpage.

In this recipe, we will create a page with a report region showing the application users and a chart region with the number of roles used. The two regions will be displayed next to each other.

Getting ready

Just make sure that theme 1 is the active theme.

How to do it...

1. In the application builder, go to your application.

2. Click the **Create page** button.

3. Select **Report** and in the next step, select **Classic report**.

4. Leave the page number or assign a number yourself and enter a name for the page. Click **Next**.

5. Select **Do not use tabs** and click **Next**.

6. In the text area, enter the following query:

```
select id
     ,      username
     ,      password
     ,      role
from   app_users;
[select_app_users.sql]
```

7. Click **Next**.

8. Enter a name for the region (that is, **Users**) and click **Next**.

9. In the last step, click the **Finish** button.

10. Your page has now successfully been created and you see a success message.

11. Click the **Edit page** icon.

12. In the regions section, click the **Add** icon in the upper right corner of the section.

13. Select **Chart**.

14. In the next step, select **HTML chart**.

15. In the title text item, enter **User roles**. Click **Next**.

16. In the query text area, enter the following query:

```
select null link
,       role label
,       count(id) value
from    app_users
group by role
[select_aur_role.sql]
```

    You can also use the query builder. Click the build query button to start a wizard which helps you to create your query.

17. Click the **Create region** button.

18. The region will be created and you now have two regions. When you run the page, you will see that the chart region is positioned below the **Users** region. Maybe you want to place the region next to the Users region. That can be done in several ways.

19. Click the **Edit page** button at the bottom of the page.

20. In the **Regions** section, click on the **User roles** link to edit the region.

21. In the user interface section, select **2** in the **Column list** box.

22. Click the **Apply changes** button and run the page to see how it looks.

23. You can see that the regions are displayed next to one another. There is also another way to control the position of the regions.

24. Click the **Edit page** button at the bottom of the page.

25. In the templates section, click on the **Page template** link.

26. In the definition section you see HTML code for the header, the body, and the footer of the page. To see how this actually looks you could use an HTML editor and copy-paste the code in the editor. However, you can also get a preview of the template. Click on the **Preview template** link in the tasks section on the right side. You can see a preview that is a little bit more clear when you go to the page, click on the **User** roles link in the regions section, and click on the flashlight that is located after the **Display** point list box in the User interface section.

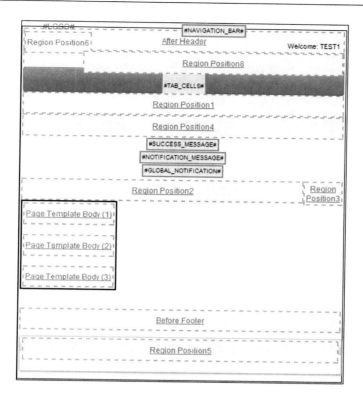

In this preview for theme 1, you can see the region position 2 and region position 3 are positioned next to each other but that region position 3 is smaller. Let's see how this looks when we position the chart region on region position 3:

1. Close the preview pop-up window and go back to your page.

2. In the regions section, click on the **Users region** to edit the region.

3. In the user interface section, select **Page template region position 2** in the **Display Point** list box.

4. Click the **Apply changes** button.

5. In the regions section, click on the **User roles** link to edit the region.

6. In the user interface section, select **Page template region position 3** in the **Display Point** list box. Select **1** in the **Column** list box (we changed this to 2 in the beginning of this recipe). Click the **Apply changes** button.

7. Run the page and see what the page looks like.

How it works...

The screenshot shown in the previous paragraph shows the various positions in the region. You can also see these positions in the display point list box in the user interface section when you click on a region in the application builder.

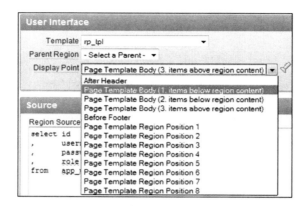

In this way you can control where the content of a region is displayed. If you position two regions at the same position, like we first did in this recipe, the last region will be displayed below the first region. You can put them next to each other by using the column list box, which you can find behind the display point list box in the user interface section. The first region will be positioned in column 1 and the second region will be positioned in column 2.

There's more...

Alternatively, you can change the entire layout, just by changing the HTML code in the template. So, if you would like to display the success message at the bottom of the page, go to the definition section of the template and enter the substitution string #SUCCESS_MESSAGE# in the footer text area.

By the way, did you notice that in theme 1, region position 5 by default is displayed twice, one time in the body and the second time in the footer? This means that if you set a region's display point to region position 5, you will see this region twice!

3
Extending APEX

In this chapter, we will cover:

- ► Adding JavaScript code to your application
- ► Creating a tag cloud with AJAX
- ► Creating visual effects with JavaScript libraries
- ► Enhancing your application with the Google API
- ► Including Google maps
- ► Embedding multimedia objects in your application
- ► Creating a region selector
- ► Sending mail via APEX
- ► Uploading and downloading files
- ► Calling APEX from an Oracle form

Introduction

In the first two chapters, we described the tasks to create a basic APEX web application. In this chapter, we will extend our application with some nice features such as visual effects, a tag cloud, and a Google map.

Many of these features are made possible with the use of JavaScript. JavaScript enables dynamic features such as dynamic list of values, drag and drop functionality, different effects on popping-up and disappearing of items.

Since APEX 4.0, many of these JavaScript features can be built using plug-ins. However, for some features you still need to use JavaScript. By the way, you also need to have good knowledge of JavaScript if you want to make use of the extensive possibilities of Google maps.

Adding JavaScript code to your application

JavaScript can also be used for client validation. We will build a validation on the salary field. When the user raises the salary by more than 10 percent, an alert box will appear where the user can confirm the salary.

Getting ready

Make sure you have a tabular form based on the EMP table. At least the salary column should be present in the form.

How to do it...

1. In the application builder, go to the page based on the EMP table.
2. In the regions section, click on the **edit Report** link.

3. Click on the **edit icon** (the pencil) near the salary column.

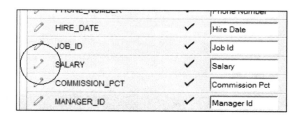

4. In the column attributes section, enter the following in the **element attributes** text field:

```
onfocus=remember_oldsal(this.value); onchange=validate_
sal(this.id,this.value);
```
[1346_03_01.txt]

5. Click the **Apply changes** button and after that, click the **Apply changes** button again.
6. In the page section, click the **edit** icon.

7. In the HTML header and body attribute section, enter the following in the HTML header text area:

```
<script type="text/javascript">
  var oldsal = 0;
  function remember_oldsal(salary)
  {
    oldsal = salary;
  }

  function validate_sal(sal_id, salary)
  {
    if (salary > (oldsal * 1.10))
    {
      var r = confirm("Are you sure you want to change this salary
                                              to " + salary);
      if (r == false)
      {
        $("#"+sal_id).val(oldsal);
      }
    }
  }
</script>
```

[1346_03_02.txt]

The header now contains two JavaScript scripts and one variable declaration. This variable declaration is necessary because if the variable had been declared in a function, it wouldn't have been accessible. The function REMEMBER_OLDSAL copies the salary when the user navigates to the salary field. The function VALIDATE_SAL calculates the old salary raised by 10 percent and if the new salary is greater than the old salary plus 10 percent, a pop-up alert is displayed. If the cancel button is clicked (r == false), the value of the variable oldsal is copied to the salary column. Otherwise, do nothing and leave the newly entered salary.

8. Click the **Apply changes** button.

9. Run the form and see what happens if you change a salary by more than 10 percent.

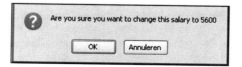

How it works...

Everything you put in the HTML header will be presented in the HTML header of the page. You can see this by right-clicking on the page and selecting view source. You will then see the HTML code which is used to present the page. On the top of the code, you can see your JavaScript code.

The JavaScript functions can be called from objects in the webpage. For example, you can call a JavaScript function when the user navigates to a text item or when the body of a webpage is loaded.

Items can be identified by an ID or a name and you can get or set the value of items with the jQuery function $("#ITEM").val(), like:

```
Variable = $("#P18_ID").val();
```

Before APEX 4, you had to use:

```
Variable = document.getElementById(id).value;
```

You can also put values into the items with this function:

```
$("#P18_ID").val(5000);
```

Or, before APEX 4:

```
document.getElementById(id).value = 5000;
```

And you can also use the jQuery syntax to copy values between items:

```
$("#P18_NAME").val($("#P18_TEXT").val());
```

In APEX you can add a call to a JavaScript function in the element attributes of the item.

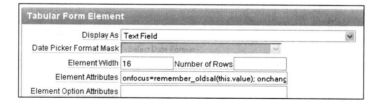

There's more...

There are various ways to include JavaScript code in the page. You can put JavaScript code in the HTML header of the page or the region but you can also put some JavaScript code in the item. Go to the item and type your code in the HTML section.

Since APEX 4, working with JavaScript has been made easy with the use of dynamic actions, region display selectors and plug-ins. This recipe is included to show how JavaScript works in APEX but if you can, use the new features. They will save you a lot of work.

Creating a tag cloud with AJAX

AJAX is an abbreviation of **Asynchronous JavaScript and XML**. AJAX is a method of communication between a client and the server where the website resides. AJAX makes it possible to dynamically respond to actions on the client side. For example, it is possible to directly check an e-mail address while you are typing! Or set the color of an object when clicking on another object. AJAX is mostly used to dynamically fetch data from the server to use in the webpage.

Until APEX 4.0, using AJAX in your webpage was really advanced programming with JavaScript. As from APEX 4.0, it is a lot easier to use AJAX with the help of dynamic actions. We will make a page with a tag cloud and a region where you can see the news articles. When you click on a tag in the tag cloud, APEX will show the articles which are related to the selected tag. This information is an AJAX call and is implemented using a dynamic action.

Getting ready

We will create a new page. Make sure you have created and have access to the tables APP_NEWS, APP_TAGS, and APP_TGS_NWS.

How to do it...

1. Go to your application and click the **Create page** button.
2. Select **Blank page**.
3. Enter a page alias, for example **tagnews**. Click **Next**.
4. Enter a name for the page. For example **News articles by tags**. Click **Next**.
5. Select **No**. Click **Next**.
6. Click **Finish**.
7. Click the **Edit page icon**.
8. In the regions section, click the **Add icon**.
9. Select **PL/SQL dynamic content**.
10. Enter a title for the region, in this case **Tag cloud**. Click **Next**.

11. In the PL/SQL source text area, enter the following code:

```
declare
  --
  cursor c_tags is
    select tns.tgs_id
    ,       tgs.tag
    ,       count(tns.tgs_id) num_of_times
    from   app_tgs_nws tns
    ,       app_tags    tgs
    where  tgs.id = tns.tgs_id
    group by tns.tgs_id, tgs.tag
    order by 1;
  --
  l_min_num number(3);
  l_max_num number(3);
  l_size    number(2);
  l_multiplx number(2);
begin
  select min(num_of_times) min_num
  ,       max(num_of_times) max_num
  into   l_min_num, l_max_num
  from   (select tns.tgs_id
          ,       tgs.tag
          ,       count(tns.tgs_id) num_of_times
          from   app_tgs_nws tns
          ,       app_tags    tgs
          where  tgs.id = tns.tgs_id
          group by tns.tgs_id, tgs.tag);
  --
  l_multiplx := round(72/l_max_num);
  --
  for r_tags in c_tags
  loop
    l_size := round(l_multiplx * r_tags.num_of_times);
    sys.htp.print (q'!<a onmouseover="this.style.
cursor='pointer';" onclick=document.getElementById("PXX_TAG").
value="!'||r_tags.tag||'";
style="font-size:'||to_char(l_size)||'px; text-decoration:
none;">'||r_tags.tag||'</a>');
    sys.htp.print ('  ');
  end loop;
end;
```

[1346_03_05.txt]

Replace XX in PXX_TAG with the page number. The `onmouseover` event is necessary to change the cursor as if it were pointing to a link. The `onclick` event copies the value of the tag that is clicked on to the hidden item PXX_TAG. This is needed to build the query. The item will be referenced in the dynamic action. But first, we need to create the item.

1. Click the **create region** button. The tag cloud region is now ready. Now we will create the hidden item.

2. In the items section, click the **add icon**.

3. Select **hidden**. Click **next**.

4. In the item name text item, enter the name PXX_TAG where XX is the page number you are creating. You can see the page number in the first line in the create item section.

5. In the region list box, select the tag cloud region you just selected. Click **Next two times**.

6. Click the **Create item** button. The hidden item is ready. Now we will create the region for the news articles.

7. In the regions section, click the **add** icon.

8. Select **HTML**.

9. Again, select **HTML** and click **next**.

10. Enter a title for the region, for example **Related articles**. Click **Next**.

11. Leave the region source empty and click the **Create region** button.

12. The last step is the creation of the dynamic action.

    In the dynamic actions sections, click the **add** icon.

13. Select **Advanced**.

14. Enter a name for this action, for example **show_articles**. Click **Next**.

15. In the event list box, select **Click**.

16. In the selection type list box, select **Region**.

17. In the region list box, select the **tag cloud** region. Click **Next**.

18. In the action list box, select **Set value**. A settings section appears.

19. In the set type list box, select **PL/SQL function body**.

20. In the PL/SQL function body text area, enter the following code:

```
declare
cursor c_nws is
select title
,      text
from   app_news
where  upper(text) like '%'||upper(:PXX_TAG)||'%';
--
```

```
l_text varchar2(32000) := '';
begin
for r_nws in c_nws
loop
l_text := l_text || '<h1>' || r_nws.title || '</h1>';
l_text := l_text || '<br>';
l_text := l_text || replace(r_nws.text,:PXX_TAG,'<b>'||:PXX_
TAG||'</b>');
l_text := l_text || '<br>';
l_text := l_text || '<br>';
end loop;
return l_text;
end;
[1346_03_06.txt]
```

Replace the xx in the :PXX_TAG by the page number. This script loops through the records of a query. The query selects the records where the text contains the tag the user clicked on. The results of the query are displayed using the htp.p function.

1. In the page items to submit text field, enter **PXX_TAG** where XX is the page number.

2. In the Escape Special Characters list box, select **No**. Click **Next**.

    In the next step we must set the affected objects.

3. In the selection type list box, select region. In the region list box, select the **HTML region (related articles)**. Click the **Create** button.

4. In the processes section, click the **Add** icon.

5. Select **PL/SQL**. Click **Next**.

6. Enter a name for the PL/SQL process, for example **populate_tags**.

7. In the point list box, select **On Load – Before Header**. Click **Next**.

8. In the PL/SQL text area, enter the following code:

```
declare
  cursor c_app_tags
  is
    select id
    ,      tag
    from   app_tags
    order by id;
  --
  cursor c_instr(b_tag in varchar2)
  is
    select id
    ,      instr(upper(text),upper(b_tag)) tag_found
    from   app_news;
```

```
begin
  delete from app_tgs_nws;
  --
  for r_app_tags in c_app_tags
  loop
    for r_instr in c_instr(r_app_tags.tag)
    loop
      if r_instr.tag_found > 0
      then
        insert into app_tgs_nws
        values (r_app_tags.id,r_instr.id);
      end if;
    end loop;
  end loop;
  --
  commit;
end;
```
[1346_03_25.txt]

This piece of code populates the intersection table between APP_NWS and APP_TAGS. First the table is truncated, and then the code loops through the text of the APP_NWS table to search for the tags from the table APP_TAGS. If it finds a match, a row is inserted into the APP_TGS_NWS table. This process is started each time the user enters this page. In this way, changes in the APP_NWS table are immediately visible. So when a row is inserted into the APP_NWS table with a text which contains something like "APEX", the tag cloud will show the APEX tag bigger. Click the **Create process** button.

The page is now ready. Run the page and see how the articles change when you click on a tag.

How it works...

We use the <a> tag where we put some extra JavaScript code. First there is the onmouseover event, which changes the cursor style to pointer (the "hand"). Second there is the onclick event, which copies the tag to the hidden item.

In the dynamic action, a PL/SQL function is executed which loops through a cursor of a query that selects all records with articles related to the tag (the like operator is used). In the dynamic action, the set value function is used to replace the contents of the affected region by the contents of the variable l_text.

Actually the affected region, related articles, is a div and the dynamic action is an AJAX process which retrieves the data from the server (the query) and puts them in the div. In JavaScript you would use the following for divs:

```
$('divid').html("some text or HTML code");
```

And you would use the following for items:

```
$('#P_ITEM').val('some text');
```

The last case is similar to a dynamic action where the affected object is an item.

You can test all this yourself:

1. Go to the page and click on the **edit** icon in the page section.
2. Create a JavaScript function.
3. In the HTML header and body attribute, enter the following in the HTML header text area:

```
<script type="text/javascript">
function set_div(){
document.getElementById("dynamicdiv").innerHTML = "This is some
text in a div";
}
</script>
```
[1346_03_07.txt]

4. Click the **Apply changes** button.
5. Assign an ID for the **related articles** div (region):
6. Click on the related articles region. In the attributes section, enter **dynamicdiv** in the static ID text field. Click the **Apply changes** button.

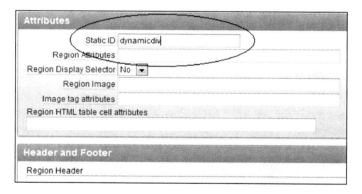

Create a text item:

1. In the items section, click on the **add** icon.
2. Select **text field**. Click **Next**. In the item name text field, enter a name and in the Region list box, select the **tag cloud** region. Click **Next** three times. Click the **Create item** button.

3. Click on the newly created item. In the element section, enter the following in the HTML form element attributes:

```
onblur=set_div();
```

[1346_03_08.txt]

The `onblur` event fires when the user navigates out of the item, by the tab key, the enter key, or by clicking the mouse pointer somewhere else.

4. Click the **Apply changes** button.

Run the page. Click on the item you just created and navigate out of the item using the tab or enter key. The div should show the text "This is some text in a div". This is just an example to show you what a dynamic action actually does. Don't mind the strange `onblur` event on the item to trigger an event. An `onclick` event was not possible as the entire tag cloud had an `onclick` event triggering the dynamic action to set the related articles region.

The static ID for the div is necessary, otherwise APEX generates its own ID, which looks something like "R431819100396833156". And then you have to find the div ID using the page source of the webpage.

Creating visual effects with JavaScript libraries

JavaScript libraries can be used to make your webpage catchy. You can use JavaScript libraries to pop up or disappear items. But JavaScript libraries can also be used when you want to implement drag and drop functionality.

There are several JavaScript libraries. The most well-known JavaScript library is JQuery. In Apex 4.0, JQuery is built-in and can be directly accessed so you don't have to download and install it. However, when you want to use a JavaScript library like Scriptaculous, you have to download and install it.

Since jQuery is built-in, we will use it to demonstrate how to make an accordion. We will create an accordion where we put some information in. By clicking in the accordion, you can see the different sections. This recipe is made with a little help from a blogpost from Patrick Wolf.

Getting ready

We will use the `APP_EVENTS` table so make sure this table is accessible.

How to do it...

First we create a region template:

1. Go to shared components | **Templates.**
2. Click the **Create** button.
3. Select region and click **Next**.
4. Select **From scratch** and click **Next**.
5. Enter a name for the region, for example **accordion**.
6. In the template class list box, select **Custom 1**.
7. Click the **Create** button.
8. In the list of templates, click the **accordion** template.

Region	accordion	2	3 hours ago	admin	-	-	4		
	Borderless Region	0	7 weeks ago	test1	-	-	20		
	Borderless Region	0	-	-	-	-	11		
	Borderless Region	0	7 weeks ago	admin	-	-	18		
	Borderless Region	0	24 hours ago	admin	-	-	4		
	Bracketed Region	0	7 weeks ago	admin	-	-	18		
	Bracketed Region	0	7 weeks ago	test1	-	-	20		

9. In the definition section, enter the following in the **Template** text field:

```
<div id="#REGION_STATIC_ID#" #REGION_ATTRIBUTES#>
#BODY##SUB_REGION_HEADERS##SUB_REGIONS#
</div>
<link rel="stylesheet" href="#IMAGE_PREFIX#libraries/jquery-
ui/1.8/themes/base/jquery.ui.accordion.css" type="text/css" />

<script src="#IMAGE_PREFIX#libraries/jquery-ui/1.8/ui/minified/
jquery.ui.accordion.min.js" type="text/javascript"></script>

<script type="text/javascript">
apex.jQuery(function() {
apex.jQuery("##REGION_STATIC_ID#").accordion();
});
</script>
[1346_03_26.txt]
```

10. The explanation of the code comes in the "How to" section. In the Sub Regions section, enter the following code in the Template text field:

```
<h3><a href="#">#SUB_REGION_TITLE#</a></h3>
<div>#SUB_REGION#</div>
```

    [1346_03_27.txt]

11. Click the **Apply changes** button.

12. The template is ready now. The next step is to create a region and a sub-region.

13. Go to the page where you want the accordion to appear.

14. In the regions section, click the **Add** icon.

15. Select **HTML** and click **Next**.

16. Again select **HTML** and click **Next**.

17. Enter a title for the region, for example **accordion**.

18. In the region template list box, select **accordion** (that is the template we just created).

19. Click **Next**.

20. Click the **Create region** button.

That was the region. Now we will create the sub-region:

1. In the regions section, click the **Add** icon.

2. Select **HTML** and click **Next**.

3. Again select **HTML** and click **Next**.

4. Enter a title for the sub-region, for example **Welcome**.

5. In the region template list box, select **No template**.

6. In the parent region list box, select the parent region we just created, **Accordion**.

7. Click **Next**.

8. In the HTML region source, enter some text.

9. Click the **Create region** button.

That was the first slice. Now we will create a second slice:

1. In the regions section, click the **Add** icon.

2. Select **Report** and click **Next**.

3. Select **sql report** and click **Next**.

4. In the Title text field, enter **Events**.

5. In the region Template list box, select **No template**.

6. In the parent region list box, select the parent region we created, **accordion**.

7. Click **Next**.

8. In the query text area, enter the following query:

```
select event
,        location
from     app_events;
[1346_03_28.txt]
```

9. Click the **Create region** button.

10. The accordion is ready now. Run the page and see what it looks like.

How it works...

This recipe consists of three parts: first we create a template of type region. Second, we create a region and sub-regions. The region is the placeholder for the accordion and the sub-regions are the slices. In the template we put some HTML and JavaScript code that is needed to reference the jQuery containing the code for the accordion, and to call the accordion function.

In the template, the `div` gets the ID from the `#REGION_STATIC_ID#` substitution variable. The accordion function uses that ID to render the accordion on the proper region. The jQuery call to the accordion includes the div ID, prefixed by the hash-sign ('#'). That is why you see two hash signs in the call to the accordion:

```
apex.jQuery("##REGION_STATIC_ID#").accordion();
```

The first is the hash prefix, the second is the enclosing hash sign of the substitution variable.

The displayed data has to conform to the following layout:

```
<div id="accordion">
    <h3><a href="#">seminar</a></h3>
    <div>30-MAR-2010: Apex day, Zeist, Netherlands</div>
    <h3><a href="#">workshop</a></h3>
    <div>07-JUN-2010: APEX 4.0 workshop</div>
</div>
```

The first line and the last line are part of the parent region. Everything in between is part of the sub-region (the slices). In the example above, you see two slices. Since the `<h3>` tag, the `<a>` tag and the`<div>` tag are in the template, you only have to put the text into the sub-region to display as desired.

There's more

You can make the accordion dynamic by using a PL/SQL dynamic content region where you use `sys.htp.p` to display the data, including the `<h3>`, `<a>`, and `<div>` tags:

1. In the regions section, click the **Add** icon.
2. Select **PL/SQL dynamic content**.
3. Enter a title for the region, for example **Events**.
4. In the region template list box, select the **accordion** template.
5. Click **Next**.
6. In the PL/SQL source text area, enter the following code:

```
declare
  cursor c_aet is
    select rownum line
      ,        event_type
      ,        event_date
      ,        event
      ,        location
      from   (select decode(row_number() over (partition by event_
type order by event_type),1,event_type,null) event_type
      ,          event_date
      ,          event
      ,          location
            from app_events);
begin
  for r_aet in c_aet
  loop
    if r_aet.event_type is not null
    then
      if r_aet.line != 1
      then
        sys.htp.p('</div>');
      end if;
      sys.htp.p('<h3><a href="#">'||r_aet.event_type||'</a></
h3>');
      sys.htp.p('<div>');
    end if;
```

```
        sys.htp.p('<b>'||to_char(r_aet.event_date,'DD-MM-YYYY')||'</
b>'||': '||r_aet.event||', '||r_aet.location);
        sys.htp.p('<br>');
    end loop;
end;
```
[1346_03_29.txt]

This code selects from the `APP_EVENTS` table and displays the date and the event. Therefore it uses `sys.htp.p` to display the data, including the necessary tags. By using the accordion template, everything will be displayed in an accordion.

You can select the slices by clicking on them. However, you can change the call to the accordion so that you only have to hover over the slices instead of clicking them. In the accordion template, change the following line:

```
apex.jQuery("##REGION_STATIC_ID#").accordion();
```

Change it to:

```
apex.jQuery("##REGION_STATIC_ID#").accordion({event:"mouseover"});
```

Besides the accordion, jQuery offers other cool "widgets", like a slider or a progress bar. For more information, take a look at `http://www.jquery.com`.

Enhancing your application with the Google API

In the previous recipe, you could see how a JavaScript library like jQuery can be used within APEX. Other JavaScript libraries can also be used but they first need to be downloaded and installed. To make life easier for people who intend to use the various JavaScript libraries, Google introduced the Google API. Google put the most well-known JavaScript libraries online so you can reference them now without installing them into your own APEX environment! By the way, you can also use the JavaScript libraries in other languages like PHP or just plain HTML with JavaScript.

To demonstrate this, we will make use of the Scriptaculous library. Suppose you have the following intranet home page:

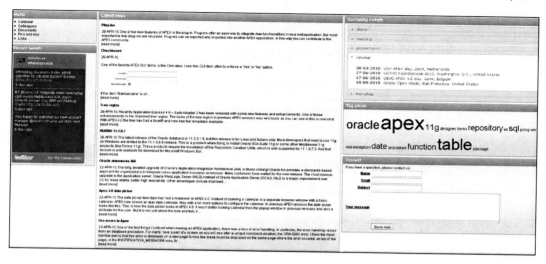

We will let the "Latest news" section pulsate on loading the homepage.

Getting ready

No preparations needed.

How to do it...

1. In the application builder, edit page 1.

2. In the page section, click on the **edit** icon.

3. In the HTML header and body section, enter the following code in the HTML header text area:

```
<script src="http://www.google.com/jsapi" type="text/
javascript"></script>
<script type="text/javascript">
google.load("prototype", "1");
google.load("scriptaculous", "1");
function pulsate_news() {
Effect.Pulsate('news', {'pulses' : 15, 'duration' : 3.0});
}
google.setOnLoadCallback(pulsate_news);
</script>
[1346_03_11.txt]
```

First, you need to load the libraries. This can be done with the `google.load()` function. The first argument is the library and the second argument is the version. In this case, we will use version 1 of the Scriptaculous Javascript library. By the way, Scriptaculous makes use of the Prototype library so this library has to be loaded first. The function `pulsate_news()` calls the pulsate effect, and the function `pulsate_news` is called by the `google.setOnLoadCallback()` function. The first argument of the `pulsate_news()` function is the IDof the affected `div`. The second argument is a list of options you can set. In this case, the news region pulsates 15 times in 3 seconds.

4. Click the **Apply changes** button.

   Now we must set the ID of the affected div to "news".

5. Click the edit region latest news.

6. In the attributes section, enter **news** in the static ID text field.

7. Click the **Apply changes** button.

8. Run the page and see the "Latest news" region pulsate.

How it works...

Load the necessary libraries with the `google.load` function. After that, create a function which calls the effect. To start the effect, use the `google.setOnLoadCallBack`. The last step is to give the affected object (a div or an item or other DOM object) an ID which will be used in the call to the JavaScript effect.

See also

For more information on the Google API or Scriptaculous, take a look at:

```
http://code.google.com/intl/nl/apis/ajaxlibs/documentation/index.
html, http://code.google.com/apis/ajax/playground/?exp=libraries or
http://script.aculo.us.
```

Including Google maps

In your APEX application, it is possible to include a Google map. A Google map can be very useful, for example, for contact details or directions. It is quite simple to include a map but you can extend the map with several functions. In former releases of APEX, you needed to create a PL/SQL dynamic region with JavaScript embedded in the PL/SQL code. Since APEX 4.0 you can use plug-ins. We will show you how to include the Google map with plug-ins. In this recipe, we will create a Google map with markers representing the locations from the APP_CUSTOMERS table.

Before, you had to request an API key in order to get the Google map working. However, the API key is not necessary anymore.

Getting ready

Make sure you have access to the APP_CUSTOMERS table.

How to do it...

First of all, you have to define a plugin.

1. In the application builder, go to your application, and click the **Shared Components** icon.

2. In the **User Interface** section, click the **Plug-ins** link.

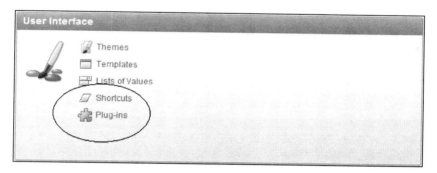

3. Click the **Create** button.

4. In the name section, enter a name in the name textfield, that is, **Google map**.

5. In the internal name textfield, enter a unique name. If you want to make your plugin publicly available, this name must be unique worldwide. In that case, it is advisable to use your company's fully qualified domain name reversed. For example, com. packtpub.apex.google_map.

6. In the type list box, select **region**.

7. Click the **create** button. The plugin has now been created and now we must define the attributes.

8. In the **Custom** attributes section, click the **Add attribute** button.

9. In the name section, enter **Width** in the label text field.

10. In the settings section, select **Integer** in the type list box.

11. Select **Yes** in the required list box.

12. In the display width text field, enter **4** and in the maximum width text field, enter **4**.

13. In the default value text area, enter **600**.

14. Click **Create** and create another.

15. In the name section, enter **2** in the attributes text field.

16. Enter **Height** in the label text field.

17. In the settings section, select **Integer** in the type list box.

18. Select **Yes** in the required list box.

19. In the display width text field, enter **4** and in the maximum width text field, enter 4.

20. In the default value text area, enter **400**.

21. Click **Create and create another**.

22. The attributes have now been defined. Now, we will enter the code which is needed to display the Google map.

23. In the source section, enter the following code in the PL/SQL Code text area:

```
function render_google_map (
p_region             in apex_plugin.t_region,
p_plugin             in apex_plugin.t_plugin,
p_is_printer_friendly in boolean )
return apex_plugin.t_region_render_result
is
cursor c_cmr is
select cust_street_address1||', '||cust_city geoloc
from    app_customers
where   cust_street_address1 is not null
order by customer_id;
--
l_width       apex_application_page_regions.attribute_01%type :=
p_region.attribute_01;
l_height      apex_application_page_regions.attribute_02%type :=
p_region.attribute_02;
l_code        varchar2(32000);
i             number(3) := 0;
begin
apex_javascript.add_library (
p_name          => 'maps?file=api&v=2',
p_directory     => 'http://maps.google.com/',
p_version       => null,
p_skip_extension => true );
--
sys.htp.p('<div id="'||p_region.static_id||'_map"
style="width:'||l_width||'px; height:'||l_height||'px"></div>');
--
```

```
l_code := 'var map = null;
var geocoder = null;
if (GBrowserIsCompatible()) {
map = new GMap2($x("'||p_region.static_id||'_map"));
map.setCenter(new GLatLng(36.902466,-84.202881), 5);
map.addControl(new GLargeMapControl());
map.addControl(new GMapTypeControl());
geocoder = new GClientGeocoder();';
--
for r_cmr in c_cmr
loop
l_code := l_code || 'geocoder.getLatLng(' ||''''||
r_cmr.geoloc ||''''||','||
'function(point) {
var baseIcon = new GIcon(G_DEFAULT_ICON);
baseIcon.shadow = "http://www.google.com/mapfiles/shadow50.png";
baseIcon.iconSize = new GSize(20, 34);
baseIcon.shadowSize = new GSize(37, 34);
baseIcon.iconAnchor = new GPoint(9, 34);
baseIcon.infoWindowAnchor = new GPoint(9, 2);
var letteredIcon = new GIcon(baseIcon);
letteredIcon.image = "http://www.google.com/mapfiles/
marker'||chr(65+i)||'.png";
markerOptions = { icon:letteredIcon };
var marker = new GMarker(point,markerOptions);
map.addOverlay(marker);
});';
i := i + 1;
end loop;
--
l_code := l_code || '}';
--
apex_javascript.add_onload_code (p_code => l_code);
--
return null;
end render_google_map;
```

[1346_03_12.txt]

This code will be explained in the next paragraph.

24. In the **Callbacks** section, enter **render_google_map** in the Render Function Name text field.

25. Click the **Apply changes** button. The plugin has now been created and can now be used within our webpage.

26. In the application builder, go to your application.

27. Click the **Create page** button.

28. Select **Blank page**.

29. In the page alias text field, enter a name, for example **Google map**. Click **Next**.

30. Enter a name for the page and click **Next**.

31. Select **No tabs** and click **Next**.

32. Click the **Finish** button to confirm.

The page has now been created. Now you can create a region with the Google map.

1. Click **Edit page**.

2. In the regions section, click the **Add** icon to create a new region.

3. Select **Plug-ins**.

4. Select the plugin you just created and click **Next**.

5. Enter a title for the region. Click **Next**.

6. In the next step, enter the width and the height of the map. The default values are shown but you can enter other dimensions. Click **Next**.

7. Click the **Create region** button.

Now the region with a Google map has been created. To show the actual addresses of the markers we will now create a reports region.

In the regions section, click the **Add** icon.

1. Select **Report** and click **Next**.

2. In the report implementation dialog, select **SQL report**.

3. Enter a title for this region, for example **Locations**. Alternatively, you can select **2** in the column list box, if you want to display the report next to the map. Click **Next**.

4. In the query text area, enter the following query:

```
select chr(64+rownum) label
,      cust_first_name
,      cust_last_name
,      cust_street_address1
,      cust_city
,      cust_state
,      cust_postal_code
from app_customers
order by customer_id
[1346_03_13.txt]
```

5. Click the **Create region** button.

6. The page is ready now. Run the page to see the result.

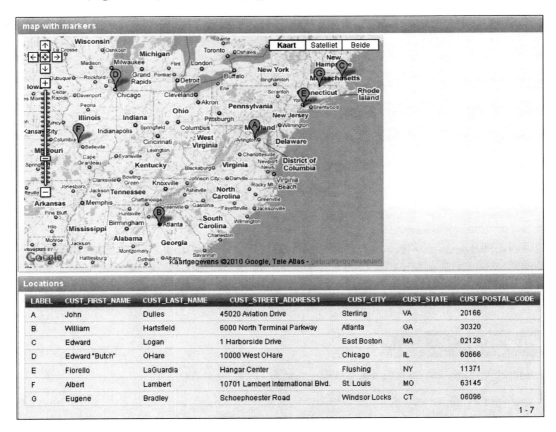

LABEL	CUST_FIRST_NAME	CUST_LAST_NAME	CUST_STREET_ADDRESS1	CUST_CITY	CUST_STATE	CUST_POSTAL_CODE
A	John	Dulles	45020 Aviation Drive	Sterling	VA	20166
B	William	Hartsfield	6000 North Terminal Parkway	Atlanta	GA	30320
C	Edward	Logan	1 Harborside Drive	East Boston	MA	02128
D	Edward "Butch"	OHare	10000 West OHare	Chicago	IL	60666
E	Fiorello	LaGuardia	Hangar Center	Flushing	NY	11371
F	Albert	Lambert	10701 Lambert International Blvd.	St. Louis	MO	63145
G	Eugene	Bradley	Schoephoester Road	Windsor Locks	CT	06096

1 - 7

How it works...

For this recipe we make use of a region type plug-in. The plug-in contains the code to put a map in the region. This code is PL/SQL with JavaScript embedded. The JavaScript code is the actual code to put the map on the screen.

The function `render_google_map` starts with a cursor with the query on table `app_customers`. The street address and the city are concatenated so that this can be used in the JavaScript code. In the declare section, you also see the attributes which were created with the plug-in: width and height. They are referenced using the `apex_plugin` types.

The code starts with a call to `apex_javascript.add_library`. In this call, the URL for the Google map is built. The next step is the creation of a div. This div is given an ID and this will be remembered so that the Google map API can put the map in this div. In the div, the width and the height attributes are used to define the size of the map.

In the JavaScript code, a new map is created with the generated ID. This map is centered using the `map.setCenter` command where the coordinates and the zoomlevel are set. The `map.addControl` sets the navigational buttons and the zoombuttons on the upper left side of the map. The geocoder is used to search the location which is fetched from the query. This is done with the `geocoder.getLatLng` function. The base icon functions define the markers on the map. For every character there is an image available on `www.google.com`. For example, if you want to put a marker with the letter A on the screen, use the following:

```
http://www.google.com/mapfiles/markerA.png
```

The `map.addOverlay` function sets the marker on the map.

This JavaScript code is put in a variable and will be used in the call to `apex_javascript.add_onload_code`.

There's more...

The Google maps API offers a lot of possibilities. You can make markers clickable so that a balloon with the location details will be shown. You can also use overlay functions like a path which graphically connects locations with a colored line. For more information take a look at the Google maps api website.

See also

For more information on plug-ins, see *Chapter 5, APEX Plug-ins*.

If you want to learn more from the Google Maps api, take a look at `http://maps.google.com` and `http://code.google.com/intl/us/apis/maps`.

Embedding multimedia objects in your application

Flash or shockwave plugins or YouTube videos can add that sparkling touch to webpages. It is nice to know that it is possible to include these multimedia objects into APEX webpages. Actually, it is quite simple to implement. To demonstrate this, we will create a webpage where a user can select a movie from a select list and see the requested video.

Getting ready

Make sure you have access to the `APP_VIDEOS` table and that the table contains some records to test.

How to do it...

1. In the application builder, click the **Create page** button.
2. Select **Blank page**.
3. Enter a page alias, that is, **Videos**. Click **Next**.
4. Enter a name for the page, that is, **Videos**. In the optional HTML regions section, enter a name in the first text field, that is, **select video**. Click **Next**.
5. Select **No tabs** and click **Next**.
6. Click **Finish** to confirm the settings.

The page has now been created, together with an HTML region. Now we will create a select list and a PL/SQL dynamic region.

1. Click the **Edit page** icon.
2. In the items section, click the **Add** icon.
3. Select **Select list**.
4. Enter a name for the select list. For example **PXX_VIDEO** (XX is the page ID). Click **Next**.
5. Click **Next** (leave the options as they are).
6. In the "page action when value changed" select list, select **Submit page**. Click **Next**.
7. Click the **Create dynamic list of values** link. A pop-up window appears.
8. Select the table/view owner and click **Next**.
9. In the table or view text field, select **APP_VIDEO**. You can use the button next to the field to select a table or view. Click **Next**.
10. In the display column list box, select **Name**. In the return value list box, select **URL**. Click **Next**.
11. Click the **Finish** button.
12. Click **Next**.
13. In the last step, click the **Create item** button.

Now we will create the PL/SQL dynamic region.

1. In the regions section, click the **Add** icon.
2. Select **PL/SQL dynamic action**.
3. Enter a title for the region, that is, **showvid**.
4. In the region template list box, select **No template**.
5. In the parent region list box, select **selectvideo** (that is the region you just created). Click **Next**.

6. In the pl/sql source text area enter the following code:

```
Sys.htp.p('<object width="640" height="385">');
Sys.htp.p('<param name="movie" value="'||:PXX_VIDEO||'&hl=nl_
NL&autoplay=1&fs=1&">');
Sys.htp.p('</param>');
Sys.htp.p('<param name="allowFullScreen" value="true">');
Sys.htp.p('</param>');
Sys.htp.p('<param name="allowscriptaccess" value="always">');
Sys.htp.p('</param><embed src="'||:PXX_VIDEO||'&hl=nl_
NL&autoplay=1&fs=1&" type="application/x-shockwave-flash" al
lowscriptaccess="always" allowfullscreen="true" width="640"
height="385">');
Sys.htp.p('</embed>');
Sys.htp.p('</object>');
[1346_03_14.txt]
```

Explanation of the code:

The PL/SQL code makes use of the htp.p function to output HTML and JavaScript to the screen. The result is the same code you should get when you want to embed a YouTube video.

And the code looks like the following:

```
<object width="640" height="385">
<param name="movie" value="http://www.youtube.com/v/vwx814B9ed8&hl=nl_
NL&fs=1&">
</param>
<param name="allowFullScreen" value="true">
</param>
<param name="allowscriptaccess" value="always">
</param>
<embed src="http://www.youtube.com/v/vwx814B9ed8&hl=nl_NL&fs=1&"
type="application/x-shockwave-flash" allowscriptaccess="always"
allowfullscreen="true" width="640" height="385">
</embed>
</object>
```

[1346_03_15.txt]

First, the object tag tells APEX that a multimedia object like an image or a movie will be included in the webpage. The size of the object can be set with the width and height parameters. The next step in the code is the declaration of parameters. The `allowscriptaccess` parameter is necessary to enable playing a video on a different website than `youtube.com`. The embed tag is the actual inclusion of the multimedia object. Src is the source of the object. In this case, the source is a URL to a movie at `youtube.com`. All this code will be showed as HTML using the `htp.p` function. To be able to use this code to show more videos, the select list will be concatenated to the code.

Well, the code has been entered, so click the **Create region** button.

The page is now ready. Run the page and see the result.

How it works...

This webpage makes use of the embedded code which you can get from the YouTube website. We could have put this code into an HTML region that works too. But in that case, the URL of the YouTube video is hardcoded and cannot be changed by the user. With the use of the `htp.p` function you can make the code dynamic by concatenating the URL.

In the recipe, you could also see that the PL/SQL dynamic region has a parent HTML region. This is done to make it look as if all the objects are put together into one region, which looks better.

You can pass some more parameters to the player such as autoplay, genie menu (showing related videos after playing the video), enable full screen mode, or start in High Definition (HD) whenever available.

There's more...

In this recipe, we showed you how to embed a YouTube movie in your webpage. It is also possible to embed other plugins such as a Flash plugin, a Twitter widget, or a weather widget. Websites like Twitter offer you the HTML code which you have to include in your webpage and similar to this recipe, you can use the `htp.p` function to send this HTML code to the screen.

You can also make a region plugin and give it some attributes such as movie, object width, and object height.

See also...

For more information on the Youtube API, take a look at
`http://code.google.com/apis/youtube/player_parameters.html`

Creating a region selector

Sometimes a webpage can be very chaotic, especially when there are many items on the screen. In that case, it may be a good idea to group items into logical sections. The sections can be displayed separately to save room for the rest of the items. We will make a webpage where the user can edit the user profile. This user profile will be divided into three categories: person, communication, and favorites. The user will be able to click on a button just to see only the category the user is interested in.

Getting ready

We will use the table APP_USER_PROFILES, so make sure this table exists and is accessible.

How to do it...

First, make a form based on a table:

1. Click the **Create page** button.
2. Select **Form**.
3. Select **Form on a table or view**.
4. Select the table/view owner and click **Next**.
5. Enter the name of the table. You can use the button next to the field to select the table. Click **Next**.
6. Enter a page name, for example, **User profile**.
7. Enter a region title, for example, **user**.
8. In the region template list box, select **APEX 4.0 – Reports region**. Click **Next**.
9. Select **Do not use tabs** and click **Next**.
10. Select the primary key column of the table. In this case it is named **ID**. Click **Next**.
11. Select **Exisiting trigger** and click **Next**.
12. Select **All columns** and click **Next**.
13. In the next step, you can enter different names for the button labels. Click **Next**.
14. Enter the page numbers APEX should navigate to after the user has clicked the cancel or create button. For example, you can enter page 1 for the cancel button, which means that APEX returns to page 1 if the user clicks on the cancel button. Click **Next** to continue.
15. Click **Finish** to confirm.

The page is now ready but we will now split the various items into three categories.

1. Click the **Edit** icon.
2. Create a new region (click the **Add** icon in the region section).
3. Select **HTML**.
4. In the type of region, select **HTML**.
5. Enter a title for the region. We will call this region **Person**.
6. In the region template list box, select **APEX 4.0 – Region without title**. Click the **Create** button.
7. Repeat the steps two more times: one for the **Communication** and one for the **Favourites**. In the end, you should have four regions: **User**, **Person**, **Communication**, and **Favourites**.
8. Make sure you switch to **tree view**.

9. Drag the items **ID, gender, birthday,** and **rel_status** to the **Person** region.

10. Drag the items **email, home_phone, mobile_phone, work_phone, Skype_name, msn, twitter,** and **nickname** to the **Communications** region.

11. Drag the items **Interests, favourite_music, favourite_movies,** and **favourite_books** to the **Favourites** region.

Now we have three regions with items from the APP_USER_PROFILES table. It will look like the following:

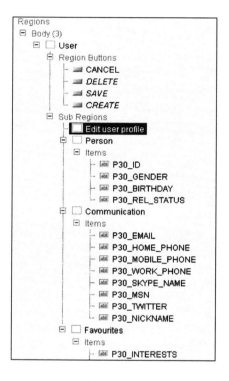

In order to create a region selector, we will have to indicate that the regions can be selected by the region selector.

1. In the regions section, click on the **edit region** link for the **Person** region.

2. In the attributes section, select **Yes** in the **Region display selector**.

3. Click the **Apply changes** button.

4. Apply the same for the **Communication** and the **Favorites** regions.

The last step is to create a region selector.

1. In the regions section, click the **Add** icon to create a new region.
2. Select **Region display selector**.
3. Enter a name for the region title, for example, **Edit user profile**.
4. Click the **Create** button.

The region display selector is now ready but we will include the region in the User region so that it looks like this all is part of one region:

1. Click the **Region display selector region** in the regions section.
2. In the user interface section, select the **User** region in the **Parent region** list box.
3. Click the **Apply changes** button.

Now we will do the same for the three other regions:

1. Click the **Person** region in the regions section.
2. In the user interface section, select the user region in the **Parent region** list box.
3. In the template list box, select **APEX 4.0 – Region without title**.
4. Click the **Apply changes** button.
5. Repeat this step for the other regions: **Communication** and **Favorites**.
6. The page is ready now. Run the page and try it out.

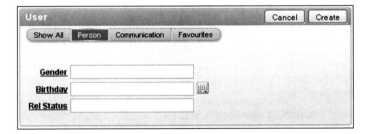

How it works...

The region display selector is actually an unnumbered list. This list contains list items and each list item has a reference to a region. In HTML, this looks like the following:

```
<ul id="96054411561206575_RDS" class="apex-rds">
<li class="apex-rds-first apex-rds-selected"><a href="#SHOW_
ALL"><span>Show All</span></a></li>
<li><a href="#R96048122465171863"><span>Person</span></a></li>
<li><a href="#R96048531469174507"><span>Communication</span></a></li>
```

```
<li class="apex-rds-last"><a href="#R96050120519180839"><span>Favourit
es</span></a></li>
</ul>
```

The `<a>` tag has a reference to a region. The regions are actually `div`s with an ID. You can find the ID's in the code behind the hash ("#") sign. You can assign your own ID by entering your own ID in the static ID text field in the attributes section of the region. In that case, you would have seen something like this:

```
<li><a href="#person"><span>Person</span></a></li>
```

You can also see the `<span>` tag. A `div` and a `span` are almost identical, with the difference that a `div` applies to a section of a document of the page and a `span` applies to the inline text but keeps the formatting of the outside text. That is the default behavior but this can be changed by the use of cascading style sheets.

Furthermore, you saw that the three regions with items have the region without title template. This is done because otherwise you would have seen the entire region including the title, which is too much information in this little space.

The three regions with items and the region display selector all have the same parent: the User region. This is not necessary. You can also display them as separate regions.

Sending mail via APEX

Sending mail is an important feature in a web application. You can use it when you want to confirm something. Or when you want to send information to the user, or the user wants to send your company an e-mail with an inquiry. In this recipe, we will make a section on the homepage where users can request information via e-mail.

Getting ready

Your database should be able to send outbound e-mails. Therefore, check your database if it is configured for sending e-mails.

How to do it...

1. In the application builder, go to **page 1** of your application.
2. In the **Regions** section, click the **Add** icon to create a new region.
3. Select **HTML**.
4. Select **HTML** again. This time it's for the type of HTML region.
5. Enter a title for this region. For example, **Contact**. Click **Next**.

6. In the text area, enter the following text: **If you have any questions, please mail us**.

7. Click the **Create region** button.

8. In the items section, click the **add** icon to create a new item.

9. Select **text field**. Click **Next**.

10. Enter a name for this item. In our case, this would be P1_NAME.

11. In the region list box, select the region you just created. Click **Next**.

12. Enter a name for the label. Click **Next two times**.

13. Click the **Create item** button.

14. The first item is now ready. You should also create the following items using the steps above:

    P1_EMAIL
    P1_SUBJECT
    P1_TEXT.

15. But for this last item, select **text area** instead of text field as the item type.

16. Next create a button. In the buttons section, click the **Add** icon.

17. Select the region for this button. In our case, we select the region we just created. Click **Next**.

18. Select **Displayed among this region's items** as the position.

19. Enter a name for this button, for example **P1_SENDMAIL**.

20. Check the **Beginning on new line** checkbox.

21. In the label field, enter **Send mail** for this button.

22. In the button style listbox, select **HTML button**.

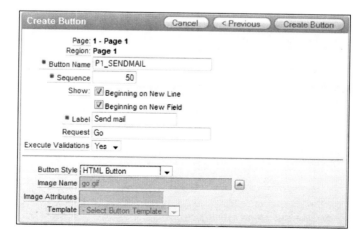

23. Click the **Create** button.

We now have a region with the necessary text items and a button to send the mail. Now we must create the process.

1. In the processes section in the middle of the screen, click the **Add** icon.
2. Select **Send E-mail** and click **Next**.

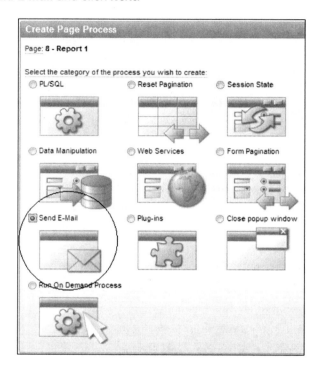

3. Enter a name for this process. Click **Next**.
4. In the **From** field, enter **&P1_EMAIL.** (with the dot at the end).
5. In the **To** field, enter your company's e-mail address.
6. In the **Subject** field, enter **&P1_SUBJECT.** (with the dot at the end).
7. In the **Body Plain Text** field, enter **&P1_TEXT.** (with the dot at the end).
8. Further, you can choose to have APEX send the mail immediately by selecting **Yes** in the **Send immediately** list box at the bottom.

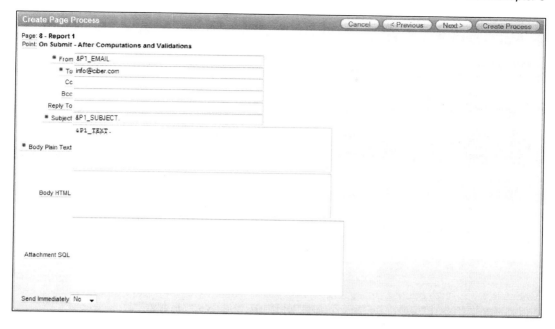

9. Click **Next**.

10. Enter a success message and a failure message. Click **Next**.

11. In the "when button pressed" list box, select the button you just created.

12. Click the **Create process** button.

The contact region with items and a send button is now ready. Run the form and try to send an e-mail.

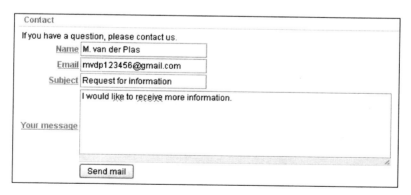

How it works...

The actual work is done by the `apex_mail.send` function and this function is called in the page process. This page process is of type **Email** and all you have to do is enter all details in the text fields. However, you can make it dynamic by using the substitution variables like **&P1_NAME**. Don't forget the dot at the end.

Uploading and downloading files

Sometimes, it is very handy to be able to upload and download files in a web application. For example, an intranet site where users can upload their own images, or a product catalog with images of the products. We will make a webpage where users can upload and download important documents such as templates of letters, fax sheets, telephone directories, and so on.

Getting ready

Make sure you have access to the `APP_DOCUMENTS` table. Also make sure the directory parameter in the call to `bfilename` points to an existing directory and that at least read access is granted. To create a directory with read access, execute the following commands (under the sys or system user) in sqlplus:

```
Create directory <<directory>> as 'c:\documents';

Grant read on directory <<directory>> to <<user>>;
```
[1346_03_17.txt]

Here, `<<directory>>` is the name of the directory you want to create in the database. This is a virtual directory and you can give it any name. `<<user>>` is the name of the Oracle user the read rights should be granted to. You can also use public if you want all users to be able to read from that directory.

How to do it...

1. In the application builder, go to your application and click the **create page** button.
2. Select **Report** and then select **Classic report**.
3. Enter a page name for the report, for example, **Documents**.
4. Select **Do not use tabs** and click **Next**.

5. In the PL/SQL text area, enter the following query:

```
select  id
    ,       description
    ,       filename
    ,       dbms_lob.getlength("DOC_CONTENT") doc_content
from    app_documents
```
[1346_03_18.txt]

6. Click **Next**. In the next step, click **Next**.

7. Click **Finish** to confirm the creation of the report.

    The report is ready but you have to do one more thing.

    Click the **edit** icon.

8. In the regions section, click on the **Edit report columns** link.

9. In the column attributes section, click on the **edit** icon right before the column named `doc_content`.

10. In the column formatting section, enter the following in the number/date format text field:

```
DOWNLOAD:APP_DOCUMENTS:DOC_CONTENT:ID:
```
[1346_03_19.txt]

11. The format mask must be filled with parameters in the following order and separated by colons :

```
DOWNLOAD:<TABLE_NAME>:<BLOB COLUMN NAME>:<PRIMARY KEY COLUMN
NAME>:
```
[1346_03_20.txt]

12. Alternatively, you can use the **Blob download format mask** link below the number/date format text field.

13. Click the **Apply changes** button. The page is ready now. Run the page to test the download.

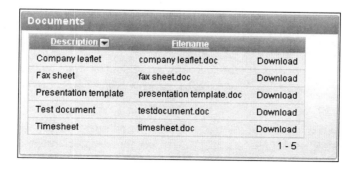

So far, we have seen the download page. To make an upload page, follow these steps:

1. In the application builder, go to your application and click the **Create page** button.
2. Select **Form**.
3. Select **Form on a table or view**.
4. Click **Next**.
5. In the table/view name text field, enter the name of the table. In our case, enter here **APP_DOCUMENTS**.
6. In the next step, enter a page name and a region name. Click **Next**.
7. Select **Do not use tabs** and click **Next**.
8. Select the primary key column of **APP_DOCUMENTS**, ID and click **next**.
9. Select **existing sequence** and in the sequence list box select the sequence **DCM_SEQ**.
10. Click **Next**.
11. In the select columns list box, select **DESCRIPTIONS**, **DOC_CONTENT**, and **FILENAME**. Click **Next**.

12. In the next step, leave the options as they are and click **Next**.
13. Enter the IDs of the pages APEX should navigate to when submitting or canceling. Click **Next**.
14. Click **Finish** to confirm. The page is almost ready now. Click the **Edit** icon.
15. In the items section, click the **doc_content** item.
16. In the source section, enter the following in the source value text area:

    DOC_CONTENT:MIMETYPE:FILENAME:CONTENT_LAST_UPDATED::

    [1346_03_21.txt]

    The parameters represent the blob column, the column containing the mimetype (this indicates what type of file has been uploaded, for example, image or wordpad), the column containing the filename, and the column containing the date last updated.

    By the way, you can also use the **Blob** download format mask link below the text area to enter the source value.

Click the **Apply changes** button. The page is ready now. Run the page to see the result.

How it works...

You just created an upload page and a page where you can download files. As you can see in the upload page, the blob column is represented by an item of type file browse. At runtime, this field gets a button which shows a file dialog on clicking. If the record already contains an uploaded file, you will also see a download link which makes it possible to download the file.

In the report page with the download link, there are two important things. First, the column in the query. For the blob column, the function `dbms_lob.getlength()` is used. Second, the column formatting needs a special type of formatting. These two things make APEX put a download link on the screen.

There's more...

We discussed the uploading and downloading of files that are stored in a blob in a table. You can also download files from the filesystem on the server.

Create a page with a HTML region with nothing in it.

In that page, create an on load-before header page process of type PL/SQL and include the following code:

```
declare
  l_name     varchar2(100) := 'testdocument.doc';
  l_filename bfile;
  v_length   number(8);
begin
  l_filename := bfilename('DIR',l_name);
  v_length   := dbms_lob.getlength(l_filename);
  --
  begin
    owa_util.mime_header('application/octet',false);
    sys.htp.p ('Content-length: ' || v_length );
    sys.htp.p('Content-Disposition: attachment; filename="'||l_
name||'"');
    owa_util.http_header_close;
    wpg_docload.download_file(l_filename);
```

```
exception
  when others then
    raise;
  end;
end;
```
[1346_03_22.txt]

This script uses the function `bfilename` to locate the file. The `owa_util.mime_header` function indicates the mimetype of the file to be downloaded. This mimetype tells APEX what type of file is to be downloaded. The `htp.p` function is used to pass the length of the file and the filename. The actual download starts with the call to the function `wpg_docload.download_file()`.

Since the page process is an on load-before header process, the download of the file will start as soon as you run this page. You don't want that so you have to make another page or take an existing page and create a link to the download page.

Calling APEX from an Oracle Form

Sometimes you may want to call an APEX webpage from within an Oracle Form. For example, when you want to redirect the user to another system which is built in APEX. Or the user wants to show a report which was already created in APEX – there's no need to create it twice and by the way, calling an Oracle Report is basically the same as calling an APEX webpage. With the Form's built-in `web.show_document`, it is possible to call a webpage from within a Form. We will make use of this function to demonstrate how to call an APEX report (an overview of customers with a Google map) from an Oracle Form.

Getting ready

Make sure you have a running Forms environment. Open an existing form from where you want to call an APEX webpage.

Have a look at your APEX URL. You can find it in the upper region of your browser and it looks like this:

The URL starts with the hostname followed by the port number. The host and the port number are separated by a colon. After `apex/` you can see "f?". APEX always starts with this and after the question mark you see `p=4550`. P is a parameter and stands for the application ID. In this case, you see application 4550. That is actually the APEX builder (yes, the APEX builder is also an application). After that you see several more numbers, all separated by a colon.

The number directly after the application ID is the page ID. After the page ID comes the session ID. You don't need to remember this number as APEX generates this ID every time you call this page. After the session ID, you can pass more parameters, even your own page items with their values.

Now that you know this, you can easily build your URL when you want a certain page in your APEX application to be called by an Oracle form. Suppose your application ID is **12133** and the page ID you want to call is **10**. And let's say your APEX host is apexhost on port **8000**, then your URL must be:

```
http://apexhost:8000/apex/f?p=12133:8
```

Remember this URL as you need it later in the recipe.

How to do it...

1. In your Form, create a **button**.
2. Under this button, create a **WHEN-BUTTON-PRESSED** trigger.
3. In the trigger, enter the following code:

```
web.show_document('http://apexhost:8000/apex/f?p=12133:10','_
blank');
```

[1346_03_23.txt]

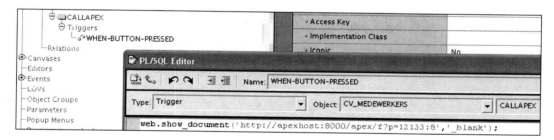

As you can see, the first parameter in the web.show_document function is the URL we just built.

Basically, that's all. Compile the trigger and the form and run it.

How it works...

With the Forms built-in `web.show_document` you can call a webpage from within Oracle Forms. `Web.Show_document` has two parameters. The first parameter is the URL of the called website. The second parameter sets the location of the called webpage.

Parameter	Meaning
`_blank`	Webpage will be shown in a separate browser window
`_self`	Webpage will replace the Forms application in the browser
`<framename>`	Webpage will be shown in a frame named <framename> in a HTML page

There's more...

The called webpage in APEX can contain items. These items can be filled with values you pass from the Oracle Form. Suppose you have a webpage with an overview of the customers and you only want to see the customers from the United States, you could do the following, provided that in the APEX page an item exists that is called `P8_COUNTRY` and this item is used in the where-clause of the query (that is, where `country = :p8_country`):

Replace the code in the when-button-pressed trigger with the following code:

```
declare
  l_country varchar2(100) := 'United States';
  l_url     varchar2(255) := 'http://apexhost:8000/apex/f?p=12133:8:::
NO::P8_COUNTRY:';
begin
  l_url := l_url || l_country;
  web.show_document(l_url,'_blank');
end;
```
[1346_03_24.txt]

Explanation: The seventh parameter is the name of the item which can be given a value when calling the page. After the item name and the colon comes the value of the item, in this case, United States.

You can also make a webpage where Forms and APEX are integrated together. And it is possible to pass parameters into both directions. You can find a lot of blogs on the internet regarding this subject.

4

Creating Websheet Applications

In this chapter, we will cover:

- ▶ Creating a websheet application
- ▶ Creating a page in a websheet
- ▶ Adding a navigation section to a page
- ▶ Implementing a datagrid
- ▶ Allowing multiple users access to a websheet
- ▶ Creating an enhanced datagrid from a spreadsheet

Introduction

When Application Express was first introduced as HTML-DB at the beginning of the century, it was positioned as a Microsoft Access killer. This was because of the fast and easy way data-centric applications could be created, just like in Access, but centralized and having all the benefits of a multi user, consistent way of manipulating data.

In APEX 4.0, a new type of application is introduced called Websheets and developers have already described it as the Excel killer.

Websheets allow multiple users to simultaneously work on the same pieces of data, without directly working on a defined data model. Instead, websheets store data in generic tables that change depending on the design of the websheet.

The biggest innovation in this is that almost every aspect of a websheet application can be altered by users instead of developers. They are easy to use and very flexible. Constraints, lists, and calculations can be added by end users, without having to use the services of a developer.

A websheet application can be published for others to use, with or without privileges to modify data or alter the Websheet itself. This multi-user environment erases the need of merging data that is a common problem in spreadsheet programs like Excel.

All this makes websheets very interesting for use in management environments to quickly have access to data.

Creating a websheet application

The first task that has to be performed is to create the application itself. In this recipe, we will show you how a basic websheet application can be created.

Getting ready

Create a user that has enough rights to create and edit websheet applications. The basic information can be entered as follows:

1. From the **Application Builder** overview, navigate to **Administration**.
2. Click on **Manage Users and Groups**.
3. Click **Create User**.
4. Enter a name (for example, WS_DEV) and an e-mail address in the appropriate fields.
5. Make sure the select list for **Team Development Access** is set to **Yes**.
6. Make sure the radio button for **User is a developer** is set to **Yes**.
7. Enter a password.
8. Click **Create User**.

How to do it...

The starting point for creating a new websheet application is the Application Builder. When you open it, you will notice that besides the standard tab for all applications, there is a specific tab for websheet applications. This tab can be clicked to get a report of all websheet applications in the workspace.

1. Click the **Create** button on any of the tabs in the Application Builder.
2. On the first page of the wizard, select **Websheet Application** and click **Next**.
3. Name the application **Sales** and enter an unused ID for the application number, or leave the proposed number as it is.

4. In the **Home Page** section, enter a text in the **Content** textarea.

Welcome to the Sales Websheet application.

Sections are the blocks that a Websheet application is built up of. To some extent, you can compare them to regions in a 'normal' APEX page.

5. This text can be just plain, but it can also be formatted. To do this, click the small arrow on the top-right of the Content area. If we hover our mouse pointer over it, the alt text will say **Expand Toolbar**.

A new area will open up, allowing many lay-out options for the text. Select the text **Sales Websheet** and click the **B** button to make it bold.

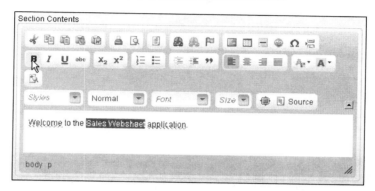

6. Click **Next**.
7. Click **Create**.

The basic websheet has now been created. When it is run, we can see that it already looks like an application, despite the fact that we haven't created any pages!

Everything about the websheet can now be managed by the users. The only influence a developer has is some of the basic properties like the logo or authentication.

To change these properties, go to the **Application Builder**, select the Websheet Application that's called **Sales** and on the following page, select **Edit Properties**.

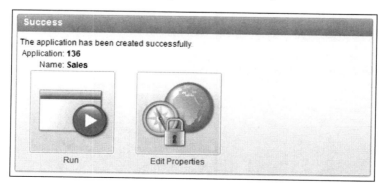

How it works

Websheets work a bit different than normal APEX applications. Instead of developers and users, there is a third user level called Websheet Developer. Users with this privilege can create and edit all aspects of the websheet application during run-time, but they cannot use the APEX Application Builder.

Besides this, websheets have three levels of internal users; readers, contributors, and administrators. More on this can be found in the recipe called *Multiple users in a websheet*.

Most of the content is added to the websheet by its users and not by the APEX developer. With that in mind, we will show some of the differences when logging into a websheet application as a normal user or as a user with Websheet Development rights. More on this can be found in the recipe called *Multiple users in a websheet* as well.

See also

In the next sections, the recipe called *Allowing multiple users access to a websheet* explains more about collaboration in a Websheet application.

Creating a page in a websheet

Websheets are prepared as a bare skeleton. The APEX developer just creates the application and leaves everything else to the end-users. One of the tasks a user can perform is creating a new page. This recipe explains how this is done.

Getting ready

Make sure there is a websheet application available to use for this recipe.

To gain access to this application, there should be a user available that has Websheet Developer rights. Log in with that user when asked to run the websheet application.

How to do it...

Run the websheet application. This will bring up the homepage of the websheet application. What immediately catches the eye is the list on the right that offers a host of possible options for the Websheet Developer.

Some of these options will come up in the next recipes, but for the moment we will concentrate on the second button labeled **New Page**. Click this button to add a page.

In the next screen, we enter the information we want on this page as shown in the following screenshot:

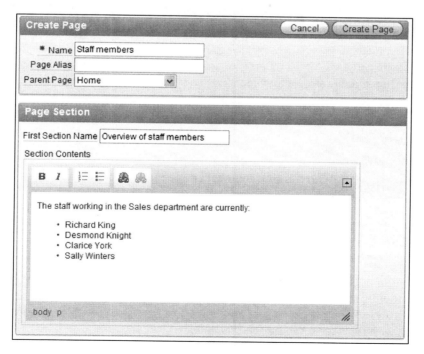

It works just the same as entering the information for the home page like we did in the previous recipe. What's new is that we now have the option to link a **Parent Page**. This will automatically generate two things; on the new page a breadcrumb is created to link to the home page and on the home page a link to the new staff members page is created.

The new staff members page itself will look like this:

Did you notice the **edit** link in the top-right corner of the page? This allows Websheet Developers to jump directly to the **Edit** window, thus speeding up the process of configuring the page.

Adding a navigation section to a page

Sections are the building blocks of websheet pages. Each page in a websheet will contain one or more sections. In the previous recipes, we've seen how creating a new page allows the Websheet Developer to create the first section.

In this recipe, we will see that there is another type of section and how it can be created.

Getting ready

As a starting point, we will use the staff members page that was created in the previous recipe.

How to do it...

1. In the menu on the right side of the page, find the button called **New Section** and click it. The familiar APEX wizard screen appears offering two options: Text and Navigation.

    Since we've seen the process of creating a Text section in the last two recipes already, we'll choose **Navigation** this time.

A navigation section is a section that allows users to navigate between pages and sections.

2. So select **Navigate** and click **Next**.
3. Select **Page Navigation** and click **Next**.
4. In the next page, set the title to **Jump to Home**.
5. By clicking the little arrow next to the **Starting Page** field, a pop-up appears offering a selection to all available pages as seen in the next screenshot. Select **Home** from the pop-up.

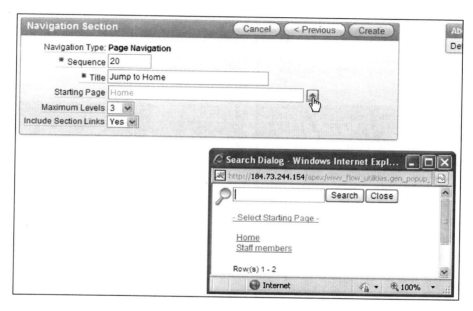

6. Leave the other fields on default and click the **Create** button.

The screen now returns to the page and allows the Websheet Developer to inspect the changes that were made.

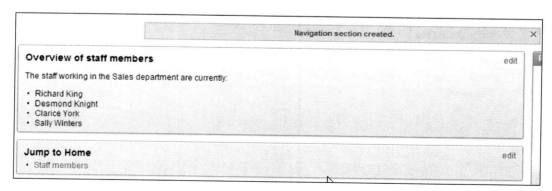

But wait! When we look at the link that has been created, we see that it doesn't navigate to the **Home** page as we would expect.

What really happened is that a link was created to all pages that have the **Home** page as a parent. This becomes clear when we create another page. Let's call it **Sales overview** and make **Home** its parent. Automatically, a new link to this page will appear in the navigation section on the **Staff members** page.

With this in mind, the title for the navigation section is a bit wrong. So click the **Edit** button on the section and rename the title to **Quick Access**.

Implementing a datagrid

Datagrids are the strong points of websheets. Websheets have been called 'Excel-killers'. If that is true, than datagrids are the weapons.

Getting ready

Make sure that there is a page available to implement the datagrid on. We can take the **Sales overview** page from the previous recipe and elaborate on that.

If you didn't create that page yet, do so before starting this recipe.

How to do it...

Let's say that the company in this example sells only one kind of product. They have no need for an elaborate database, so they would like a simple grid to monitor all sales.

1. When on the **Sales Overview** page, click the button on the right side called **New Datagrid**.

2. On the first page of the wizard, select the option **From Scratch**.

3. Next, enter the title and columns for the datagrid as shown in the following screenshot:

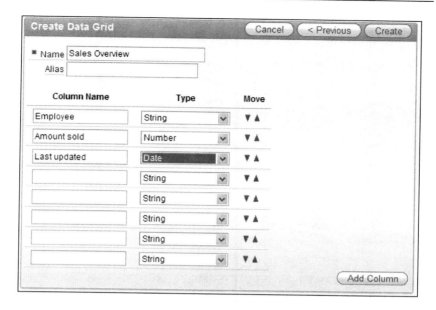

4. Click **Create**.

What we see now is an empty datagrid. To add data to the grid, press the **Add Row** button.

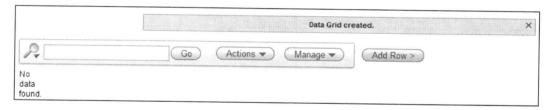

Data can now be entered into the datagrid, row-by-row.

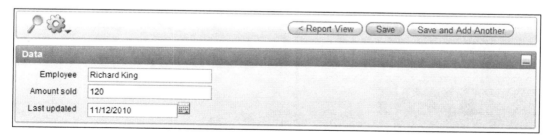

When a row is done, click **Save** to finish or click **Save and Add Another** to continue entering data.

After the last row is entered and the page is run, we will see a nice table of data quite similar to an Interactive Report in Application Express.

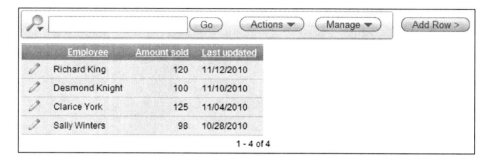

Under the **Actions** button, we can find some of the visual attributes to filter and sort the data in the grid.

Everything looks alright, so now we can put the datagrid onto the **Sales Overview** page.

1. Go to the **Sales Overview** page and click **New Section**.
2. We can see two new options: Data and Chart. Click **Data** and **Next**.
3. Now select Sales Overview from the select list at Data Grid, click **Next** and **Create**.
4. The datagrid is now added as a section to the page.

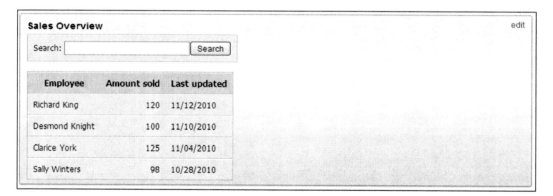

<h1>How it works...</h1>

Datagrids look like normal tables in an interactive report. But in the background they are not based on real database tables. APEX keeps the data for datagrids inside metadata-tables. That is why we don't have to define tables before creating pages with datagrids. The only drawback is that there are limitations on things like the number of columns, indexing, and so on because of that.

The recipe called *Creating a websheet application from a spreadsheet* will elaborate on this subject and show some of the advanced features of Datagrids.

Allowing multiple users access to a websheet

In this recipe, we are going to see how Access Control can be used to allow different types of users to access websheets.

Getting ready

Before starting this recipe we should have a websheet application containing multiple pages with at least a text section, a navigation section, and a datagrid.

Make sure that there are two APEX users available with websheet access; one named Richard and one named Sally. Any other name will do as well, but change the names in the rest of this recipe accordingly.

How to do it...

First, log in to the websheet application as an APEX Administrator. The role of Websheet Developer is not enough.

When you are logged in, navigate to the **Administration** page and select **Access Control**. Next, click on **Create Entry**.

In the following screen, we can create users that have different roles. These users will be added to the **Access Control List** or **ACL** for short.

- ▶ **Reader** is allowed to view content, but cannot edit
- ▶ **Contributor** is allowed to view and edit content
- ▶ **Administrator** is allowed to edit the ACL and delete the application

We will create an Administrator, a Contributor, and a Reader, so we can see the difference between the two.

1. In the **Create Entry** screen, enter **Richard** in the name field and select **Contributor** from the **Privilege** radio group.

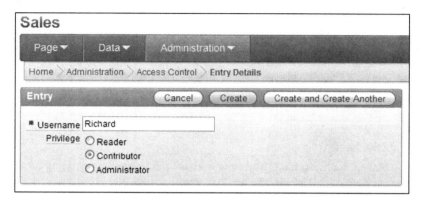

2. Click **Create and Create Another**.
3. This time enter **Sally** and select **Reader** before clicking **Create and Create Another**.
4. This last time enter the name of the APEX Administrator that you are logged in with and select **Administrator** before clicking **Create**.

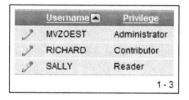

Now there are three users available to work with. Notice that APEX has changed the names to all uppercase.

The next step to be able to use the advantages of the ACL is to edit the application properties to allow use of the Access Control List.

1. Go to **Edit Properties** of the Sales Websheet application.
2. Scroll down to the **Authorization** section.
3. Set **Access Control List Type** to **Custom**.
4. Click **Apply Changes**.

Let's see what the differences are between the two users Richard and Sally.

First log in as **RICHARD**. When we look at the websheet, we can still see the **Edit** links on all the sections and all buttons in the menu on the right are also available. Richard can still navigate to the datagrid on the **Sales Overview** page and edit it.

Now log in as **SALLY**. You will immediately notice that the edit links are gone and the right side menu is a lot smaller. Sally can only read the information on the pages and cannot edit anything.

How it works...

APEX 4.0 has introduced multiple levels of access control. The old-fashioned APEX users are still available, but the introduction of websheets has also brought with it the websheet roles in the form of the **Access Control List**.

Access Control

Once authenticated to an application, access control specifies what users can do within the application. The table below identifies what capabilities different types of users will have based on the authentication being used within this application.

Category	Capability	Authentication with Access Control List			Application Express Account Authentication without Access Control List		
		Reader	Contributor	Administrator	End User	Developer	Workspace Administrator
Administration from within Application Builder							
	Create Application					X	X
	Delete Application					X	X
	Update Application Properties					X	X
	Edit Authentication					X	X
	Edit SQL Access and Suggested Objects					X	X
Run and View							
	Pages	X	X	X	X	X	X
	Data Grids	X	X	X	X	X	X
	Reports	X	X	X	X	X	X
	Annotations (files, tags, notes)	X	X	X	X	X	X
Add / Modify							
	Pages		X	X		X	X
	Sections		X	X		X	X
	Data Grids		X	X		X	X
	Data Grid Data		X	X		X	X
	Reports		X	X		X	X
	Annotations (files, tags, notes)		X	X		X	X
	Links		X	X		X	X
Administration when Running Application							
	Access Dashboard			X			X
	Access Monitor Activity			X			X
	Update Application Properties			X			X
	Maintain Access Control List			X			X

Make sure that you keep the difference in mind. Properties for APEX users have an influence on the way users can work with websheets.

The Access Control List in turn doesn't have any influence on the way users can work with other APEX applications or the application builder.

Creating an enhanced datagrid from a spreadsheet

In one of the previous recipes we created a datagrid, by defining all columns by hand. In that recipe we called datagrids a 'weapon' for the 'Excel-killer', as websheets are called.

Well if normal datagrids are weapons, then this recipe will show you a thermo-nuclear device.

We will create another datagrid, but this time we will base it on an existing Excel sheet and therefore adding many more possibilities.

How to do it...

The company that we used as an example in the datagrid recipe has decided to add two new products to their portfolio. This means that they have to do a bit more administration. Salespeople will be able to sell more types of products and this has to be recorded. Also the company wants to base the bonuses for the salespeople on the profit they make and not just on the amount of sales. In short: selling a more expensive product means a higher bonus.

To start with this administration, the company has created an Excel sheet. In this sheet each employee has a row with his or her sales per product and the bonus that is generated by those sales. Product 1 gives a bonus of 10, product 2 a bonus of 20 and product 3 a bonus of 25.

	A	B	C	D	E	F
1	Employee	Product 1	Product 2	Product 3	Last Updated	Bonus
2	Richard King	120	10	30	11-12-2010	2150
3	Desmond Knight	100	32	44	10-12-2010	2740
4	Clarice York	125	50	21	10-12-2010	2775
5	Sally Winters	98	22	160	11-12-2010	5420
6		443	114	255		13085
7						

On the bottom is a row with totals for each column.

To allow employees of the administration department to see and adjust these figures from a web environment, it is decided to put this sheet into a websheet.

1. Click the **New Datagrid** button on the right menu.
2. Select **Copy** and **Paste** in the wizard and click **Next**.

3. Name it **Extended Sales Overview** and paste the spreadsheet data directly into the available field. Be sure to only select the five data columns from the Excel sheet and not the computed columns and fields as shown in the screenshot. Keep the checkbox checked.

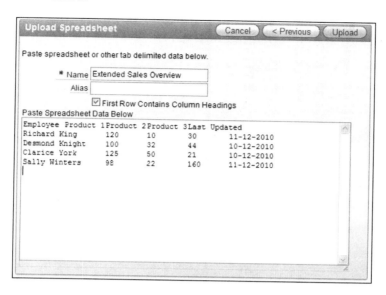

4. Now click **Upload** and the datagrid is created.

To put this new datagrid into the existing Sales Overview page, perform the following steps:

1. Click **Edit** on the existing Sales Overview datagrid section.
2. Select the delete button and click **OK** on the following pop-up to confirm the deletion.
3. Return to the **Sales Overview** page.
4. Now create a new Datagrid section, but this time, select the **Extended Sales Overview** datagrid.

There's more...

To add the **Bonus** column and **Total** fields to the datagrid, there is still some work to do.

1. Click the **Edit** link on the **Extended Sales Overview** section.
2. Click on the **Data Grid Name**.

   Now we are back at the Interactive Report for the datagrid. First, we are adding the Total fields under each of the product columns.

3. Select the **Action** button, then **Format**, and then **Aggregate.**

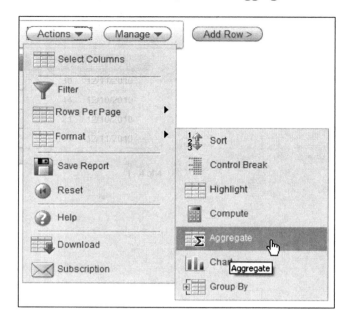

4. Under **Aggregation**, leave the default New Aggregation.

5. In **Function**, select **Sum**.

6. In **Column**, select **Product 1** and click on **Apply**.

7. Repeat these steps for Product 2 and Product 3.

8. When all three columns are done, select **Actions | Save Report**.

9. Choose **As Default Report Settings** in the **Save** field.

10. Select **Primary** and click **Apply**.

The settings are now set for all users that can view this datagrid.

To add the **Bonus** column, we have to do something else:

1. Select **Actions | Format | Computation**.
2. Enter **Bonus** as the column heading.
3. Use (B * 10) + (C * 20) + (D * 25) as the computation.
4. Click **Apply**.
5. Save the report again using **Actions | Save Report**.

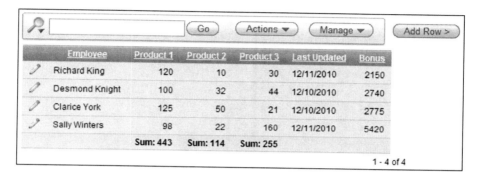

As we can see, the new column is now added.

5
APEX Plug-ins

In this chapter, we will cover:

- ▶ Creating an item type plug-in
- ▶ Creating a region type plug-in
- ▶ Creating a dynamic action plug-in
- ▶ Creating a process type plug-in

Introduction

In APEX 4.0, Oracle introduced the plug-in. A plug-in is an extension to the existing functionality of APEX. The idea behind plug-ins is to make life easier for developers. Plug-ins are reusable and can be exported and imported. In this way it is possible to create functionality which is available to all APEX developers. It is also possible to install and use them without having knowledge of what is inside the plug-in.

APEX is actually a program that converts your settings from the APEX builder to HTML and JavaScript. For example, if you created a text item in the APEX builder, APEX converts this to the following code (simplified):

```
<input type="text" id="P12_NAME" name="P12_NAME" value="your name">
```

When you create an item type plug-in, you actually take over this conversion task of APEX and you generate the HTML and JavaScript code yourself by using PL/SQL procedures. That offers a lot of flexibility because now you can make this code generic so that it can be used for more items.

The same goes for region type plug-ins. A region is a container for forms, reports, and such. The region can be a div or a HTML table. By creating a region type plug-in, you create a region yourself with the possibility to add more functionality to the region.

There are four types of plug-ins:

- Item type plug-ins
- Region type plug-ins
- Dynamic action plug-ins
- Process type plug-ins

In this chapter, we will discuss all four types of plug-ins.

Creating an item type plug-in

In an item type plug-in you create an item with the possibility of extending its functionality. To demonstrate this, we will make a text field with a tooltip. This functionality is already available in APEX 4.0 by adding the following code to the HTML form element attributes text field in the Element section of the text field:

```
onmouseover="toolTip_enable(event,this,'A tooltip')"
```

But you have to do this for every item that should contain a tooltip. This can be made more easy by creating an item type plug-in with a built-in tooltip. And if you create an item of type plug-in, you will be asked to enter some text for the tooltip.

Getting ready

For this recipe, you can use an existing page with a region where you can put some text items on.

How to do it...

1. Go to **Shared Components | User Interface | Plug-ins**.

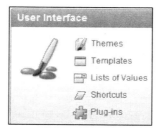

2. Click the **Create** button.
3. In the name section, enter a name in the name text field. In this case, we enter **tooltip**.

4. In the internal name text field, enter an internal name. It is advised to use your company's domain address reversed to ensure the name is unique when you decide to share this plug-in. So, for example, you can use **com.packtpub.apex.tooltip**.

5. In the source section, enter the following code to the PL/SQL code textarea:

```
function render_simple_tooltip (
p_item                    in apex_plugin.t_page_item
, p_plugin                in apex_plugin.t_plugin
, p_value                 in varchar2
, p_is_readonly           in boolean
, p_is_printer_friendly in boolean )
return apex_plugin.t_page_item_render_result
is
l_result             apex_plugin.t_page_item_render_result;
begin
if apex_application.g_debug
then
apex_plugin_util.debug_page_item (
    p_plugin                 => p_plugin
,    p_page_item             => p_item
,    p_value                 => p_value
,    p_is_readonly           => p_is_readonly
,    p_is_printer_friendly => p_is_printer_friendly);
end if;
--
sys.htp.p('<input type="text" id="'||p_item.name||'" name="'||p_
item.name||'" class="text_field" onmouseover="toolTip_enable(event
,this,'||''''||p_item.attribute_01||''''||')">');
--
return l_result;
end render_simple_tooltip;
```

[render_simple_tooltip.sql]

This function uses the `sys.htp.p` function to put a text item (`<input type="text"`) on the screen. On the text item, the `onmouseover` event calls the function `tooltip_enable()`. This function is an APEX function and can be used to put a tooltip on an item. The arguments of the function are mandatory.

The function starts with the option to show debug information. This can be very useful when you have created a plug-in and it doesn't work. After the debug information the `htp.p` function puts the text item on the screen, including the call to `tooltip_enable`. You can also see that the call to `tooltip_enable` uses `p_item.attribute_01`. This is a parameter that you can use to pass a value to the plug-in. That is the following step in this recipe.

6. The function ends with the return of `l_result`. This variable is of type `apex_plugin.t_page_item_render_result`. For the other types of plug-in there are also dedicated return types, for example, `t_region_render_result`.

7. Click the **Create** button.

8. The next step is to define the parameter (attribute) for this plug-in. In the **Custom Attributes** section, click the **Add Attribute** button.

9. In the **name** section, enter a name in the label text field, for example tooltip.

10. Ensure that the attribute text field contains the value **1**.

11. In the settings section, set the type to **text**.

12. Click the **Create** button.

13. In the callbacks section, enter **render_simple_tooltip** into the render function name text field.

14. Click the **Apply changes** button.

15. The plug-in is ready now. The next step is to create an item of type tooltip plug-in.

16. Go to a page with a region where you want to use an item with a tooltip.

17. In the items section, click on the add icon to create a new item.

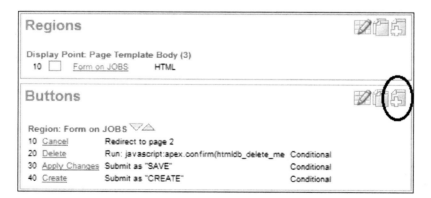

18. Select **Plug-ins**.

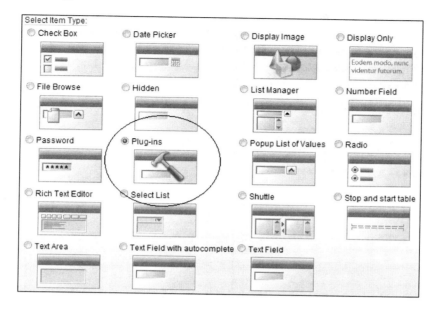

19. Now you will get a list of available plug-ins. Select the one we just created, **tooltip**. Click **Next**.

20. In the item name text field, enter a name for the item, for example **tt_item**.

21. In the region select list, select the region you want to put the item in. Click **Next**.

22. In the next step, you will get a new option. It's the attribute you created with the plug-in. Enter the tooltip text here. Click **Next**.

23. In the last step, leave everything as it is and click the **Create item** button.

24. You are ready now. Run the page. When you move your mouse pointer over the new item, you will see the tooltip.

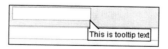

How it works...

As stated before, this plug-in actually uses the function `htp.p` to put an item on the screen. Together with the call to the JavaScript function `toolTip_enable` on the `onmouseover` event, this makes this a text item with a tooltip, replacing the normal text item.

There's more...

The tooltips shown in this recipe are rather simple. You could make it look better, for example, by using the Beautytips tooltips. Beautytips is an extension to jQuery and can show configurable help balloons. Visit `http://plugins.jquery.com` to download Beautytips. We downloaded version 0.9.5-rc1 to use in this recipe.

1. Go to **Shared Components** and click the **plug-ins** link.
2. Click the tooltip plug-in you just created.
3. In the source section, replace the code with the following code:

```
function render_tooltip (
p_item                in apex_plugin.t_page_item,
p_plugin              in apex_plugin.t_plugin,
p_value               in varchar2,
p_is_readonly         in boolean,
p_is_printer_friendly in boolean )
return apex_plugin.t_page_item_render_result
is
l_result             apex_plugin.t_page_item_render_result;
begin
if apex_application.g_debug
then
apex_plugin_util.debug_page_item (
    p_plugin                => p_plugin
,   p_page_item             => p_item
,   p_value                 => p_value
,   p_is_readonly           => p_is_readonly
,   p_is_printer_friendly   => p_is_printer_friendly);
end if;
```

[render_tooltip.sql]

The functions also starts with the debug option to see what happens when something goes wrong.

```
--Register the javascript and CSS library the plug-in uses.

  apex_javascript.add_library (
p_name      => 'jquery.bgiframe.min',
p_directory => p_plugin.file_prefix,
p_version   => null );
apex_javascript.add_library (
p_name      => 'jquery.bt.min',
p_directory => p_plugin.file_prefix,
p_version   => null );
```

For more information on this tooltip, go to: `http://plugins.jquery.com/project/bt`.

Creating a region type plug-in

As you may know, a region is actually a div. With the region type plug-in you can customize this div. And because it is a plug-in, you can reuse it in other pages. You also have the possibility to make the div look better by using JavaScript libraries. In this recipe, we will make a carousel with switching panels. The panels can contain images but they can also contain data from a table. We will make use of another jQuery extension, Stepcarousel.

Getting ready

You can download `stepcarousel.js` from `http://www.dynamicdrive.com/dynamicindex4/stepcarousel.htm`. However, in order to get this recipe to work in APEX, we needed to make a slight modification in it. So, `stepcarousel.js`, `arrowl.gif`, and `arrow.gif` are included in the download bundle of this book.

How to do it...

1. First, we will create the plug-in. Go to shared components and click on the **plug-ins** link.
2. Click the **Create** button.
3. In the **Name** section, enter a name for the plug-in in the Name field. We will use **Carousel**.
4. In the Internal name text field, enter a unique internal name. It is advised to use your domain reversed, for example, **com.packtpub.carousel**.
5. In the type list box, select **Region**.
6. In the **Source** section, enter the following code in the PL/SQL code text area:

```
function render_stepcarousel (
p_region              in apex_plugin.t_region,
p_plugin              in apex_plugin.t_plugin,
p_is_printer_friendly in boolean )
return apex_plugin.t_region_render_result
is
cursor c_crl is
select id
,       panel_title
,       panel_text
```

```
,        panel_text_date
from    app_carousel
order by id;
--
l_code varchar2(32767);
begin
```
[render_stepcarousel.sql]

The function starts with a number of arguments. These arguments are mandatory but have a default value. In the declare section, there is a cursor with a query on the table APP_CAROUSEL. This table contains several data to appear in the panels in the carousel.

```
--
add the libraries and stylesheets
--
apex_javascript.add_library (
p_name      => 'stepcarousel',
p_directory => p_plugin.file_prefix,
p_version   => null );
--
--Output the placeholder for the region which is used by the
Javascript code
```
[Render_stepcarousel.sql]

The actual code starts with the declaration of stepcarousel.js. There is a function, APEX_JAVASCRIPT.ADD_LIBRARY to load this library. This declaration is necessary but this file needs also to be uploaded in the next step. You don't have to use the extension .js here in the code.

```
--
sys.htp.p('<style type="text/css">');
--
sys.htp.p('.stepcarousel{');
sys.htp.p('position: relative;');
sys.htp.p('border: 10px solid black;');
sys.htp.p('overflow: scroll;');
sys.htp.p('width: '||p_region.attribute_01||'px;');
sys.htp.p('height: '||p_region.attribute_02||'px;');
sys.htp.p('}');
--
sys.htp.p('.stepcarousel .belt{');
sys.htp.p('position: absolute;');

sys.htp.p('left: 0;');
sys.htp.p('top: 0;');
sys.htp.p('}');
```

```
sys.htp.p('.stepcarousel .panel{');
sys.htp.p('float: left;');
sys.htp.p('overflow: hidden;');
sys.htp.p('margin: 10px;');
sys.htp.p('width: 250px;');
sys.htp.p('}');
--
sys.htp.p('</style>');
```
[render_stepcarousel.sql]

After the loading of the JavaScript library, some style elements are put on the screen. The style elements could have been put in a Cascaded Stylesheet (CSS) but since we want to be able to adjust the size of the carousel we use two parameters to set the height and width. And the height and the width are part of the style elements.

```
--
sys.htp.p('<div id="mygallery" class="stepcarousel" style="overflow:
hidden"><div class="belt">');
--
for r_crl in c_crl
loop
sys.htp.p('<div class="panel">');
sys.htp.p('<b>'||to_char(r_crl.panel_text_date,'DD-MON-YYYY')||'</
b>');
sys.htp.p('<br>');
sys.htp.p('<b>'||r_crl.panel_title||'</b>');
sys.htp.p('<hr>');
sys.htp.p(r_crl.panel_text);
sys.htp.p('</div>');
end loop;
--
sys.htp.p('</div></div>');
```
[render_stepcarousel.sql]

The next command in the script is the actual creation of a div. Important here is the name of the div and the class. The stepcarousel searches for these identifiers and replaces the div with the stepcarousel. The next step in the function is the fetch of the rows from the query in the cursor. For every line found, the formatted text is placed between the div tags. This is done so that stepcarousel recognizes that the text should be placed on the panels.

```
--Add the onload code to show the carousel
--
l_code := 'stepcarousel.setup({
galleryid: "mygallery"
,beltclass: "belt"
,panelclass: "panel"
```

```
,autostep: {enable:true, moveby:1, pause:3000}
,panelbehavior: {speed:500, wraparound:true, persist:true}
,defaultbuttons: {enable: true, moveby: 1, leftnav: ["'||p_plugin.
file_prefix||'arrowl.gif", -5, 80], rightnav: ["'||p_plugin.file_
prefix||'arrowr.gif", -20, 80]}
,statusvars: ["statusA", "statusB", "statusC"]
,contenttype: ["inline"]})';
--
apex_javascript.add_onload_code (p_code => l_code);
--
return null;
end render_stepcarousel;
```
[render_stepcarousel.sql]

The function ends with the call to `apex_javascript.add_onload_code`. Here starts the actual code for the stepcarousel and you can customize the carousel, like the size, rotation speed, and so on.

1. Click the **Create** button.

2. In the callbacks section, enter the name of the function in the return function name text field. In this case, it is **render_stepcarousel**.

3. In the files section, upload the files **stepcarousel.js**, **arrowl.gif** and **arrowr.gif**.

> For this purpose, the file `stepcarousel.js` has a little modification in it. In the last section (setup:function), `document.write` is used to add some style to the div. Unfortunately, this will not work in APEX, as `document.write` somehow destroys the rest of the output. So, after the call, APEX has nothing left to show, resulting in an empty page. `Document.write` needed to be removed and the style elements need to be added in the code of the plug-in:
>
> ```
> sys.htp.p('<div id="mygallery" class="stepcarousel"
> style="overflow:hidden"><div class="belt">');
> ```

In this line of code you see `style='overflow:hidden'`. That is the line that actually had to be included in `stepcarousel.js`. This command hides the scrollbars.

1. After you have uploaded the files, click the **Apply changes** button. The plug-in is ready and now we can use it in a page.

2. Go to the page where you want this stepcarousel to be shown.

3. In the regions section, click the **Add** icon.

4. In the next step, select **Plug-ins**.

5. Select **Carousel**.

6. Click **Next**.

7. Enter a title for this region, for example **Newscarousel**. Click **Next**.

8. In the next step, enter the height and the width of the carousel. To show a carousel with three panels, enter **800** in the **width** text field. Enter **100** in the **height** text field. Click **Next**.

9. Click the **Create region** button.

10. The plugin is ready. Run the page to see the result.

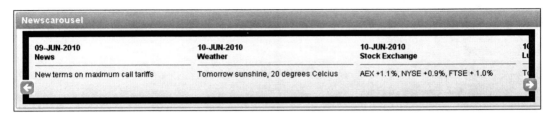

How it works...

The stepcarousel is actually a div. The region type plug-in uses the function `sys.htp.p` to put this div on the screen. In this example, a div is used but for the region, but also a HTML table can be used. An APEX region can contain any HTML output but for the positioning, mostly a HTML table or a div is used, especially when layout is important within the region.

The `apex_javascript.add_onload_code` starts the animation of the carousel. The carousel switches panels every three seconds. This can be adjusted (pause:3000).

See also

For more information on this jQuery extension, go to `http://www.dynamicdrive.com/dynamicindex4/stepcarousel.htm`.

Creating a dynamic action plug-in

A dynamic action is a piece of code that can handle page events (onchange, onclick, and so on). It is actually the APEX implementation of JavaScript event handling. For example, you can show or hide an item or a region on a specific moment. And that moment can be, for example, when a user clicks an item with the mouse, or when a user enters some text in an item. These moments are called events. There are several events which we already described in the recipe "Controlling the display of regions and items with dynamic actions" in *Chapter 1, Creating a basic APEX application*.

A dynamic action plug-in offers the same functionality but you can customize the appearance of the affected objects. In this recipe, we will show you how you can make a dynamic action plug-in which changes the color of a text item when a user enters some text in another text item.

Getting ready

No preparations are needed, except that you have an existing page with a region where you can put the items from this recipe on.

How to do it...

1. In the application builder, go to **Shared Components | Plug-ins**.
2. Click the **Create** button.
3. In the name section, enter a name for the plug-in, for example **setcolor**.
4. In the Internal name text field, enter a unique name, for example, **com.packtpub. setcolor**. In the type list box, select **Dynamic action**.
5. In the category list box, select **Miscellaneous** (use this category to easily find the plug-in back in the categorized action listbox later on in the recipe).
6. In the source section, enter the following code into the PL/SQL code text field:

```
function render_setcolor (
p_dynamic_action in apex_plugin.t_dynamic_action,
p_plugin         in apex_plugin.t_plugin )
return apex_plugin.t_dynamic_action_render_result
is
l_result apex_plugin.t_dynamic_action_render_result;
begin
l_result.javascript_function := 'function(pAction){this.
affectedElements.css("color", this.action.attribute01);}';
l_result.attribute_01        := p_dynamic_action.attribute_01;

return l_result;
end render_setcolor;
[render_setcolor.sql]
```

This piece of code starts with the declaration of the function with its parameters. The return value should be of type `apex_plugin.t_dynamic_action_render_result`. This return type contains the call to the built-in JavaScript function `this.affectedElements.css()`, which can change the style attributes of an object in the webpage, in this case a text item. The value of the color is set by the parameter `p_dynamic_action.attribute_01`.

7. In the **Callbacks** section, enter **render_setcolor** into the render function name text field.

8. In the **Standard attributes** section, check the **For Item(s)** and the **Affected Element Required** checkbox.

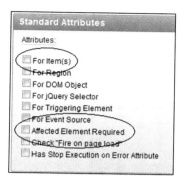

9. Click the **Create** button.

10. In the **Custom Attributes** section, click the **Add Attribute** button.

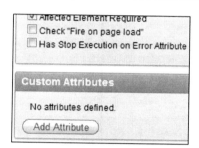

11. In the name section, enter **color** into the label text field.

12. Click the **Create** button.

13. Click the **Apply changes** button.

The plug-in is ready and now we will create two text items, one for triggering the event and one that is going to be the affected item.

1. Go to an existing page where you want to put this.

2. In the items section, click the **Add** icon.

3. Select **Text field**.

4. Enter a name for the text field, for example **PX_EVENT** (replace **X** by the page ID).

5. Click **Next** three times.

6. Click the **Create item** button to finish the create item wizard.

7. Again in the items section, click the add icon.

8. Select **Text field**.

9. Enter a name for the text field, for example **PX_TEXT** (replace X by the page ID).

10. Click **Next** two times.

11. Click **Create item**.

The two items are ready now. The last thing we have to do is to create the dynamic action.

1. In the dynamic actions section in the lower left corner, click the **Add** icon.

2. Select **Advanced**.

3. Enter a name for the dynamic action, for example **set_color**. Click **Next**.

4. In the **Items** text field, enter the name of the event item, **PX_EVENT** (replace X by the page id).

5. In the condition list box, select **Equal to**.

6. In the value text area, enter **SEMINAR**. Click **Next**.

7. In the action list box, select our newly created plug-in, **setcolor[Plug-in]**.

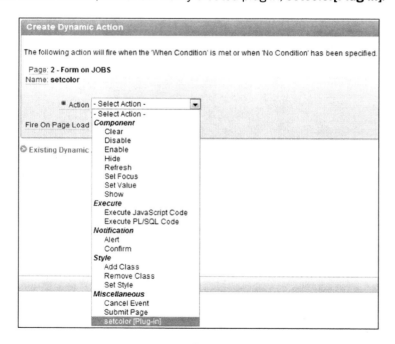

8. In the color text field, enter a color, for example, blue. Click **Next**.

9. In the false action select box, again select the new plug-in, **setcolor(Plug-in)**.

10. In the color text field, enter another color, green. Click **Next**.

11. In the selection type list box, select **Item**.

12. Click on the item **PX_TEXT** (replace X by the page ID) and click on the single arrow in the middle of the shuttle. Click the **Create** button.

13. You are ready now. Run the page and see what happens when you enter **SEMINAR** in the event text field.

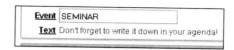

How it works...

This dynamic action plug-in works just as the normal dynamic actions except that there is a new action. Instead of show or hide, we now give the affected object a certain color, simply by changing the style of the object. We could have used some other style, for example font-weight instead of color. In that case, don't use the color names (blue and green) but bold and normal.

Creating a process type plug-in

A process type plug-in extends the functionality of a page process. This can be anything but it is typically used for APEX built-ins or Internet functionalities like e-mail sender or Twitter update. The benefit of this is that the process type plug-ins can be reused. We will create a process type plug-in which changes the language by using the APEX_UTIL.SET_SESSION_LANG built-in. There are more ways to change the session language but in this recipe, we will use this built-in in a page process to demonstrate how it works.

Getting ready

Make sure you have an existing webpage with a region.

How to do it...

1. Go to shared components and click **Plug-ins**.

2. Click the **Create** button.

3. In the name section, enter **set_language** in the name text field.

4. In the internal name text field, enter a unique name, for example **com.packtpub. set_language**.

5. In the type list box, select **Process**.

6. In the PL/SQL code text area, enter the following code:

```
function set_language (
p_process in apex_plugin.t_process,
p_plugin  in apex_plugin.t_plugin )
return apex_plugin.t_process_exec_result
is
Dynamic Attribute mapping
l_language    varchar2(50) := p_process.attribute_01;
l_result      apex_plugin.t_process_exec_result;
begin
Set session language
apex_util.set_session_lang(l_language);
Set success message
l_result.success_message := 'Session language switched to '||l_
language;
return l_result;
end set_language;
```
[set_language.sql]

The function starts with two arguments, which are necessary but have a default value. The return type is `apex_plugin.t_process_exec_result`. The actual switch is done by `APEX_UTIL.SET_SESSION_LANG`.

1. In the callbacks section, enter **set_language** in the execution function name.

2. Click the **Create** button.

3. In the custom attributes section, click the **Add Attribute** button.

4. In the name section, enter **Language** in the label text field.

5. Click the **Create** button. The process type plug-in is ready. Now we will create a text item and a button to start the process.

6. Go to your application and click on the page you want to edit.

7. In the processes section, click the add icon.

8. Select **plug-ins**.

9. Select the plug-in we just created, **set_language**.

10. Enter a name for this plug-in, for example, **setlang**. Click **Next**.

11. In the language text field, enter **&PX_LANGUAGE.** (replace X by the page ID).

12. Click the **Create process** button.

13. In the items section, click the add icon.

14. Select the **Select list**.

15. Enter **PX_LANGUAGE** (replace X by the page id) in the item name text field.

16. In the region select list, select the region you want to put this item on. Click **Next** two times.

17. In the create item section, set the **Page action when value changed** list box to **Submit Page**. Click **Next**.

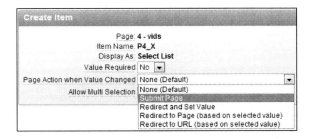

18. Click the **Create or edit static List of Values** link.

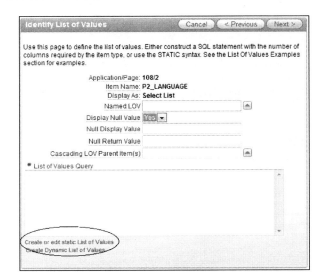

19. In the pop-up window, enter the following languages in both columns:

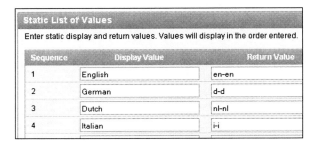

20. Click the **Apply** button.
21. Click **Next**.
22. Click the **Create item** button.

The process type plug-in and the page are ready now. Run the page and test the plug-in.

How it works...

The only thing this plug-in does is a call to `apex_util.set_session_lang` with a language abbreviation.

There's more...

See `http://download.oracle.com/docs/cd/B19306_01/server.102/b14225/applocaledata.htm#i634428` for a list of country and language codes.

6

Creating Multilingual APEX Applications

In this chapter, we will cover the following topics:

- ▶ Creating a translatable application
- ▶ Using XLIFF files
- ▶ Switching languages
- ▶ Translating data in an application

Introduction

The consequence of publishing applications on the web is that anyone from anywhere in the world (and beyond since they have the Internet on the International Space Station) can view your work. When your target audience is in one country, a single language is often enough. But what can you do when you want to serve your website to many international visitors in their native tongue?

Application Express offers built-in functionality to translate applications, without having to rebuild the application completely.

This chapter is about how we can fully translate an application using those built-ins and adding something of ourselves to easily switch between languages.

Creating a translatable application

An application needs to be altered before translations will work. It has to know for instance that it is going to be translated, by setting some properties.

This recipe will show how an application can be prepared for translations.

Getting ready

To start with this recipe we will need a new application. We will use the EMP and DEPT tables to build a straightforward application with minimal effort.

1. In the Application Builder, click **Create** to start making a new application.
2. Select **Database** as the Application Type and click **Next**.
3. Select **From Scratch** and click **Next**.
4. Name the application **HR Multilingual**. Leave the Application ID and other options on their default values and click **Next**.
5. Select the Page Type: **Report and Form**.
6. Enter **EMP** as the **Table Name**.
7. Select the Implementation Classic and click **Add Page**.
8. Repeat these steps to add a Report and Form for the DEPT table.
9. Press **Create** to finalize the application using Theme 1 or click **Next** and follow the wizard to select another theme. When you do that, remember to keep the language on English.

We now have an application with five pages; one Login page and a Report and Form page for both the EMP and DEPT tables.

When we run the application, we will see the application in English as can be expected. We are now ready to implement the functionality that is necessary to make this a multilingual application.

How to do it...

Now that we have an application at our disposal, we can start to prepare it for translations. The first step that we have to take is that we have to tell the application how it will know what language to use. This is going to require a special application item.

1. First navigate to the Application overview and click the button that is labeled **Edit Application Properties**.

2. Go to the tab **Globalization**.

3. Set the property **Application Language Derived From** to **Item Preference (use item containing preference)**.

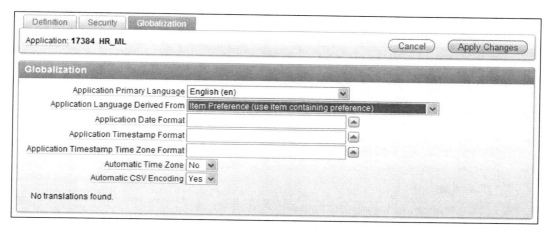

APEX now knows that it can derive the language to show the page in from a special application item. But this item still has to be created. To do this, follow the next steps:

1. Go to **Shared Components**.

2. Under **Logic** click on **Application Items**.

3. Click on the **Create** button.

4. Enter the name **FSP_LANGUAGE_PREFERENCE** for the item and leave all other properties on their default value.

5. Click **Create** to finish.

The item is called FSP_LANGUAGE_PREFERENCE, because APEX recognizes that name as an item reserved for application languages. When a page is rendered, APEX checks the FSP_LANGUAGE_PREFERENCE item to see in what language the page has to be shown.

There is a snag in this process. Because of the way Application Express builds up its page, a change in the FSP_LANGUAGE_PREFERENCE item is not immediately visible. Whenever the language is changed, the page has to be reloaded to show the result.

To make this happen, we will add an Application Process that will handle the reloading of the page:

1. Return to **Shared Components**.

2. Under **Logic** click on **Application Processes**.

3. Click the **Create** button.

4. Enter the name **set_language**.

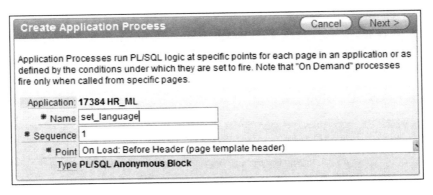

5. Select **On Load: Before Header (page template header)** at the **Point** property to trigger the process as soon as possible on the page.

6. Click **Next**.

7. In the Process Text, enter the following PL/SQL code:

```
begin
owa_util.redirect_url('f?p='||:APP_ID||':'||:APP_PAGE_ID||':'||:
APP_SESSION);
end;
```

8. In the **Error Message** box, enter **Process cannot be executed** and click **Next**.

We choose to start this process when a page is called using a special Request. This will be defined with the following steps:

1. As the **Condition Type**, select **Request = Expression 1**.

2. In the textarea that appears enter **LANG** (all uppercase).

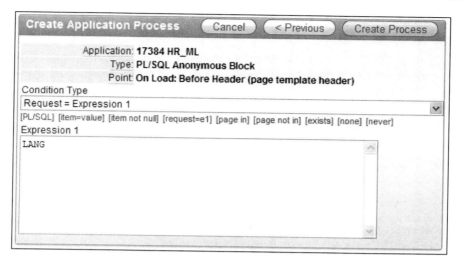

3. Click **Create Process** to finish.

When we now review the list of application processes, we can see the new process has been added to the list.

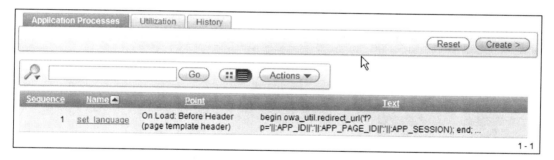

The application is now ready to be translated. Everything is in place to run it in any language imaginable.

To call the application in another language, change the URL of your application to the following:

```
http://yourdomain:port/pls/apex/f?p=&APP_ID.:&PAGE_ID.:&SESSION_
ID.:LANG:NO::FSP_LANGUAGE_PREFERENCE:nl
```

This example will call the chosen page in the application and show it in the Dutch language instead of in English. To select another language change the property nl at the end of the URL to your desired language code.

See also

Now that we have a translatable application, we can start on the translation itself. The application is still only available in English, so we will have to create a translated version of the application in another language.

This will be shown in the recipe called *Using XLIFF files*.

Next to that we can only call the application in other languages by changing the FSP_LANGUAGE_PREFERENCE item in the URL. We should create a more user-friendly way to navigate to different languages.

This topic will be covered in the recipe called *Switching languages*.

Item preference is not the only way of telling an application how to get it's language. A new option in APEX 4.0 is 'Session'. The recipe called *Translating data in an application* will show how to use this. It will also show an example of translating the data in an application.

Using XLIFF files

One of the world's most recognized standards in localization is the XLIFF format. XLIFF is the abbreviation for **XML Localisation Interchange File Format**. As the name explains, it's an XML standard and it has been adopted by Application Express as the format in which different language files can be exported from and imported into APEX applications.

This recipe will show how we can use XLIFF to quickly translate an application from its default language to a new language.

Getting ready

Start with the translatable application that we have built in the first recipe of this chapter. By doing that, we have a good and clean starting point for the first translation.

How to do it...

1. Navigate to **Shared Components**.

   At the bottom of the page we can see a section called **Globalization**. This section holds all options that are needed to translate the current application.

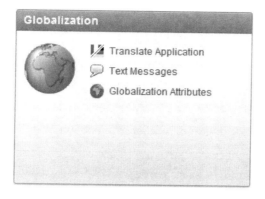

2   Click on the link that is labelled **Translate Application**.

This will open up a new page with several options to use when translating an application. In fact, it's a list of all steps necessary to fully translate the application in APEX.

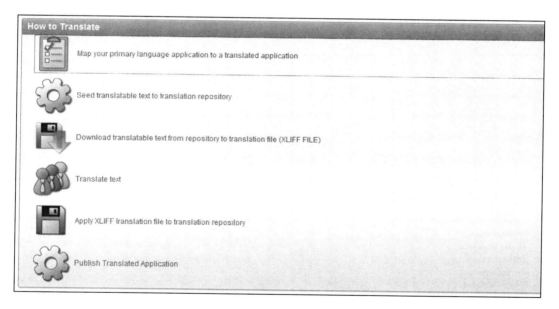

3.   Click on the first link **Map your primary language application to a translated application**. This will tell APEX the new language that is going to be used.

4.   Click the **Create** button.

5.   Enter a new application ID that is not yet used by your APEX environment.

6.   Select the language code that you want to translate to. In this example, we will use 'Dutch (Netherlands) (nl)'.

7. Click **Create**.

   The fundament for the new translation is now in place and we can proceed to the next step.

8. Return to the Application Translation Home by clicking on the **Translate** link in the breadcrumb.

9. Click the second step called **Seed Translatable Text** to translation repository.

10. Select the **Language Mapping** that we just created.

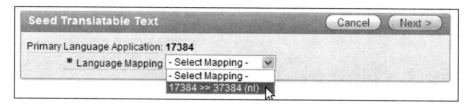

11. Click **Next**.

12. Click **Seed Translatable Text**.

This will create entries in the APEX repository for every translatable text in the application. These entries will be used later to generate the XLIFF files.

After the seeding process is completed, APEX shows an overview with summaries of all relevant figures. Click **Done** to close this screen.

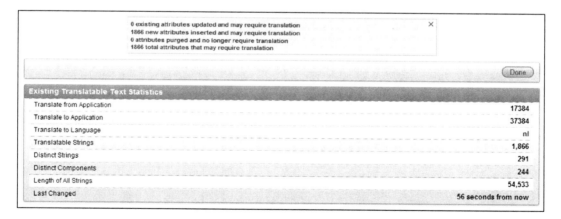

1. Return to the Application Translation Home again by clicking on the **Translate** link in the breadcrumb.

2. Click the third step called **Download translatable text from repository to translation file (XLIFF FILE)**.

   The following screen offers two options; download an XLIFF file for the complete application or download a file for a specific page. We will use the second option to get a feeling of what is required to use an XLIFF file.

3. In the bottom section called **Download XLIFF file for Application Page** use the first select list to select the application we are working on.

4. In the second select list select page **101 Login**.

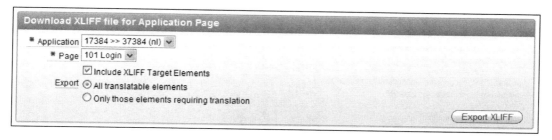

5. Press the button **Export XLIFF**.

6. Use the dialogs to save the file to a location on the hard drive.

   The XLIFF file has now been downloaded and is ready to be edited. This is the fourth step in the Translation process.

7. Use your file browser program to locate the downloaded `.xlf` file and open it for editing in your favourite text editor.

8. Scroll down to the bottom and find the entries with `Username` and `Password`. Change the text between the 'target' tags to the following:

```
<source>Username</source>
<target>Gebruikersnaam</target>

<source>Password</source>
<target>Wachtwoord</target>
```

By changing these two entries, we will at least be able to see the changes. Feel free to change all other translations as well to see the effect on the login page, but this is not necessary for this recipe.

We will now upload the altered file back into APEX.

1. Save the XLIFF file and return to the APEX Application Translation Home.

2. Click on the fifth step called **Apply XLIFF translation file to translation repository**.

3. Click the button labelled **Upload XLIFF**.

4. Enter the title **en_nl_translation** and use the **Browse** button to find the `.xlf` file that we have just edited.

5. Click **Upload XLIFF File**.

6. Click on the title of the XLIFF file we just uploaded.

7. In the next screen, select the translation mapping to apply the XLIFF file to.

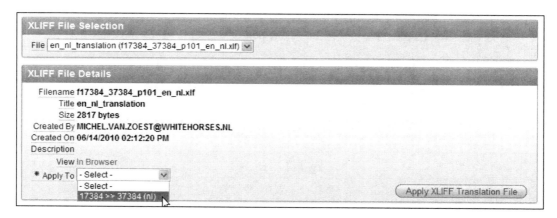

8. Click **Apply XLIFF Translation File** to finish connecting the file to the mapping.

9. In the next screen, select the translation mapping again in the select list labelled **Publish Application Translation**. Note that this is equal to Step 6 in the list on the Application Translation Home.

10. Click **Publish Application**.

We are done with the translation of all APEX texts in this application.

How it works...

All translatable text is saved in the Application Express Repository. It's possible to directly alter these entries by navigating to a special page.

1. Go to **Shared Components**.

2. Go to **Translate Application**.

3. In the bottom section called **Translation Utilities**, click on the item **Manually Edit Translation Repository**.

From there, we can select the right mapping and if desired a single page. Because this is an Interactive Report, we can use filters and other features to find the desired text to translate.

The quickest way to translate a lot of text is still using the XLIFF file. Because this is an international standard, an XLIFF file can be handled by any translation service.

An XLIFF file is always built the same way; a header and a body. The first part of the header shows some information about the file, the original application, and the translation target application. Because this is commented, it will not be used by a processing application.

```
<?xml version="1.0" encoding="UTF-8"?>
<!--
    ******************
    ** Source     :  17384
    ** Source Lang:  en
    ** Target     :  37384
    ** Target Lang:  nl
    ** Filename:     f17384_37384_en_nl.xlf
    ** Generated By: MICHEL.VAN.ZOEST@WHITEHORSES.NL
    ** Date:         15-JUN-2010 14:05:34
    ******************
-->
```

The second part of the header shows the version of the XLIFF standard that is used. The latest specification version is 1.2, but APEX still uses 1.0 by default.

```
<xliff version="1.0">
```

The third part of the header holds some more information about the file, the source language, and the target language. This information is used by APEX when importing the file.

```
<file original="f17384_37384_en_nl.xlf" source-language="en" target-
language="nl" datatype="html">
<header></header>
```

After the header the body starts.

```
<body>
```

The following part is repeated for every text in the APEX repository: an identification for the item that holds the text, a source in the original language, and a target in the new language.

```
<trans-unit id="S-2-27846723888160713-17384">
<source>Logout</source>
<target>Uitloggen</target>
</trans-unit>
```

Finally, the file is closed.

```
</body>
</file>
</xliff>
```

There is one thing that you will always have to keep in mind when using XLIFF files for translating an application. Every time something is changed in the application, you will have to repeat the process of seeding, exporting, translating, and importing. Otherwise, not all changes will be visible in the translated version of the application.

So when the translating itself is done by an external company, it would be wise to send them the XLIFF file after the application in the default language is completely done. This could save a lot of money.

Switching languages

In the past two recipes, we have changed a standard application so that it can be translated and we performed the translation itself. In this recipe, we will add something that will make switching between languages much easier for users.

Getting ready

To start this recipe, we will need an application that has been translated like the application we created in the past two recipes.

How to do it...

The best place to create a language switch is a place that is visible at all times. In this case, we will use the navigation bar. Since this bar is in the header of our application, it is visible on all pages; ideal for our purposes.

1. Navigate to the **Shared Components**.
2. In the **Navigation Section** find the **Navigation Bar Entries** and click it.
3. There should already be an entry called **Logout** in place.
4. Click the **Create** button.
5. Confirm that the option **From Scratch** is selected and click **Next**.
6. Select **Navigation to URL** and click **Next**.
7. Enter **English** as the Entry Label and click **Next**.
8. In the next page, enter the following for the properties:
   - **Target is a: Page in this application**
   - **Page: &APP_PAGE_ID.** (do not forget the dot at the end)
   - **Request: LANG**
   - **Set these items: FSP_LANGUAGE_PREFERENCE**
   - **With these values: en**

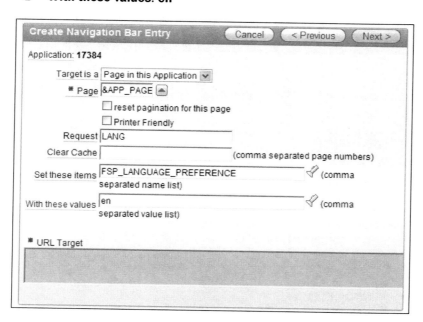

9. Click **Next**.
10. Click **Create**.

We have now created a link in the navigation bar that will direct users to the English part of the application. To create a link to the Dutch version of the application, repeat these steps but change the Entry Label to 'Nederlands' and set **With these values** to **nl** instead of **en**.

Remember to run the XLIFF translation steps again to make sure the new text is available in both languages.

When we now run the application, we can see that two entries are available in the navigation bar.

Clicking on **Nederlands** will show the application in Dutch and clicking on **English** will change it back to the English language.

Translating data in an application

Besides the application labels, there is more to translate in an application. Data for instance.

In this recipe, we will see an example of this. To accomplish this, we will use a built-in way of translating the session language that is new in APEX 4.0.

Getting ready

Start by creating some new database objects. Remember that this is a crude setup. In a production environment, this should be more elaborate.

First, we will create a copy of the EMP table, but with a change. The JOB column will now be called JOB_NO and it's content will reference to a EMP_JOB_TITLES table.

```
create table EMP_LANG
(
  empno     NUMBER(4) not null,
  ename     VARCHAR2(10),
  job_no    NUMBER,
  mgr       NUMBER(4),
  hiredate DATE,
```

```
   sal        NUMBER(7,2),
   comm       NUMBER(7,2),
   deptno     NUMBER(2)
);
```
[emp_lang.sql]

Also create the EMP_JOB_TITLES table. This table contains a LANGUAGE column that will hold the language in which the job_title is entered for that row.

This also means that job_no is not a unique column in this table, but job_no in combination with language is the unique key.

```
create table EMP_JOB_TITLES
(
   job_no     NUMBER,
   job_title  VARCHAR2(32),
   language   VARCHAR2(10)
);
```
[emp_job_titles.sql]

Next, it will need data. First the EMP_JOB_TITLES. This script will fill the table with the original 5 job titles from the EMP table with language 'en' and add 5 translations in Dutch for the same titles.

```
insert into EMP_JOB_TITLES (job_no, job_title, language)
values (1, 'PRESIDENT', 'en');
insert into EMP_JOB_TITLES (job_no, job_title, language)
values (2, 'MANAGER', 'en');
insert into EMP_JOB_TITLES (job_no, job_title, language)
values (3, 'ANALYST', 'en');
insert into EMP_JOB_TITLES (job_no, job_title, language)
values (4, 'CLERK', 'en');
insert into EMP_JOB_TITLES (job_no, job_title, language)
values (5, 'SALESMAN', 'en');
insert into EMP_JOB_TITLES (job_no, job_title, language)
values (1, 'Directeur', 'nl');
insert into EMP_JOB_TITLES (job_no, job_title, language)
values (2, 'Manager', 'nl');
insert into EMP_JOB_TITLES (job_no, job_title, language)
values (3, 'Analist', 'nl');
insert into EMP_JOB_TITLES (job_no, job_title, language)
values (4, 'Klerk', 'nl');
insert into EMP_JOB_TITLES (job_no, job_title, language)
values (5, 'Verkoper', 'nl');
```
[emp_job_titles_data.sql]

For the `EMP_LANG` table, copy the data from the `EMP` table, but replace the contents of the `JOB` column with the reference number as it was entered in the `EMP_JOB_TITLES` table (for example; `PRESIDENT` will become 1, `CLERK` will become 4).

Some examples of this data are:

```
insert into EMP_LANG (empno, ename, job_no, mgr, hiredate, sal, comm,
deptno)
values (7839, 'KING', 1, null, to_date('17-11-1981', 'dd-mm-yyyy'),
5000, null, 10);
insert into EMP_LANG (empno, ename, job_no, mgr, hiredate, sal, comm,
deptno)
values (7698, 'BLAKE', 2, 7839, to_date('01-05-1981', 'dd-mm-yyyy'),
2850, null, 30);
```
[emp_lang_data.sql]

The `emp_lang_data.sql` script contains 12 more rows.

How to do it

When there is a datamodel available that allows data to be saved in multiple languages, the hardest part is writing smart queries to get this data out in the right language for the user. We will create a page based on such a query for our simple datamodel.

The first step is getting the application ready. To use the **Session** option, take the following steps.

1. Go to the **Application Properties**.
2. Go to the **Globalization** tab.
3. In the select list **Application Language Derived From** select **Session**.
4. Click **Apply Changes**.

   Next step is to create a page based on a language-driven query.

5. On the application overview, click **Create Page**.
6. Select **Report** and click **Next**.
7. Select **Classic Report** and click **Next**.
8. Enter a number and name for the page and click **Next**.
9. Select **Do Not Use Tabs** and click **Next**.

10. Enter the query that will drive the Page.

```
select emp.empno
, emp.ename
, job.job_title
, emp.hiredate
, emp.sal
from emp_lang emp
, emp_job_titles job
where emp.job_no = job.job_no
and upper(job.language) = upper(apex_util.get_session_lang)
```

11. Click **Next** a few times until the **Finish** button appears and click it.

To test the changes, Run the page by altering the URL to accept a p_lang parameter like so:

```
http://server:port/apex/f?p=app_id:page_id:session&p_lang=en
```

Empno	Ename	Job Title	Hiredate	Sal
7369	SMITH	CLERK	17-DEC-80	1900
7499	ALLEN	SALESMAN	20-FEB-81	1600
7521	WARD	SALESMAN	22-FEB-81	1250
7566	JONES	MANAGER	02-APR-81	2975
7654	MARTIN	SALESMAN	28-SEP-81	1250
7698	BLAKE	MANAGER	01-MAY-81	2850
7782	CLARK	MANAGER	09-JUN-81	2450
7788	SCOTT	ANALYST	09-DEC-82	3200
7839	KING	PRESIDENT	17-NOV-81	5000
7844	TURNER	SALESMAN	08-SEP-81	1500
7876	ADAMS	CLERK	12-JAN-83	1100
7900	JAMES	CLERK	03-DEC-81	950
7902	FORD	ANALYST	03-DEC-81	3000
7934	MILLER	CLERK	23-JAN-82	1300

For the Dutch language, enter the URL like this:

```
http://server:port/apex/f?p=app_id:page_id:session&p_lang=nl
```

Empno	Ename	Job Title	Hiredate	Sal
7369	SMITH	Klerk	17-12-80	1900
7499	ALLEN	Verkoper	20-02-81	1600
7521	WARD	Verkoper	22-02-81	1250
7566	JONES	Manager	02-04-81	2975
7654	MARTIN	Verkoper	28-09-81	1250
7698	BLAKE	Manager	01-05-81	2850
7782	CLARK	Manager	09-06-81	2450
7788	SCOTT	Analist	09-12-82	3200
7839	KING	Directeur	17-11-81	5000
7844	TURNER	Verkoper	08-09-81	1500
7876	ADAMS	Klerk	12-01-83	1100
7900	JAMES	Klerk	03-12-81	950
7902	FORD	Analist	03-12-81	3000
7934	MILLER	Klerk	23-01-82	1300

How it works

Using the **Session** option for Globalization, allows developers to take advantage of some additional built-in functions and procedures.

1. `apex_util.set_session_lang(p_lang in varchar2)`
   - This procedure will set the language for the session to the value in the parameter
2. `apex_util.get_session_lang`
   - This function will get the current session language. It can also be called using the variable v('BROWSER_LANGUAGE')
3. `apex_util.reset_session_lang`
   - This procedure will clear the session language

In this recipe we took advantage of the apex_util.get_session_lang procedure to retrieve the correct job titles in our report. It doesn't take a lot of imagination to see the possibilities of this kind of construction. We have now seen how to put translatable data into a separate table and making it unique by combining an ID column like the JOB_NO column in our example to a LANGUAGE column.

Of course this can be used for any kind of data. Just remember to keep a keen eye on the performance of your application.

7
APEX APIs

In this chapter, we will cover the following topics:

- ▶ Updating a table with the hidden primary key
- ▶ Reading a checkbox programmatically
- ▶ Creating help functionality with `apex_application.help`
- ▶ Counting clicks with `apex_util.count_clicks`
- ▶ Setting default item settings with `apex_ui_default_update`
- ▶ Creating a background process with `apex_plsql_job`

Introduction

APEX 4.0 comes with a set of application programming interfaces (APIs). These APIs help the APEX developer to programmatically change the settings you would normally do in the APEX builder. The APIs offer a lot of flexibility and speed in developing web applications. Especially when you have to do a lot of repeating actions in the APEX builder, the APIs can be very useful.

In this chapter, we will show you how to use some of the APIs. For more information, refer to the APEX API reference which is included in your APEX 4.0 download.

Updating a table with the hidden primary key

`APEX_ITEM` is a PL/SQL package that you can use to programmatically put items on the screen. The package also contains a function to put hidden items on the screen. Hidden items are items that are placed in a webpage but are not visible. However, they can contain a value. In this way, you can make each row in a report unique. We will make an updatable report which makes use of the `APEX_ITEM` API.

Getting ready

Make sure you have access to the table APP_EVENTS.

How to do it...

First, we will make a classic report based on the APP_EVENTS table.

1. In the application builder, click the **Create page** button.
2. Select **Report**.
3. Select **Classic report**.
4. Enter a name for the page and click **Next**.
5. Select **Do not use tabs** and click **Next**.
6. In the text area, enter the following query:

```
select apex_item.hidden(1,id)||apex_item.text(2,event) appevent
,       apex_item.date_popup(3,rownum,event_date,'dd-mm-yyyy')
event_date
,       apex_item.text(4,location) location
,       apex_item.text(5,event_type) event_type
from    app_events;
```
[1346_07_01.txt]

7. Click **Next**.
8. You can enter a region name. After that, click **Next**.
9. Click **Finish**. The report has been created and we are now going to edit it.

10. Click the **Edit Page** icon.
11. Click on the **Report** link in the regions section to edit the report attributes.
12. Click on the **Edit** icon (the pencil) to edit the first column.
13. In the column attributes section, select **Standard Report Column** in the **Display As** listbox.

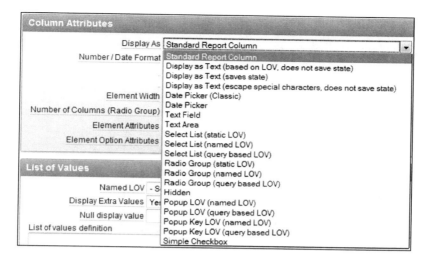

14. Click the **Apply changes** button.

15. Repeat these steps for the other three columns and click the **Apply changes** button to return to the page definition.

Now we will make a button and a page process to enable the saving of data.

1. In the buttons section, click the **Add** icon.

2. Select a region for the button and click **Next**.

3. Select **Create a button in a region position** and click **Next**.

4. Enter a name for the button, for example **Save**. Enter a label for the button. You can enter here **Save** as well. Click **Next**.

5. Select **Bottom of region** and click **Next**.

6. In the action list box, select **Submit Page.** Click **Create** button.

7. In the **Processes** section, click the **Add** icon.

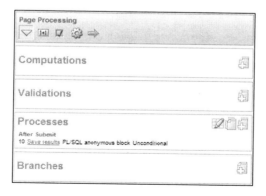

8. Select **PL/SQL**.

9. Enter a name for the page process. You can enter here **save_results**. Click **Next**.

10. In the text area, enter the following code:

```
begin
for i in 1..apex_application.g_f01.count
loop
update app_events
set     event       = apex_application.g_f02(i)
,       event_date  = to_date(apex_application.g_f03(i),
                                    'dd-mm-yyyy')
,       location    = apex_application.g_f04(i)
,       event_type  = apex_application.g_f05(i)
where   id          = to_number(apex_application.g_f01(i));
end loop;
end;
```

[1346_07_2.txt]

11. Click the **Create process** button.

12. The page is ready. Run it and try to change some values in the page. Then try to save by clicking the **Save** button.

How it works...

With APEX_ITEM you can put an item on the screen. The first parameter in the function (hidden, text, or date_popup) is the index which you can use to find the item back. Let's say you use the following command to put an item on the screen:

APEX_ITEM.TEXT(2,'COLUMN_NAME')

When submitted, the values of the APEX items will be stored in the PL/SQL array APEX_APPLICATION.G_F0X. Then you can find this item back with:

APEX_APPLICATION.G_F02(i).

Where i is the row indicator in case you are working with a multi row tabular form.

Furthermore, you can use the first variable to do some aggregate functions like count. Use it in the following way:

APEX_APPLICATION.G_F01.COUNT.

Note that the example in this recipe only handles existing rows.

Reading a checkbox programmatically

In the previous recipe, we saw that we can use APEX_ITEM and APEX_APPLICATION to programmatically display and control items. We can also create and manipulate a checkbox. In this recipe, we will show you how to use the APEX_ITEM.CHECKBOX function and how to avoid problems. We will use the previous recipe and extend it with a checkbox.

A checkbox is a special kind of item on a webpage. It can either be checked or unchecked. But APEX doesn't know the unchecked state and therefore it replaces the unchecked value with null. Since APEX_APPLICATION is an array, null values will not be stored in APEX_APPLICATION. But if you try to look up the value of a certain row, you might get a no data found error.

Getting ready

Make sure you have a working events page from the previous recipe. Add a column to the table APP_EVENTS by entering the following in SQLplus:

```
Alter table app_events
Add oracle_event varchar2(1);
```

[1346_07_03.txt]

How to do it...

We will make a change to the page from the previous recipe.

1. Go to the page you created in the previous recipe.
2. In the regions section, click the **Report region** link.
3. Replace the region source with the following:

```
select apex_item.hidden(1,id)||apex_item.text(2,event) appevent
,       apex_item.date_popup(3,rownum,event_date,'dd-mm-yyyy')
event_date
,       apex_item.text(4,location) location
,       apex_item.text(5,event_type) event_type
,       apex_item.checkbox(6,id,decode(nvl(oracle_event,'N'),'Y','C
HECKED',null)) oracle_event
from    app_events
```

[1346_07_04.txt]

The difference with the query in the previous recipe is that there is one extra column: APEX_ITEM.CHECKBOX. The third argument is the decode, which sets the checkbox to be checked if the value is 'Y'. If the value of ORACLE_EVENT is 'N' or empty, the checkbox is unchecked. However, in APEX, you cannot speak of an unchecked status. The checkbox is either checked or null. This is an HTML restriction. And this is exactly the point you need to pay attention to. However, besides the checked status, a checkbox can also get a value and in this query the checkbox gets the value of the ID column of the APP_EVENTS table. We will use that later on in the recipe.

1. Click the **Apply changes** button.

2. Click on the **Report** link in the regions section.

3. Click on the **Edit** icon (the pencil) next to the column ORACLE_EVENT.

4. In the column attributes section, select **Standard report column** in the **Display as select** list.

5. Click the **Apply changes** button.

6. Click the **Apply changes** button again.

7. In the processes section in the middle of the screen, click the SAVE_RESULTS link.

8. Replace the code in the process text area with the following:

```
declare
   type            t_event is table of varchar2(10) index by
                                         binary_integer;
   v_event         t_event;
   l_index         number(3);
   l_oracle_event varchar2(10);
begin
   -- use a pl/sql table to put the 'Y' in the
   -- right index
   for a in 1..apex_application.g_f06.count
   loop
     if apex_application.g_f06.exists(a)
     then
       l_index := to_number(apex_application.g_f06(a));
       v_event(l_index) := 'Y';
     end if;
   end loop;
   --
   -- Loop through the records
   for i in 1..apex_application.g_f01.count
   loop
      -- if the pl/sql table contains a value for this
      -- row, oracle_event has to be set to 'Y'. Otherwise
      -- leave oracle_event to null
```

```
if v_event.exists(to_number(apex_application.g_f01(i)))
then
  l_oracle_event :=
          v_event(to_number(apex_application.g_f01(i)));
else
  l_oracle_event := null;
end if;
--
update app_events
set     event          = apex_application.g_f02(i)
,       event_date     = to_date(apex_application.g_f03(i),
                                  'dd-mm-yyyy')
,       location       = apex_application.g_f04(i)
,       event_type     = apex_application.g_f05(i)
,       oracle_event   = l_oracle_event
where   id             = to_number(apex_application.g_f01(i));
  end loop;
end;
```
[1346_07_05.txt]

This code is different from the code in the previous recipe. You can see that the ORACLE_EVENT is added to the update statement. Furthermore, you can see that a PL/SQL table (V_EVENT) is used to store the checked values. APEX_ITEM.CHECKBOX only stores the checked values. This means that when the checkboxes of rows 1, 3 and 5 are checked, the array for the checkbox, apex_application.g_f06, contains only three values. But when you try to read the value of the fifth row, you will get an error message. Contrary to, let's say event (with the apex_application.g_f03 array), you cannot get the value of the checkbox of a certain row.

To make this clear, have a look at the following table. You can see that the arrays for the ID and the EVENT column contain the correct values for each row. But the array for the checkbox shows the checked state for the first three rows where it should be checked for the rows 1, 3, and 5.

Index value	Value of ID column Array	Value of EVENT column array	Value of Checkbox array
1	2	ODTUG...	Checked (1)
2	3	OBUG...	Checked (3)
3	4	OOW...	Checked (5)
4	5	Dinner...	
5	6	Knowledge session...	

To avoid this, we use a PL/SQL table (V_EVENT) that only stores a value for the rows that contain a checked checkbox. We already saw that in the query each checkbox gets the value of the ID column. This value is used as index for the PL/SQL table V_EVENT. Later on in the code, where APEX loops through the array for the ID column, APEX checks whether V_EVENT contains a value for that particular index (ID). If so, the column ORACLE_EVENT should be updated with 'Y'.

1. Click the **Apply changes** button.
2. The page is ready. Run it, check some checkboxes, and see if it works.

Creating help functionality with apex_application.help

To support a user-friendly interface, applications can be enhanced with a help-functionality. In APEX, you can easily build a context-sensitive help. You can place a help link in the navigation bar so that it is available on every page in the application.

Getting ready

Make sure you have an existing application with some pages where you can show some help.

How to do it...

First, let's create the help page:

1. In the application builder, click the **Create page** button.
2. Select **Blank page**.
3. Enter a page number and an alias. Click **Next**.
4. Enter a name for the help page. Click **Next**.
5. Select **No tabs** and click **Next**.

6. Click **Finish**.

   The page has now been created. Click the **edit** page icon to continue.

7. In the regions section, click the **Add** icon.

8. Select **PL/SQL Dynamic content**.

9. Enter a title. Click **Next**.

10. In the PL/SQL source text area, enter the following code:

```
APEX_APPLICATION.HELP(
p_flow_id => :APP_ID,
p_flow_step_id => :REQUEST,
p_before_region_html => '<p><br/><table bgcolor="#33BED8" width="1
00%"><tr><td><b>',
p_after_prompt_html  => '</b></p>  ');
```
[1346_07_06.txt]

This piece of code calls the APEX built-in APEX_APPLICATION.HELP, which shows the help. This help is customizable by using parameters. You can find an overview of the parameters at the end of this recipe. In the previous example, you can see that the parameter P_BEFORE_REGION_HTML and P_AFTER_PROMPT_HTML are used to display a help with a header with a background color #33BED8 (blue).

You can also see the parameters P_FLOW_ID and P_FLOW_STEP_ID. Those are the two parameters to indicate the application and the page where the call comes from. To pass these parameters, :APP_ID and :REQUEST are used.

11. Click the **Create region** button.

    The region has now been created and the help page is ready now. Next, we will enter some help text and create a link in the navigation bar.

12. Go to a page where you want to enter the help text.

13. In the page section, click the link behind the page name.

14. Click on the **Show all** tab.

15. Go to the help section and enter some help text in the text area.

16. Click the **Apply changes** button.

17. If you have items on the page click on the item and go to the help text section.

18. Enter some help text in the text area.

19. Click the **Apply changes** button.

20. Repeat these steps for the other items on the page.

21. Go to shared components, **Navigation Bar Entries** (navigation section in the upper-right corner).

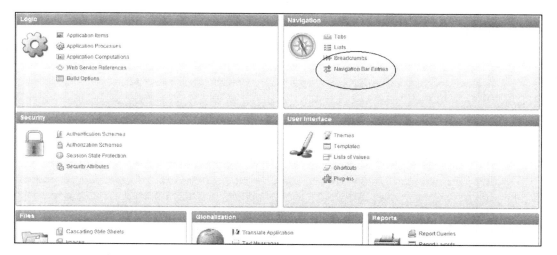

22. Click the **Create** button.

23. Select **From scratch** and click **Next**.

24. Select **Navigation to URL** and click **Next**.

25. Enter help in the entry label text field and click **Next**.

26. In the target list box, select **URL**.

27. In the URL target text area, enter the following:

```
javascript:popupURL('f?p=&APP_ID.:<PAGE>:&SESSION.:&APP_PAGE_
ID.');
```

[1346_07_07.txt]

Where <PAGE> is the page number of the help page you just created.

28. Click **Next**.

29. Click the **Create** button.

The help functionality is ready now. To offer a complete help, check that help text is entered at every page and every item.

When you run a page you will see that the navigation bar contains a help link. Clicking on this link will show you a pop-up window with the help text.

> **Help page**
>
> Use this page to add, modify or delete employees.
>
> **Form on EMP**
>
> **Empno**
>
> The employee's ID
>
> **Ename**
>
> The name of the employee.
>
> **Job**
>
> The job title of the employee.
>
> **Mgr**
>
> The employee ID of the manager of this employee.
>
> **Hiredate**
>
> Date hired.
>
> **Sal**
>
> The employee's salary.
>
> **Comm**
>
> The employee's commission. This field is only applicable if the employee is a Salesman.
>
> **Deptno**
>
> The ID of the department the employee works for.

How it works...

In this example, we make use of the APEX_APPLICATION.HELP built-in. The built-in collects the help information and shows it in a pop-up window. The call to APEX_APPLICATION.HELP comes from within a PL/SQL dynamic region. It gets the information from the help link. The help link in the navigation bar contains the URL to the help page and contains the session ID and the page ID so that these two variables can be passed to the call to APEX_APPLICATION.HELP.

You can also use a region of type Help to get the same result. However, with the built-in, you can customize with colors and other formatting options.

There's more...

The APEX_APPLICATION.HELP function has the following parameters:

Parameter	Meaning
P_REQUEST	Not used.
P_FLOW_ID	The ID of the application.
P_FLOW_STEP_ID	The ID of the page.
P_SHOW_ITEM_HELP	Show item help. Default Yes.
P_SHOW_REGIONS	Show region headers. Default Yes.
P_BEFORE_PAGE_HTML	Use HTML code between page level help text and item level help text.
P_AFTER_PAGE_HTML	Use HTML code at the end of the page.
P_BEFORE_REGION_HTML	Use HTML code before every region section. Ignored if P_SHOW_REGIONS is No.
P_AFTER_REGION_HTML	Use HTML code after every region section. Ignored if P_SHOW_REGIONS is No.
P_BEFORE_PROMPT_HTML	Use HTML code before every item label for item level help. Ignored if P_SHOW_ITEM_HELP is No.
P_AFTER_PROMPT_HTML	Use HTML code after every item label for item level help. Ignored if P_SHOW_ITEM_HELP is No.
P_BEFORE_ITEM_HTML	Use HTML code before every item help text for item level help. Ignored if P_SHOW_ITEM_HELP is No.
P_AFTER_ITEM_HTML	Use HTML code after every item help text for item level help. Ignored if P_SHOW_ITEM_HELP is No.

Counting clicks with apex_util.count_click

Sometimes you want to keep statistics on your web application, for example, to measure the level of interest in the application. Or you may want to log when a user clicks a certain link in the application. In that case, you could use the APEX_UTIL.COUNT_CLICK function. We will show you how to use this function in the following recipe.

Getting ready

We will create a section on a page, for example page 1, with the latest news. Just a few words of the news article is displayed. Below the text is a link, **[read more]**, which redirects the user to the complete news article. Make sure you have a page where you can create a news section.

How to do it...

1. In the application builder, go to the page where you want to put the news section on.

2. In the regions section, click the **Add** icon.

3. Select **PL/SQL dynamic content**.

4. Enter a title for the region, for example, **news**. Click **Next**.

5. In the PL/SQL source text area, enter the following:

```
declare
cursor c_nws is
select id
,       title
,       date_published
,       substr(text,1,300)||'...' text
from    app_news;
--
l_url VARCHAR2(255);
l_cat VARCHAR2(30);
l_workspace_id VARCHAR2(30);
begin
for r_nws in c_nws
loop
l_url := 'http://host:port/apex/f?p=&APP_ID.:2:&APP_SESSION.::NO::
P2_ID:'||r_nws.id;
l_workspace_id := TO_CHAR(APEX_UTIL.FIND_SECURITY_GROUP_ID('WS'));
l_cat := 'news';
--
htp.print('<h1>'||r_nws.title||'</h1>');
```

```
htp.print(r_nws.date_published);
htp.print(r_nws.text);
htp.print('<br>');
htp.print('<a href="http://host:port/apex/z?p_url=' || l_url
|| '&p_cat=' || l_cat || '&p_workspace=' || l_workspace_id ||
'">[read more]</a>');
end loop;
end;
```

[1346_07_08.txt]

In the code there is a cursor with a query on the APP_NEWS table. The code loops through the records found and displays the first 300 characters. This is done using the htp.print function. After that, a link with the text **[read more]** will be displayed. Again, this is done using the htp.print function. However, in the link you can find the APEX function, which is used to count the clicks. In the code you see the link:

```
http://host:port/apex/z?p_url=...
```

Where host is the name of the host where APEX resides and port is the port number used by APEX. Furthermore, you see "z?p_url=". Z is the shortcut name for APEX_UTIL.COUNT_CLICK. Behind the function call you can see a number of parameters which can be used to distinguish the different links. The most important parameters are p_url, which passes the URL APEX should navigate to, and p_cat, which passes the category (you can choose any name). In this case, the URL is a link to another page in the application. We use the &APP_ID and &SESSION_ID to dynamically determine the application ID and session ID. The ID of the page as well as the other parameters you might possibly need must be entered by yourself. In this case, the news article ID is passed in the URL. WS is the name of the workspace.

6. Click **Next**.

7. Click **Create region**.

The region is now ready. Run the page and hover with the mouse over the [read more] link below a news article. In the bottom status bar of your browser you will see the link to the news article. You will see that this link starts with the call to "z", or the APEX_UTIL.COUNT_CLICK function. Try to click on a link. At first sight nothing special happens except that APEX redirects to the page where the news article will be shown. However, use SQLplus or an IDE like SQL developer and query on the APEX_WORKSPACE_CLICKS view. This view is accessible for all Oracle users so you should be able to query it. You can use the following query:

```
select workspace
,       category
,       apex_user
,       to_char(clickdate,'DD-MM-YYYY HH24:MI:SS')
,       click_id
,       clicker_ip
,       workspace_id
```

```
from    apex_workspace_clicks
order by clickdate desc;
```
[1346_07_09.txt]

This query retrieves all rows from the view and displays the data in date descending order. The date is shown together with the timestamp to be able to see exactly when a link has been clicked.

How it works...

APEX_UTIL.COUNT_CLICK is actually a function which can be called either via the URL or via a call in a PL/SQL procedure. You can also use z as a shortcut. The function actually inserts a line in the apex_workspace_clicks view. The function has more parameters:

Parameter	Meaning
P_url	The URL to which to navigate
P_cat	A category to distinguish between different links
P_id	Secondary id to associate with the click
P_user	The application user ID
P_workspace	The workspace name

There's more...

You can also use a PL/SQL procedure to directly call the count_clicks function:

```
declare
  p_name varchar2(100) := 'apx_usr';
begin
  apex_util.count_click(
    p_url         => 'http://host:port/apex/f?p=<app>:<page>:
                      &SESSION_ID.',
    p_cat         => p_name,
    p_id          => null,
    p_user        => owa_util.get_cgi_env('REMOTE_ADDR'),
    p_company     => apex_util.find_security_group_
id('YOURWORKSPACE'));
end;
```
[1346_07_10.txt]

Where <app> is the id of your application and <page> is the id of the page. Make a page process and use this code. Use a button to call this page process. APEX will redirect to the link in p_url and insert a line in APEX_WORKSPACE_CLICKS.

If you use a list to use as a menu, you can use the built-in count click mechanism:

1. Go to shared components and click on the lists link in the navigation section.

2. Click on an existing list. You will get an overview of links included in this list. Click on a link.

3. Click on the **Click Counting** tab.

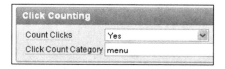

4. In the **Count Clicks** list box, select **Yes**.

5. In the **Click Count Category** text field, enter a category name. You can choose any name, as long as it is unique within the application so that you can find it back in the APEX_WORKSPACE_CLICKS view. This view shows a row for each call to APEX_UTIL.COUNT_CLICK. You can view the workspace, the workspace ID, the category, the date and time of the moment the user clicked, the APEX user, and the IP address.

Setting default item settings with apex_ui_default_update

When you create a form or a report, most of the time this is done with the help of a wizard. It is very easy for the most common things but if you want a different width of a text item, other than the default width, you have to do this afterwards. When you have a lot of items on your screen this could be very cumbersome. In this recipe, we will show you how to set the default width of columns with the APEX_UI_DEFAULT_UPDATE.UPD_ITEM_DISPLAY_WIDTH procedure. We will set the default width of column EVENT in table APP_EVENTS to 200.

Getting ready

Before you can use this function, the table needs to be included in the APEX dictionary. The view APEX_UI_DEFAULTS_COLUMNS holds the columns and their default width. You can add your table to this dictionary view by doing the following:

1. In APEX, go to **SQL workshop.**

2. Click **Utilities**.

3. Click **User interface defaults**.

4. Click the **Manage table dictionary** button.

5. Click the **Synchronize** button on the right side of the screen.

6. You will see a small report which shows the objects with defaults and the objects without defaults. Click the **Synchronize defaults** button. When APEX is ready, you will see a success message. All the tables in the schema that is linked to your workspace are now in the APEX dictionary.

7. You can also synchronize in SQL plus. Log in as the table owner and issue the following command:

```
exec apex_ui_default_update.synch_table('APP_EVENTS');
```
[1346_07_11.txt]

The only difference is that in the APEX builder, all tables will be included at once and in SQL plus you have to do this for every table separately (OK, you could write a script).

If you ignore these steps, the table with the columns you wish to set the default width for might not be in the APEX dictionary, and the steps in the next paragraph will lead to a "ORA-20001: UI Default update failed - there is no associated table" error message.

How to do it...

1. Go to SQL plus or an IDE where you can enter SQL commands. Log in to the schema where your tables for the APEX application reside.

2. Enter the following command:

```
begin
apex_ui_default_update.upd_item_display_width(
p_table_name    => 'APP_EVENTS'
,p_column_name   => 'EVENT'
,p_display_width => 200);
end;
/
```
[1346_07_12.txt]

This small procedure calls the APEX_UI_DEFAULT_UPDATE.UPD_ITEM_DISPLAY_WIDTH function and sets the display width of column EVENT in table APP_EVENTS to 200.

3. To demonstrate the default width of the EVENT column, go to the application builder, go to your application, and click the **Create page** button.

4. Select **Form**.

5. Select **Form on a table or view**.

6. Select the table or view owner and click **Next**.

7. In the **Table/view name** text field, enter the name of the table, in this case **APP_EVENTS**. Click **Next**.

8. Change the page number or the page name or the region title or change nothing at all and click **Next**.

9. Select **Do not use tabs** and click **Next**.

10. In the **Primary key** list box, select the primary key column of the APP_EVENTS table. In this case it is ID, so select **ID** and click **Next**.

11. Select **Existing sequence**. In the **Sequence** list box, select the sequence used for this column. In this case, select APP_AET_SEQ and click **Next**.

12. Select **All columns** and click **Next**.

13. If you want, you can change the button labels. When you're done, click **Next**.

14. Enter the page numbers where this page should navigate to after clicking on the buttons. You can also use the current page number. Click **Next**.

15. Click **Finish**.

16. Run the page and you will see that the Event text item has a width of 200.

How it works...

The call to the function actually updates the APEX dictionary view. You can see that when you do a query on APEX_UI_DEFAULT_COLUMNS where table_name is APP_EVENTS and column name is EVENT:

```
select  table_name
,       column_name
,       label
,       display_width
,       display_in_form
from    apex_ui_defaults_columns
where   table_name  = 'APP_EVENTS'
and     column_name = 'EVENT';
```
[1346_07_13.txt]

The result is as follows:

	TABLE_NAME	COLUMN_NAME	LABEL	DISPLAY_WIDTH	DISPLAY_IN_FORM
1	APP_EVENTS	EVENT	Event	200	Y

The display width is adjusted to 200.

There's more...

The `APEX_UI_DEFAULT_UPDATE` package contains more functions to set default values of tables or columns, for example form region title, item format mask and labels.

Creating a background process with apex_plsql_job

APEX supports running background processes. This can be useful, for example, when you want to postpone all reports printing to evening hours or you want to e-mail some information to a large number of e-mail addresses. After submitting the job, the user can continue working with the application and is able to monitor the job. This recipe will show you how to submit a background process. We will create a button on a report page which shows an overview of all upcoming events. When the user clicks the button, a background process is submitted which starts a procedure that sends the overview to a number of e-mail addresses.

Getting ready

Make sure you have a report of all upcoming events. If you don't have it, create one:

1. In the application builder, click the **Create page** button.
2. Click **Report**.
3. Click **Classic report**.
4. Enter a page number or a page name. Click **Next**.
5. Select **Do not use tabs** and click **Next**.
6. Enter the following query:

```
select  id
    ,       title
    ,       date_published
    ,       text
from    app_news;
[1346_07_14.txt]
```

7. Click **Next**.
8. Click **Next**.
9. Click **Finish**. The report is ready now and you can choose to run it or edit it.

How to do it...

We will now edit the report. We will create a button and a PL/SQL page process.

1. Click the **Edit page** icon.

2. In the buttons section, click the add icon.

3. Select a region for the button. In this case, there is only one region which is already selected. Click **Next**.

4. Select **Create a button in a region position**. Click **Next**.

5. Enter a name for the button, for example **mail events**. Click **Next**.

6. Click **Next**.

7. Click **Create button**.

8. In the **Processes** section, click the add icon.

9. Select **PL/SQL**.

10. Enter a name for the page process, for example **Sendevents**. Click **Next**.

11. In the text area, enter the following code:

```
declare
l_sql VARCHAR2(4000);
l_job NUMBER;
begin
l_sql := 'begin'||
'  -- here goes your code to send emails'||
'  app_mail.send_mail;'||
'end;';
l_job := apex_plsql_job.submit_process(p_sql    => l_sql
,p_status => 'Send mail job started');
end;
```
[1346_07_15.txt]

12. Click **Next**.

13. Now you can enter a success message and a failure message, if desired. Click **Next**.

14. In the **When button pressed** list box, select **mail_events**. Click the **Create process** button.

15. You are ready now to test it. Run the page and click the **Mail events** button.

How it works...

When the user clicks the button, the page process is started. The page process submits a job using the `APEX_PLSQL_JOB.SUBMIT_PROCESS` function.

There's more...

You can monitor the job using some other functions in the `APEX_PLSQL_JOB` package. There is the `TIME_ELAPSE` function which shows you how long the job already is running and you can use `UPDATE_JOB_STATUS` to set the status of the job.

Using Webservices

8

In this chapter, we will cover:

- ► Creating a SOAP webservice reference
- ► Creating a REST webservice reference
- ► Building a page based on a webservice reference

Introduction

Data-centric applications can have many different architectures. In some of these architectures, the data is not even in the database itself. In these cases, a possible scenario can be that the data is collected by calling webservices.

Essentially, a webservice provider offers a way for external applications to unlock its data, but not give away total access to its database (or other datasources).

A call to a webservice will have to satisfy certain standards as set by the **World Wide Web consortium (W3C)**. Since the fourth version of Application Express, it provides the possibility to natively call two of these standards: **Simple Object Access Protocol (SOAP)** and **Representational State Transfer (REST)**. But, by using a little more PL/SQL and XML DB, it's possible to use any type of webservice in APEX.

In this chapter, we are going to create some examples of how to use webservices in APEX.

Creating a SOAP webservice reference

As explained in the introduction of this chapter, SOAP stands for Simple Object Access Protocol. It is a standard that defines how the message that calls the webservice should be defined and how the answer is returned. Both messages are in XML.

SOAP webservices can be defined in so-called **Web Service Description Language** (**WSDL** for short) documents. By reading a WSDL, an application knows what webservices are available, how to call them, and what response it can expect back. APEX uses the information in a WSDL document to generate the SOAP messages, without the developer having to do any programming.

In this recipe, we are going to show how we can call a SOAP webservice, using built-in functionality of Application Express.

Getting ready

Have an application ready. It doesn't have to be empty, as long as we can add new pages.

Also make sure that if you are working on an Oracle 11g database, that the host of each webservice that we are going to use is entered into the **Access Control List** (**ACL**) for the APEX user.

The ACL is a structure to allow access to network services. In earlier versions of the database, access was essentially granted to all services or none. In 11g this has been changed, so it is now possible to allow fine grained access to selected network services.

To allow the `APEX_040000` user access to a network service like a webservice, we can use the following script:

```
begin
   dbms_network_acl_admin.create_acl (acl         => 'acl_user.xml'
                                     ,description => 'Description'
                                     ,principal   => 'APEX_040000'
                                     ,is_grant    => true
                                     ,privilege   => 'connect'
                                     ,start_date  => null
                                     ,end_date    => null);
   --
   dbms_network_acl_admin.add_privilege (acl       => 'acl_user.xml'
                                        ,principal => 'APEX_040000'
                                        ,is_grant  => true
                                        ,privilege => 'resolve');
   --
   dbms_network_acl_admin.assign_acl (acl  => 'acl_user.xml'
                                     ,host => 'name of website or host,
                                      i.e. soap.amazon.com');
   --
   commit;
end;
[1346_08_01.txt]
```

This piece of code will do three things.

- ▶ It will create a new entry in the ACL for the APEX_040000 user, to allow this user to connect to network and/or internet resources.
- ▶ It will add a privilege for the same user to resolve addresses.
- ▶ It will assign a certain hostname to the ACL entry.

So these three together will allow the APEX_040000 user to resolve a network address and connect to it.

The ACL entries can be inspected by querying the database using the following query as a DBA user:

```
select * from dba_network_acls;
```

Their associated privileges can be found by using the following query, again as a DBA user:

```
select * from dba_network_acl_privileges;
```

Instead of a single URL for the host, a wildcard ('*') can be entered. But be careful when doing this, because this will allow any APEX user to connect to any network and internet address from any APEX application or PL/SQL code.

How to do it...

In this recipe, we are going to create a page and a report based on a webservice using the information from a WSDL document.

1. Navigate to the **Web Service Reference** overview by going to **Shared Components** and **Web Service References**.
2. Click the **Create** button.

   We are now in the wizard that will guide us through the creation process. On the first screen choose **Based on WSDL** and click **Next**.

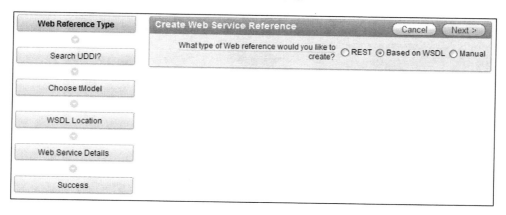

3. Select **No** when asked if we want to search a UDDI registry and click **Next**.

4. For the WSDL location, enter **http://ws.cdyne.com/WeatherWS/Weather. asmx?wsdl.**

5. Click **Next**.

6. In the following screen, change the name to **CDYNE Weather**. Leave everything else on its default value and click **Create Reference**.

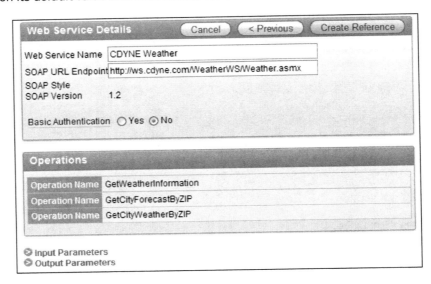

We can see that APEX has gathered some information about the webservice by calling the WSDL document. It has found the name of the webservice, its endpoint and more importantly, the available operations to use. Later in the recipe, we will use the GetCityWeatherByZIP operation.

After creating the webservice reference, APEX gives us the option to inspect it or continue directly to build a page using the reference.

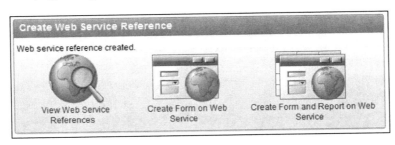

1. Click **Create Form on Web Service** to continue.

2. From the available references in the pulldown on the next page, select **CDYNE Weather**.

3. A new select list appears with the available operations. Select **GetCityWeatherByZIP** and click **Next**.

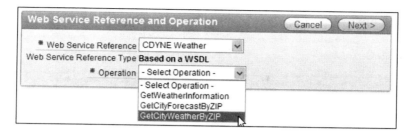

4. Application Express will now show a list of default properties. When necessary change the page number, else leave the values on their default and click **Next**.

   The next screen will allow us to create items that can be used in the webservice call. These have been generated based on the information from the WSDL. If the page number has changed, then rename the items accordingly. In this case, there is only one parameter, the input parameter to hold the zipcode for our webservice request.

5. Change the **Item Label** to **Zipcode** and click **Next**.

6. The next screen is the same principle, but for output parameters. APEX has generated 15 items—one for each possible item in the response. This screen might look a little strange, but that should be fixed in a later version of Application Express. Click **Next**.

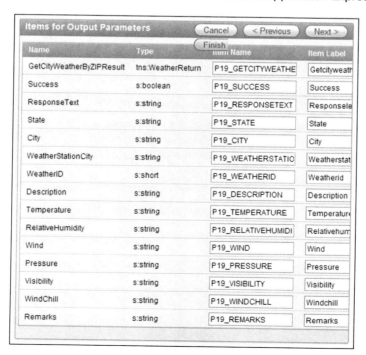

7. Select the tab that you want to use or create a new tab and click **Next**.

8. Click **Create Form** and run the Page.

You will see that APEX has created a straightforward page for us that will allow us to enter the required input parameter for the webservice. It has also created text fields for all the output parameters.

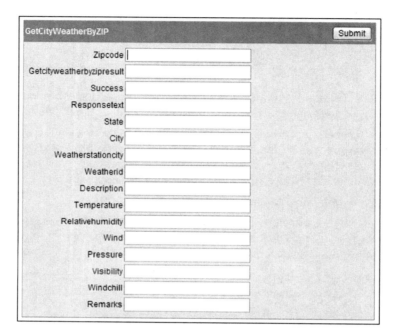

Try the webservice by entering an American zip code into the appropriate field (for the non-Americans; everybody remembers 90210 don't we?) and pressing **Submit**. This will result in the webservice returning an XML file with weather information for the chosen city. APEX automatically translates this data and enters it into the right fields on the screen.

How it works...

When we call a webservice from an APEX application, the request and response are an XML file. Thanks to built-in functionality, we don't always have to worry about the structure of these files. In a straightforward example like this, all translations to and from XML are done under the hood.

See also

In the recipe called 'Building a page on a webservice reference' we will see an example that utilizes the built-in XML DB functionality to extract data from the XML response of a Webservice.

Creating a REST webservice reference

A **Representational State Transfer** webservice or **REST** service is another kind of webservice standard. REST does not necessarily use WSDL or SOAP messaging, but can be called directly by using methods like POST and GET and other HTTP operations. So we can call a REST service directly from a URL unlike SOAP. This makes testing a lot easier.

APEX developers can use REST webservices and the wizard interface offers many possibilities for creating the call.

In this recipe, we are going to use the opportunities that APEX offers us to create a page based on a public REST webservice—the popular photo application Flickr.

Getting ready

Before starting this tutorial, create a Flickr account at http://www.flickr.com and request an API key.

How to do it...

1. Go to **Shared Components** and click on **Web Service References**.
2. Click the **Create** button.
3. Select the radio button next to REST and click **Next**.
4. In the **Name** field enter **Flickr REST service**.
5. In the URL field enter http://www.flickr.com/services/rest/.
6. Leave the rest on default and click **Next**.

In the Input parameters, we are going to enter three parameters.

1. Name the first method and click **Add Parameter**.
2. Name the second api_key and click **Add Parameter**.
3. Name the last user_id and click **Next**.
4. Enter for **XPath to Output Parameters** the string **/rsp**.
5. Click **Create** to save the webservice call.

Now we are ready to test if everything is OK.

1. Navigate back to the list of Web Service References.
2. Make sure the **Report View** is selected by pressing the corresponding button in the toolbar above the list.

3. Now click the **Test** button for our Flickr REST Service.
4. To make this work enter values for the three Input Parameters we created earlier:
   - Method = flickr.people.getPublicPhotos
   - Api_key = your Flickr API Key
   - User_id = your Flickr user id (or use mine: 52012402@N05)
5. Now click the **Test** button.

After a little wait a **Response** is returned as an XML file, containing all publicly available pictures for the selected user.

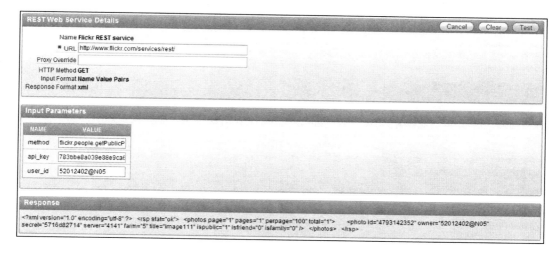

How it works...

There are a lot of other differences between REST and SOAP. Both of them have advantages. Some of these for REST are:

- ▶ It is lightweight without a lot of extra XML markup
- ▶ It has human readable results
- ▶ It's easy to build without any toolkits

The main advantages of SOAP are:

- ▶ Easier to consume (most of the time).
- ▶ Contract driven.
- ▶ There are a lot of development tools available.

The industry lately seems to be in favor of using REST for internet services. A lot of the larger companies (such as Twitter, Google, and Amazon) have chosen this standard for their webservices. SOAP still seems to be the standard for enterprise applications. But choosing REST or SOAP in a project is completely dependant on the specifications of that project.

There's more...

With the information from this recipe, it is possible to create a page to enter the required parameters and to display the response in a more readable format. We will do so in the next recipe.

Building a page on a webservice reference

Creating a standard looking page on a webservice reference is one thing. Making it more user-friendly is another. In this recipe, we are going to take a look at some of the possibilities for fine-tuning the look of the page created in the previous recipe.

Getting ready

Make sure that the Flickr REST webservice reference from the previous recipe is available.

How to do it...

Because the REST service we created earlier responds with an XML message, we can use output parameters to hold the returned data. To add these parameters, navigate to the webservice reference in Shared Components and select the Flickr REST service.

1. Find the **REST Output Parameters** section and click **Add Output Parameter**.
2. In the **Name** field, enter **photo_id**.
3. In the **Path** field, enter **/photos/photo/@id**.
4. Add another parameter using values **title** and **/photos/photo/@title**.
5. Add a third parameter using values **secret** and **/photos/photo/@secret**.

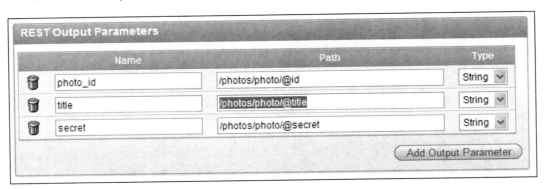

6. Click **Apply Changes** at the top of the screen.

We are now going to create a Form and Report based on these new parameters.

1. Go to the **Application Builder**.
2. Click the **Create Page** button.
3. Select Form and click **Next**.
4. Select Form and Report on Web Service and click **Next**.

5. Select the Flickr REST service and the operation **doREST** and click **Next**.

6. Keep all defaults and click **Next**.

7. Check all boxes next to the Result parameters to select them all and click **Next**.

8. Create a new tab for this page and click **Next** until we reach the confirmation page.

9. Click **Create Form and Report**.

Now we can run the page to see the result. In the input fields, use the same values that we used in the previous recipe to compare the outcome.

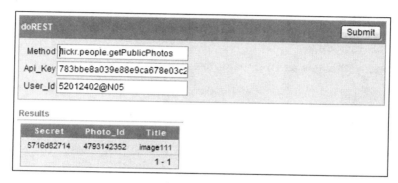

Keep in mind that this will only work correctly if the response contains a single record, else APEX will throw an error. For this to be corrected, we have to change the generated query that extracts the data out of the XML response. We will do that later in this recipe.

To make this page a little more user-friendly, we will make some changes to the way the fields are displayed. First of all, not all input parameters need to be shown. Method and Api_Key will always be the same, so we will make them hidden parameters.

1. Go to Application Builder and open the page we created for this webservice call.

2. Under **Region | Body | doREST** find the item for **METHOD**.

3. Right-click the **METHOD** item and click **Edit**.

4. Change **Display as** to **Hidden** using the select list.

5. Change **Default Value** to **flickr.people.getPublicPhotos**.

6. Click **Apply Changes**.

7. Now find the API_KEY item and click **Edit**.

8. Again change **Display as** to **Hidden**.

9. Change **Default Value** to your Flickr API_KEY.

10. Click **Apply Changes**.

If we run the page now, we can see that only the User_id field is left on the screen. The other values will be sent to the webservice call without the user having to input them.

The Report could also use a little makeover. Let's make the **PHOTO_ID** column a clickable link to the Flickr page for the photo.

1. Find the **Results** region and expand all **Report Columns**.

2. Right-click on the Photo_id column and click **Edit**.

3. Scroll down to the **Column Link** section.

4. Change **Link Text** to **#photo_id#**.

5. Change Target to URL.

6. Change URL to http://www.flickr.com/photos/&P17_USER_ID./#photo_id#. If the user_id item is named differently in your situation, change that part of the URL accordingly.

7. Click **Apply Changes** and run the page again.

Clicking on the data in the Photo_Id column will redirect to the Flickr page for the photo.

How it works...

The extraction of data from the XML response is done by making use of the XML-DB functionality of the Oracle database. Most of the time we won't see a lot of this when we are creating simple request/response pages. In this recipe, we've seen a hint of this when we extracted data using paths like /photos/photo/@id. This path is directly related to the structure of the XML response.

In the next section, we will see a more elaborate way to extract date from this XML.

There's more...

Remember that we promised to solve the problem with more users that have more than one photo attached? We're going to do that now.

To understand the problem, we need to look at the XML response that we are getting from Flickr. The following is an example from a user that has two photos available to show:

```
<?xml version="1.0" encoding="utf-8" ?>
<rsp stat="ok">
  <photos page="1" pages="1" perpage="100" total="2">
    <photo id="5155098679" owner="52012402@N05" secret="3f51a3dc69"
server="4042" farm="5" title="image074" ispublic="1" isfriend="0"
isfamily="0" />
    <photo id="4793142352" owner="52012402@N05" secret="5716d82714"
server="4141" farm="5" title="image111" ispublic="1" isfriend="0"
isfamily="0" />
  </photos>
</rsp>
```
[1346_08_03.xml]

As we can see, the XML has three nodes: rsp, photos, and photo. And that is exactly the problem here. Because the generated code from APEX is only told that there is a single 'photo' node, it will fail when a second 'photo' is found. For that to be corrected, we have to tell APEX to look a level higher and loop through everything that is found underneath that level.

1. Go to the **Edit Page** screen, right-click on the **Results** region, and click **Edit**.

2. Change the query to the following:

```
select extractValue(value(t),'*/@page') "page"
     , extractValue(value(ti),'*/@secret') "secret"
     , extractValue(value(ti),'*/@id') "photo_id"
     , extractValue(value(ti),'*/@title') "title"
  from wwv_flow_collections c
     , table(xmlsequence(extract(c.xmltype001,'*/photos'))) t
     , table(xmlsequence(extract(value(t),'*/photo'))) ti
 where c.collection_name = 'P17_DOREST_RESULTS'
```
[1346_08_04.sql]

3. Now run the page again and use a `User_Id` with more than one photo in the profile.

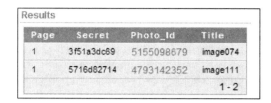

Results			
Page	Secret	Photo_Id	Title
1	3f51a3dc69	5155098679	image074
1	5716d82714	4793142352	image111
			1 - 2

And now that we are going, we can also change the page so that the image itself is shown as a thumbnail on this page itself and have the link on the page direct to the photo immediately.

1. Return to the query for the **Results** region.

2. Change the query to the following:

```
select extractValue(value(t),'*/@page') "page"
    , extractValue(value(ti),'*/@secret') "secret"
    , extractValue(value(ti),'*/@id') "photo_id"
    , extractValue(value(ti),'*/@farm') "farm"
    , extractValue(value(ti),'*/@server') "server"
    , extractValue(value(ti),'*/@title') "title"
    , '<img src="http://farm'||extractValue(value(ti),'*/@
farm')||'.static.flickr.com/'||extractValue(value(ti),'*/@
server')||'/'||extractValue(value(ti),'*/@id')||'_'||extractValue(
value(ti),'*/@secret')||'_s.jpg">' "image"
  from wwv_flow_collections c
    , table(xmlsequence(extract(c.xmltype001,'*/photos'))) t
    , table(xmlsequence(extract(value(t),'*/photo'))) ti
 where c.collection_name = 'P17_DOREST_RESULTS'
```
[1346_08_05.sql]

As we can see there are some new columns that will be selected. We need those later to create the direct link to the large image.

The last column with the "image" alias is actually some HTML code to generate an `<img>` tag for a Flickr image with size 's', which is the size of a thumbnail.

1. Now go the **Report Attributes** tab and click on the pencil icon next to the image column.

2. Under **Column attributes** change **Display as** to **Standard Report Column** and click **Apply Changes**.

   The thumbnail is now set up. Now let's change the link.

3. Click on the pencil icon next to the **photo_id** column.

4. Scroll down to the **Column Link** section and change the URL to `http://farm#farm#.static.flickr.com/#server#/#photo_id#_#secret#_b.jpg`.

5. Click **Apply Changes**.

As we are tidying up, we can also remove the columns that are not interesting from view.

1. Uncheck the checkboxes under the **Show** column for page, secret, farm and server.

2. Click **Apply Changes**.

3. Run the page to see the final results.

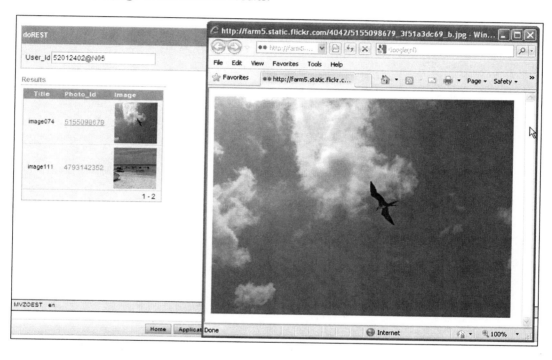

With this knowledge in hand, we can turn our APEX application into an online photo album, for example.

Publishing from APEX

9

In this chapter, we will cover:

- ▶ Exporting to a comma separated file
- ▶ Creating a PDF report
- ▶ Creating a report query
- ▶ Creating a report layout using Oracle BI publisher
- ▶ Linking the report layout to the report query
- ▶ Calling a report from a page

Introduction

Using APEX it is possible to create reports which can be displayed on the screen. However, as a user, you would also like to print the report on paper or at least get the output in some kind of digital format such as PDF or Microsoft Excel. APEX supports a number of formats your reports can be exported to. This needs a little setup work. Furthermore, you can use your output in BI Publisher. In this chapter, we will show you how to export reports and how to interact with BI Publisher.

Exporting to a comma separated file

APEX offers a standard built-in to export data to a **CSV** (**Comma Separated Value**) file. A CSV file is readable by Microsoft Excel or OpenOffice Calc. Each row contains the data of a record in a table and each value in the row is separated by a comma and represents the value of a column of the table. When export to CSV is enabled, a link is shown just below the region with the data. We will show you how to add this link.

Getting ready

You should have a working application with at least one standard report. If you don't have a report, create one. You can find a recipe for creating a simple report in *Chapter 1, Creating a Basic APEX Application.*

How to do it...

First, we will adapt the report. We will put a link on the report.

1. Go to the **Report** page.

2. In the **Regions** section, click on the **Report** link.

3. In the **Report Export** section, select **Yes** in the **Enable CSV output** list box.

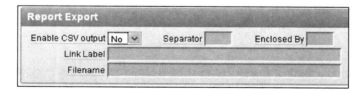

4. In the **Link Label** text field, enter **export to csv**. This text appears as a link below the region.

5. In the filename field, you can enter a filename. By default, the filename is the name of the region with the extension `.csv`.

6. Click the **Apply changes** button.

7. The link should now appear when you run the report.

When you click on the link, you will get a pop-up window asking whether you want to open the file with the program of your choice or download it to your computer.

How it works...

The link on the screen points to the same page but with an extra argument in the URL:

```
http://localhost:8000/apex/f?p=114:12:2184716804402017:FLOW_EXCEL_
OUTPUT_R435417443089863248_en
```

At the end of the URL, you see `FLOW_EXCEL_OUTPUT_R435417443089863248_en`. The large number after `FLOW_EXCEL_OUTPUT_R` is the region ID. You can find it in the view `APEX_APPLICATION_PAGE_REGIONS`. So, with the help of that view, you can make your own link. You just need the application ID and the page ID. So, for example, if you have an application with the application ID **114** and a report with the page ID **12**, and you want to add an "export to csv" link in your report, enter the following:

```
select  'http://localhost:8000/apex/f?p='||application_id||':'||page_
id||':&SESSION.:FLOW_EXCEL_OUTPUT_R'||region_id||'_en'
from    apex_application_page_regions
where   upper(source_type) = 'REPORT'
and     application_id = 114
and     page_id = 12;
```
[1346_09_01.sql]

(This is provided that APEX is installed on your local machine and that it is set to port 8000). The result will be something like this:

```
http://localhost:8000/apex/f?p=114:12:2184716804402017:FLOW_EXCEL_
OUTPUT_R435417443089863248_en.
```

This link also works even if you have set **Enable CSV output** to **No**.

If you have an interactive report, you have also the possibility to export to CSV. Click on the **Actions** button and select **Download**.

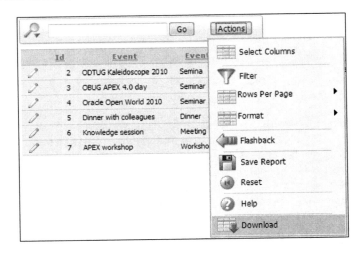

In the **Download** section you can click on the CSV icon to export the report to CSV format. To see the link, just hover over the **CSV** icon. In the status bar at the bottom of your screen you will see something like this:

```
http://localhost:8000/apex/f?p=108:15:2184716804402017:CSV:
```

So here it's even simpler to generate a download to CSV link.

Creating a PDF report

In APEX it is possible to export the data to **PDF (Portable Document Format)** format. The PDF format is created by Adobe and is widely accepted as a standard. To be able to export to PDF format, you need a report server like BI Publisher, a Java application server like Tomcat or Oracle's Weblogic with Apache FOP or a standard XSL-FO processing engine. We will discuss the interaction with Oracle BI Publisher.

Getting ready

First you need to install Oracle BI Publisher. You can download it from Oracle.com. We downloaded version 10.1.3.4.1 for Windows.

Don't make the install path too long. Otherwise the installer will fail.

After downloading and unpacking, run `setup.exe` and follow the steps in the installer. After installing, try to run BI Publisher. You can find the relevant settings such as the BI Publisher admin screen URL with the username and password and the commands to start and stop BI Publisher in the file `BI_Publisher_readme.txt`, which you can find in `<drive:>\ Orahome_1`, where `<drive:>` is your local hard drive. By default, the URL is `http:// localhost:9704/xmlpserver` if you installed BI Publisher on your own computer. If you installed BI Publisher on another computer, localhost must be replaced by the name of the other host. For this recipe, we will use the default hostname localhost and port 9704.

If the installation went OK, you should see something like the following screenshot:

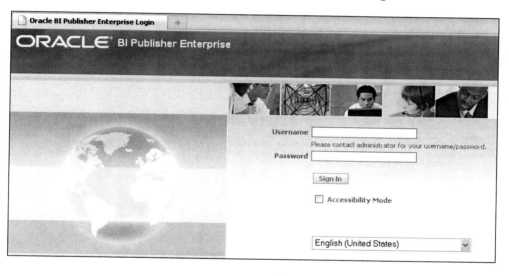

The next step is to configure APEX for BI Publisher. Therefore, you have to log in to the internal workspace as administrator.

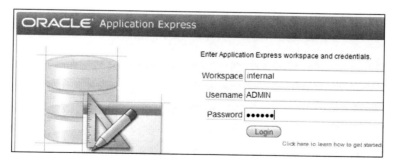

1. If you don't know the password, ask your administrator. If the password is unknown, you can change it using the `apxchpwd.sql` script, which you can find in the APEX directory. You need to execute this script as the SYS user.

2. After successful login, select **Manage Instance**.

3. In the instance settings section, click the **Instance settings** link.

4. In the report printing section, select **Advanced (requires Oracle BI Publisher)** in the **Print server** radio button.

5. In the print server host address field, enter the name of the host where BI Publisher is installed. In our case, this is the local machine, so enter here **localhost**.

6. In the print server port field, enter **9704**. That is the default port number of BI Publisher. In the print server script field, enter **/xmlpserver/convert**.

7. Click the **Apply changes** button. APEX is now configured for interaction with BI Publisher.

You should have an application with at least one report.

How to do it...

Now we will make a link below a report region which enables the user to export the report to PDF format.

1. Go to the **Report** page.

2. In the **Regions** section, click on the **Report** link.

3. Click on the **Print Attributes** tab.

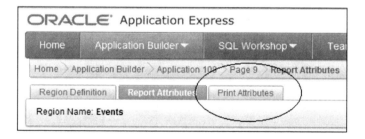

4. In the printing section, select **Yes** in the enable report printing list box.

5. In the link label field, enter a name for the link.

6. In the output format list box, select **PDF**.

7. Click the **Apply Changes** button.

8. The link is ready now. In the **Regions** section, you will see that there is a **Print** link behind the report region.

9. Click **Run** to run the report.

10. You will see a link below the report region. Click this link.

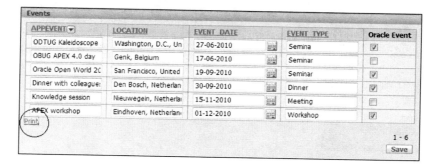

11. The result will be a pop-up window where the user can choose to save the report in PDF format or open the report using Adobe Reader. In the last case, you will see something like this:

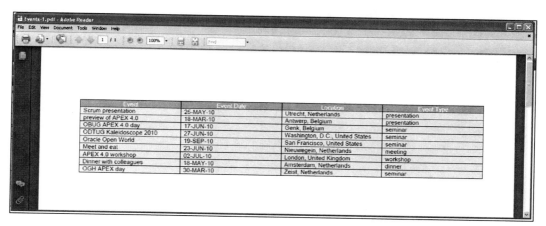

How it works...

When using the print link, APEX converts the data to an XML format and sends it to the BI Publisher engine. The convert script then converts it to PDF format and sends it back to APEX.

There's more...

The output shown is rather simple. Using BI Publisher and templates you can make more advanced and nice looking reports.

Creating a report query

The report in the previous recipe was rather simple. You see a table with headers and the data and that's it! Nothing more, nothing less. But we want a nice, good looking report with headers and footers. Fortunately, APEX offers a way to design reports with a custom layout using Microsoft Word and Oracle BI Publisher. The first step is to define the query the report should be based on. We will do that in this recipe.

Getting ready

Make sure you have access to the APP_CUSTOMERS table.

How to do it...

1. Go to **Shared Components**.

2. In the report section, click the **Report queries** link.

3. Click the **Create** button.

4. In the Report Query Name field, enter a name for the query. Enter **rq_customers**. Click **Next**.

5. In the SQL query text area, enter the following query:

```
Select cust_first_name
,          cust_last_name
,          cust_street_address1
,          cust_postal_code || ' ' || cust_city "city"
,          cust_state
From app_customers
[1346_09_02.sql]
```

6. Click **Next**.

7. In the next step, we must download the XML definition of this query. We will use that in the next recipe. Select **XML data** and click the **Download** button. Select **Save file** and click **OK**. Remember the location where you saved the file. We need the file when we want to create a layout in Microsoft Word.

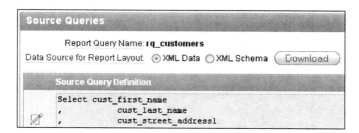

8. Go back to the APEX application builder and click **Create report query**.

9. At this point, you can test the report by clicking the **Test Report** button. You will see the same simple layout.

10. Click the **Finish** button.

11. The report query is ready now. We can use the definition in the next recipe.

How it works...

Oracle APEX creates an XML file from the query. In Microsoft Word, using the BI Publisher Desktop add-in, we can use this XML definition to create a custom layout.

Creating a report layout using Oracle BI Publisher

In this recipe, we will show you how to work with templates. We will create a report which presents data from the APP_CUSTOMERS table.

Getting ready

Make sure you have installed Oracle BI Publisher desktop. BI Publisher desktop is packed with BI Publisher Enterprise. You can find it in `<local hard drive>:\OraHome_1\xmlp\ XMLP\Tools`, assuming that you have installed Oracle BI Publisher in `\OraHome_1`. During installation, all Microsoft applications such as Word and Outlook need to be closed.

After installation, Microsoft Word is enriched with a BI Publisher add-on. How the plug-in looks depends on the version of Word.

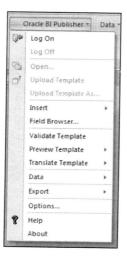

How to do it...

1. Open **Microsoft Word**.
2. Select **Add-ons**.
3. Click the **Oracle BI Publisher** tab and select **Data – Load sample XML data**.

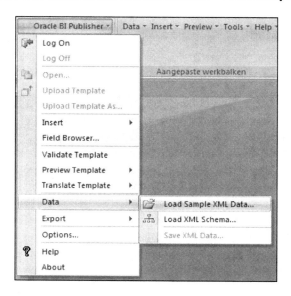

4. In the pop-up window, select the file that you just created in APEX. Click to open the file.
5. It seems that nothing happens. That is **OK**.
6. Click the Oracle BI Publisher tab again and select **Insert –Table wizard**.
7. A pop-up window with a wizard appears.

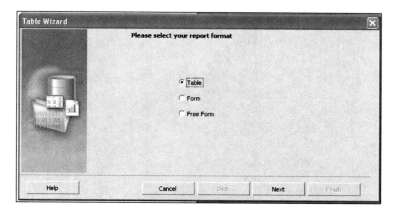

8. Select **Table** and click **Next**.

9. Click **Next**.

10. We want to select all columns, so click the button with the **double arrows**.

11. Click **Next**.

12. If desired, you can group the report in the next step. If you don't want to group, just click **Next**.

13. In the next step, you can enter the sort order. Select the column that you want to use to order the data (or leave the sort by list box empty) and click **Next**.

14. In the last step, you can enter a different name for the labels. Click **Finish**.

15. The wizard is ready now and if everything went OK, you will see a table with a header and five columns.

16. You can also add a header and a footer to the document to make it complete.

List of customers				
Cust First Name	**Cust Last Name**	**Cust Street Address1**	**City**	**Cust State**
F CUST_FIRST_NAME	CUST_LAST_NAME	CUST_STREET_ADDRESS1	city	CUST_STATE E

17. Save the report by clicking on the **Save** button. In the pop-up window that appears, select **RTF** in the **Save as** list box. In the **filename** field, enter a name for the report, for example, **customers_layout.rtf**. Select the desired map and click **Save**.

18. Close Microsoft Word. The layout is ready and saved in the `.rtf` file.

How it works...

Take a closer look at the `.rtf` file in Microsoft Word. In the second row of the table that you see, you can see the names of the columns of the report query. Just before the first column, you see an "F". Behind the last column, you see an "E". These are actually control fields. "F" stands for "for each" and "E" stands for "end". This is very important, because APEX recognizes these fields. On running the report, APEX loops through the records and replaces the columns by the values of the query.

Linking the report layout to the report query

Now that we have created a layout in Word we want to use it for our report. In this paragraph, we will show you how to upload the `.rtf` file and link the layout to a report query.

Getting ready

1. Make sure that you selected **Advanced** in the **Print server** settings. You can set these fields in the internal workspace logging in as admin.

2. After successful login, click **Manage Instance**.

3. In the **Instance settings** section, click the **Instance settings** link.

4. In the **Report printing** section, select **Advanced (requires Oracle BI Publisher)** in the **Print server** radio button.

5. Click the **Apply changes** button.

6. This step is necessary as otherwise you won't see the named columns (RTF) option in the report layout type radio group.

How to do it...

1. Go to **Shared Components— report layouts**.

2. Click the **Create** button.

3. Select **Named columns (RTF)**. Click **Next**.

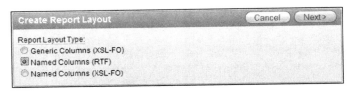

4. In the layout name text field, enter a name for the report, for example, **cmr_layout**.

5. Click the **Browse** button to upload the RTF file.

6. In the pop-up screen, select the file `customers_layout` from the map where you saved it and click **Open**.

7. Click the **Create layout** button.

8. The layout is ready. Now we must link this layout to the report query that we created in the previous recipe.

9. Go to **Shared Components | Report queries**.

10. Click on the icon of the report query **rq_customers**.

11. In the report layout list box, select **cmr_layout**.

12. You can now click on the test report button in the source queries section to see how the report and the layout look like. Otherwise, click the **Apply changes** button.

13. The report query and the report layout are ready now.

How it works...

We made a query and a layout. And now we bring them together. We uploaded the report layout that we made in Microsoft Word and modified the settings of the report query so that it should use the uploaded layout. The query should contain at least the same columns that are used in the Microsoft Word layout, no matter in what order they are. You can use more columns in the query but if they are not in the layout file, you will not see them on the report. On the other hand, if your layout file contains a column that is not in the query, the report will show an empty column.

And just to make it more complex, if you use another column in your query and you give it an alias that is the name of one of the columns in the layout file, APEX will show a report with data from that other column.

Calling a report from a page

In the previous paragraphs, we made a report query and a report layout. Since we want to call this report from a page within our application, we have to add something to the webpage like a button or a link. We will show you how to do this in this recipe.

Getting ready

In the previous recipes, you have created a report query and a report layout. Make sure they work as desired. You should also have a webpage based on the APP_CUSTOMERS table.

How to do it...

1. Go to the page based on the APP_CUSTOMERS table.
2. In the buttons section, click the **Add** icon to create a new button.
3. Select the appropriate region and click **Next**.
4. Select **Create button in a region position** and click **Next**.
5. Enter a name and a label for the button and click **Next**.
6. Click **Next**.

7. In the action select list, select **Download Printable Report Query** (after selecting this option, the **Report Query** select list appears below the **Execute Validations** select list).

8. In the **Report Query** select list, select **rq_customers**.
9. Click **Create** button.
10. The button is ready. You can run the page now and click on the button to see what happens.

		List of customers		
Cust First Name	**Cust Last Name**	**Cust Street Address1**	**City**	**Cust State**
John	Dulles	45020 Aviation Drive	20166 Sterling	VA
William	Hartsfield	6000 North Terminal Parkway	30320 Atlanta	GA
Edward	Logan	1 Harborside Drive	02128 East	MA

How it works...

Like the link for CSV export, the button in this page uses a URL to call the report. It looks like the following:

```
http://localhost:8000/apexf?p=114:0:&SESSION.:PRINT_REPORT=rq_
customers
```

You could copy this link and paste it in the address bar of your browser, provided you have a valid session ID that has to replace the &SESSION. variable. The 0 in the URL, just behind the application ID of 114, is an indicator that this is an internal application process. Normally, a page number should be entered at this place. The last part of the URL is the PRINT_REPORT argument. Here you can pass the name of the report query you would like to see. In this case, it is rq_customers.

10
APEX Environment

In this chapter, we will cover:

- ▸ Setting up a development environment using subscriptions
- ▸ Debugging an APEX application
- ▸ Debugging an APEX application remotely
- ▸ Deploying an application with SQL Developer
- ▸ Setting up version control with APEX and SVN
- ▸ Setting up a production environment with an Apache proxy
- ▸ Setting up the APEX Listener on Tomcat

Introduction

When starting with APEX development, it's important to choose the right architecture. It should be straightforward, should allow flexibility, and not need much maintenance.

This chapter contains recipes that will show how to set up and use a development environment, how to use version control, and how to deploy Application Express on a web container with the APEX Listener.

Setting up a development environment using subscriptions

The architecture of a single APEX application is simple. You create a workspace, then you create an application, and then you build pages inside this application.

But what if we anticipate more than one application in our workspace? It's possible that a company has a single corporate style for all its web applications. If we would have to create templates for this style in every single APEX application, we would lose a lot of time better spent on creating functionality in the application itself.

In this recipe, we will see how we can set up a development environment that can reuse as many elements as possible and still be flexible.

Application Express offers a feature called subscriptions. This allows developers to inherit a number of properties from one application to another. By using these subscriptions we don't have to build something like a template twice, but instead we create it once in a parent application and then use that same template in a child application by subscribing to it. Now whenever a change is made to the layout of the template in the parent application, all we have to do is update the subscriptions to rollout the changes to all child applications.

But this is not limited to templates. It can also be used for CSS files, authentication, or JavaScript and many more parts of the parent application.

In a very simple graph, the architecture would look a little like this:

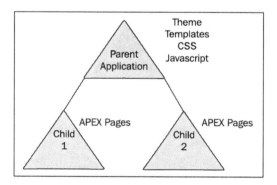

Developers can go as far with this architecture as they want. For example, if a company has a layout that is used for all web applications, but the financial department needs to add an extra region containing legal statements to some of it's pages for legal purposes, we can add another layer of child applications. So the company has a standard layout, the financial department subscribes to this standard to comply with company policy. They themselves create a standard layout for the required legal regions. The applications created by the financial department then subscribe to this new legal standard.

This would change the architecture to something like this:

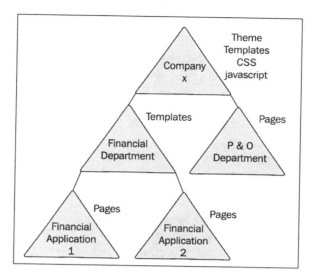

And this can go as far and deep as the developers want. Keep in mind however that pushing a master subscription will only update the first level of subscriptions. So if you want to apply a change in the master more than one level down, you have to publish the change on every level.

How to do it...

First, we have to create an application to be used as the parent.

1. Go to the Application Builder and press the **Create >** button.
2. Select **Database** and press **Next**.
3. Select **From Scratch** and press **Next**.
4. Name the application **Company Parent** and press **Next**.
5. Add a single Blank page and name it **Main** then press **Next**.
6. Select **One Level of Tabs** and press **Next** until we reach the Theme selection screen.
7. Select **Theme 1** and press **Next**.
8. Finally, press **Create** to finish.

We now have an almost empty application (except for the Main page), so let's adjust something in a template to see what happens.

1. Navigate to **Shared Components** and then to **Templates.**

2. In the list of templates, locate the one called **One Level Tabs - Right Sidebar (optional / table-based)** under the Page templates and open it.

3. In the **Definition** section, find the **Body** section. In this section, change the first `<div>` area with the id `"header"` to the following:

```
<div id="header">
  <div id="logo"><h2>Company X</h2><a href="#HOME_
LINK#">#LOGO##REGION_POSITION_06#</a></div>
  #REGION_POSITION_07#
  <div id="navbar">
    #NAVIGATION_BAR#
    <div class="app-user">#WELCOME_USER#</div>
    #REGION_POSITION_08#
  </div>
</div>
```
[1346_10_1.txt]

4. Press **Apply Changes**.

5. Now Run the Company Parent application.

You will see that the header for the Main page has been changed. It now contains the text **Company X**.

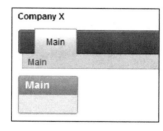

Now let's create a Child application that will subscribe to this template.

1. Go to the **Application Builder** and press the **Create** button.

2. Select **Database** and press **Next**.

3. Select **From Scratch** and press **Next**.

4. Name the application **Company Child** and press **Next**.

5. Add a single Blank page and name it **Main** then press **Next**.

6. Select **One Level of Tabs** and press **Next** until we reach the Theme selection screen.

7. To show the contrast with the Company Parent application, select **Theme 2** and press **Next** and then **Create.**

When we run this new application we can see that it's mainly blue and does not contain the name **Company X** in the header.

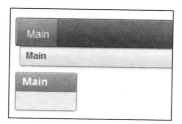

Now we are going to subscribe to the template we changed in the first part of this recipe, so we can see how this works.

1. Go to the **Shared Components** of the Company Child application and go to **Templates**.

2. Click on the **One Level Tabs - Right Sidebar (optional / table-based)** template to open it.

3. In the **Subscription** section, press the **List of Values** button next to the field labelled **Reference Master Template From**.

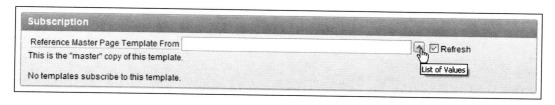

4. In the pop-up that opens, find the entry for **One Level Tabs - Right Sidebar (optional / table-based)** that corresponds to the Application ID of our Company Parent application.

5. Press **Apply Changes**.

When we now return to the template, we can see that the **Subscription** section has changed.

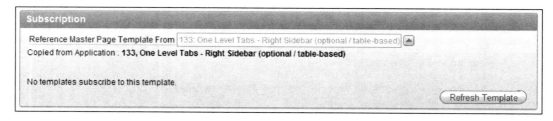

We can see that the template is now copied from our Company Parent application (in this screenshot the Application ID is **133**), and a button called **Refresh Template** has been added. This button pulls in all changes made to the master copy of the template, in fact the opposite of the publish process we will see later on in the recipe.

If we run the Main page in the Company Child application, we can see that it looks exactly like the Main page of the Company Parent application. At least, the parts that belong to our One Level Tabs region template. This proves that the copy process for the template works.

Let's return to our Company Parent application to find out if the publishing works as well.

1. Return to the Company Parent application and navigate to **Shared Components | Template** and click on the **One Level Tabs - Right Sidebar (optional / table-based)** template again.

   Let's assume that the CEO of Company X has a new marketing strategy and wants to let the world know how good the company is.

2. In the Body section change the "header" div to:

   ```
   <div id="header">
     <div id="logo"><h1>The best company in the world!</h1><a
   href="#HOME_LINK#">#LOGO##REGION_POSITION_06#</a></div>
     #REGION_POSITION_07#
     <div id="navbar">
       #NAVIGATION_BAR#
       <div class="app-user">#WELCOME_USER#</div>
       #REGION_POSITION_08#
     </div>
   </div>
   ```
   [1346_10_2.txt]

3. Press **Apply Changes**.

4. Run the Company Parent application as well as the Company Child application to see the difference.

5. Return to the Company Parent application and navigate to **Shared Components |
Template** and click on the **One Level Tabs - Right Sidebar (optional / table-based)**
template again.

In the **Subscription** section, we can see that there is a list of templates that reference
this one.

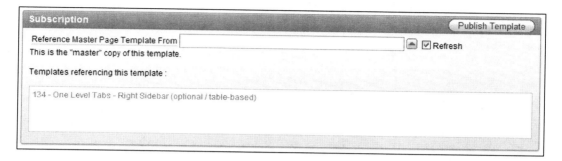

In the screenshot there is the reference from our Company Child application with
Application ID 134.

6. Press the button **Publish Template** to apply the changes to the referencing
templates.

7. Press **Refresh All** to complete the publishing.

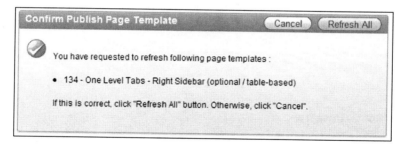

When we now run the Company Child application we can see the result. This application now
automatically looks like its parent.

Debugging an APEX application

An essential part of the development process of almost any software project is debugging. A
good debug method allows developers to exactly pinpoint problems in the application.

Application Express offers some built-in functionality to debug applications, pages, and even
items. This recipe will explain how to set up debugging on an application and how to interpret
the reports that APEX generates.

Getting ready

The only thing we need to start on this recipe is a (working) application. We will use a simple application, based on the EMP table.

Create a new application with a Form and Report (based on an interactive report) on the EMP table. That is enough to get through this recipe.

How to do it...

First of all debugging has to be enabled for the application. By default, this option is disabled. To enable debugging, follow the next steps:

1. In the **Application Builder**, select the application that we are going to debug.

2. Locate the button labelled **Edit Application Properties** near the top of the main region and press it.

3. Find the area called **Properties** and change the value of the select list called **Debugging** from **No** to **Yes**.

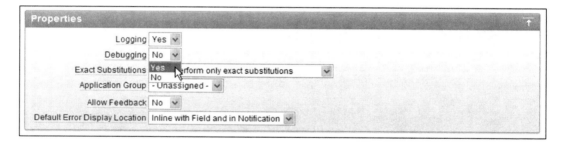

4. Press **Apply Changes**.

   Now the application is ready to be debugged.

5. Start the application.

6. In the **Developer Toolbar** at the bottom of the screen, press the button labeled **Debug**. If the steps in the first part of this recipe have gone well, then the label will change to No Debug. Otherwise an error message will appear and we have to check if debugging on the application is really set to **Yes**.

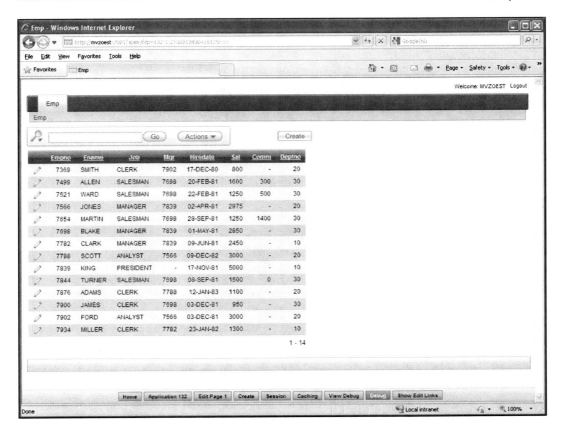

7. Perform some actions on the application, like navigating or performing a search.

8. When you navigate to a different page, the **Debug** option will turn off automatically. If you want to re-enable it, simply press the button in the Developer Toolbar again. To avoid this behaviour, we can also call the application using the value **YES** for the &DEBUG. substitution in the URL on the fifth parameter position. Buttons and links calling URLs inside the application will have to hold the substitution as well. A URL with this substitution will look like this:

```
f?p=APP_ID:APP_PAGE_ID:APP_SESSION::YES:::
```

9. Press the button labelled **View Debug** in the Toolbar. This will open up a new window with a list of actions that have been performed during the time that Debug was enabled.

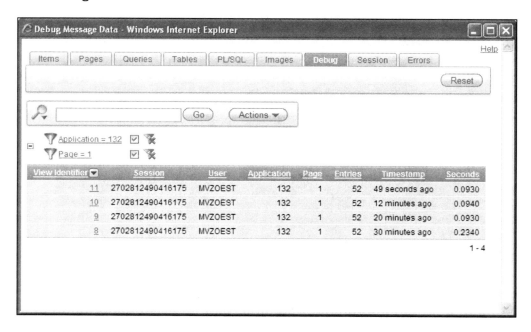

By default the current page is selected. To see debug information for other pages, deselect the filter for Page.

The list in the screenshot shows a timestamp for when the page was called, how many actions took place while loading the page (under the **Entries** column), and how many **Seconds** it took to fully load the page.

1. Press one of the links in the column **View Identifier** to see the debug information for the loading of that page.

2. Review the report that is now shown. The following screenshot shows an example of a **Save** action on the Edit page of the EMP application. Results may look different when another action or page has been selected.

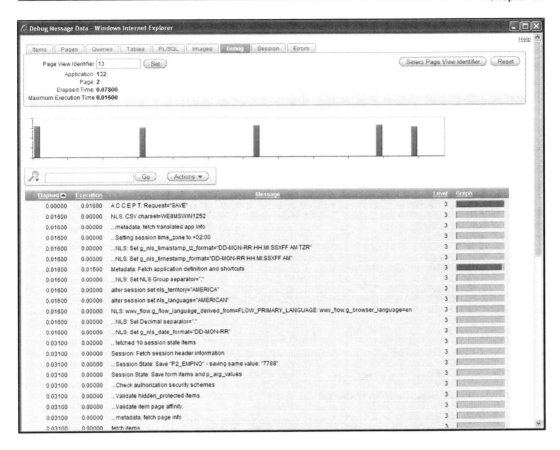

This report is made up of three regions of interest. The top region shows information about the currently selected page. Most of it is also shown in the main overview from the previous screenshot, but **Maximum Execution Time** is new. This tells us the time it took the longest process to complete, so we can quickly identify where a performance problem might exist.

In this same perspective of quickly identifying problems, the graph section can be seen. Processes taking a lot of time to load will get a higher graph bar. When hovering over a bar with the cursor, the relevant process can be identified.

The main part of the screen is occupied by a report. This report shows all processes that are executed during the load of the currently selected page.

The first column shows the elapsed time after processing the current line. The second column shows the time that the particular process took. So, for example, when we look at the line that says ...fetch session state from database, we can see that the time it took to complete that process was 0.01600 seconds, but the total loading time for all processes until that moment was 0.03100 seconds.

The total report can be used for three purposes: what happened, when it happened, and how long it took.

We can see some NLS parameters being set in lines like:

```
NLS: CSV charset=WE8MSWIN1252
```

Or

```
alter session set nls_language="AMERICAN"
```

Because we selected a **SAVE** operation to debug, we can also find a couple of lines for this as well.

```
Session State: Saved Item "P2_ENAME" New Value="SCOTT"

Session State: Saved Item "P2_SAL" New Value="3200"
```

(Variable names and values may vary).

Now, we will change the Edit page and try to find out if we can find this alteration in the debug information.

1. Go to the Application Builder and select Page 2 to edit.
2. In the Edit Emp region, add a hidden item.
3. Name it **DEBUG_TESTING** and click **Next**.
4. Set **Value Protected** to **No** and click **Next**.
5. The **Source Type** will be **SQL Query (return single value)**.
6. In **Item Source Value** enter the query: `select sysdate from dual`.
7. Press **Create Item**.

Now when we run the application and enable Debug on the pages, the information for this new item should be seen in the debug report.

To check this, press the **View Debug** button again and find the latest entry for page 2. When browsing down the debug report, you will find a line with the text `Item: DEBUG_TESTING NATIVE_HIDDEN` to show that the new item was indeed created at runtime with the rest of the page.

In the same fashion, any item loaded in a page can be found and analyzed.

There's more...

Besides the debug messages that APEX generates itself, it's also possible to create our own custom messages inside PL/SQL processes.

1. Go to Page 1 of this recipe.

2. Expand the **Before Header** node.

3. Right-click on **Processes** and press **Create**.

4. Select PL/SQL and press **Next**.

5. Enter the name **show_custom_debug** and click **Next**.

6. Enter the following code in the PL/SQL Process area and press **Create Process**:

   wwv_flow.debug('My Custom Debug Message');

7. Run the page and click the **Debug** button in the Developer Toolbar.

8. Click the **View Debug** button.

In the **Debug** screen, we can now see two entries mentioning our custom code. The first is the process itself that is being called. The second is our custom debug message.

Using this it's possible to quickly find certain pieces of code using these custom messages as a sort of bookmark. But more advanced debugging is also possible, for example, by showing the value of a variable.

1. Go back to the page and edit the show_custom_debug process.

2. Change the PL/SQL code to the following:

   wwv_flow.debug('My Custom Debug Message for: '||:APP_USER);

   This will add the username of the current logged-in user to the message.

3. Press **Apply Changes**.

4. Run the page and press the **Debug** button in the Developer Toolbar.

5. Press the **View Debug** button.

When we open the Debug window now and look for our message, we can see that it indeed changed and now shows the username.

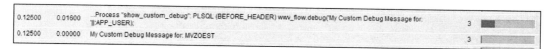

Debugging an APEX application remotely

When developing an application, you may want to see what's actually happening on page processing or running some PL/SQL code. Especially PL/SQL code that is stored in the database and called from a page within APEX, is hard to debug. However, Oracle SQL Developer offers a way to debug PL/SQL code which is called from APEX. We will show you how to do that.

Getting ready

It is important to have the latest version of SQL Developer on your computer. And that you have an application with a page that calls a PL/SQL procedure in the database. In this recipe, we take the Twitter search from Chapter 1. We will call the app_search_user procedure.

Furthermore, you need to grant some privileges:

```
grant debug any procedure to <user>;
grant debug connect session to <user>;
```

[1346_10_10.txt]

Here, <user> is the user that needs the privileges. If you use the embedded PL/SQL gateway, use ANONYMOUS, otherwise use APEX_PUBLIC_USER.

If you are running APEX on Oracle 11g database, you also need to create an **Access Control List (ACL)** and its privileges.

```
begin
   dbms_network_acl_admin.create_acl (acl           => 'acl_anm.xml'
                                      ,description => 'Description'
                                      ,principal   => 'ANONYMOUS'
                                      ,is_grant    => true
                                      ,privilege   => 'connect'
                                      ,start_date  => null
                                      ,end_date    => null);
   --
   DBMS_NETWORK_ACL_ADMIN.ADD_PRIVILEGE(acl           => 'acl_anm.xml'
                                        ,principal => 'ANONYMOUS'
                                        ,is_grant  => true
                                        ,privilege => 'resolve');
   --
```

```
   DBMS_NETWORK_ACL_ADMIN.ASSIGN_ACL(acl   => 'acl_anm.xml'
                                    ,host => '127.0.0.1'
                                    ,lower_port => 4000
                                    ,upper_port => 4000);
   --
   commit;
end;
/

begin
   dbms_network_acl_admin.create_acl (acl          => 'acl_db.xml'
                                     ,description => 'Description'
                                     ,principal   => '<dbusr>'
                                     ,is_grant    => true
                                     ,privilege   => 'connect'
                                     ,start_date  => null
                                     ,end_date    => null);
   --
   DBMS_NETWORK_ACL_ADMIN.ADD_PRIVILEGE(acl          => 'acl_db.xml'
                                       ,principal => '<dbusr>'
                                       ,is_grant  => true
                                       ,privilege => 'resolve');
   --
   DBMS_NETWORK_ACL_ADMIN.ASSIGN_ACL(acl   => 'acl_db.xml'
                                    ,host => '*');
   --
   commit;
end;
/
```
[1346_10_11.txt]

The code creates an ACL for the ANONYMOUS user and the database user who is the owner of the procedure, marked with <dbusr>. Replace it with your own database user (schema owner). The ACL for the ANONYMOUS user gives that user the privilege to connect to the localhost at port 4000, the port we will use for the remote debug session. To keep it simple, we create an ACL for the owner of the procedure with the privilege to connect to any host.

How to do it...

1. Start Oracle SQL Developer.

2. Right-click on the database connection where the procedure is stored.

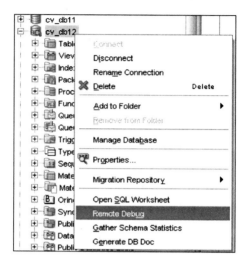

3. Select **Remote Debug**.

4. A pop-up is shown with three text fields: Port, timeout, and local address.

5. Choose a port number that is not yet assigned to any process and is not blocked by a firewall. You need this port number later.

6. Enter a number of seconds in the timeout field to indicate how long the debug session must be kept open before it automatically closes. Enter 0 to leave the session open without closing. You can leave the local address field empty.

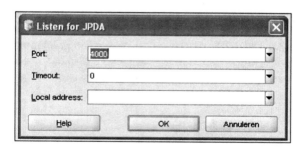

7. Click **OK** to start the debug session.

8. Click the database connection open and go to the APP_SEARCH_USER procedure.

9. Right click the procedure and select edit. The procedure is now open for editing.

10. Set some breakpoints by clicking the line number in the gutter.

11. When you are ready, click the compile for debug icon.

The procedure is now ready to be compiled. We will now create a page in APEX with a text item and a button and when the button is pressed, APEX will start the debug session.

1. Go to APEX, go to the application builder, and select the application that you want to edit.

2. Click the **Create Page** button.

3. Select blank page.

4. Click **Next**.

5. Enter a name and a title for the page. For example. 'Check Twittername'. Click **Next**.

6. Click **Next**.

7. Click **Finish**.

8. Click the **edit page** icon.

9. In the regions section, click the **add** icon to create a new region.

10. Select **HTML**.

11. Click **Next**.

12. Enter a title for the region, for example check. Click the **Create** button.

13. In the items section, click the **add** icon to create a new item.

14. Select **text**.

15. Select text field. Click **Next**.

16. Enter a name for the item, for example, P_TWITTERNAME. Click **Next**.

17. Click **Next**.

18. In the buttons section, click the **add** icon to create a new button.

19. Click **Next**.

20. Click **Next**.

21. Enter a name for the button, for example **Check name**. Click **Next**.

22. Click **Next**.

23. Click **Next**.

24. Click **Create** button.

25. Click the **create item** button.

26. In the validations section, click the **add** icon to create a new validation.

27. Select item level validation and click **Next**.

28. Select the item P_TWITTERNAME and click **Next**.

29. Select **PL/SQL**.

30. Select **Function returning error text** and click **Next**.

31. Enter a name for the validation, for example `chk_twt`. Click **Next**.

32. In the validation text area, enter the following code:

```
dbms_debug_jdwp.connect_tcp('127.0.0.1',4000);
declare
  l_result varchar2(100);
begin
  app_search_user('TWITTERUSER','password',:P_TWITTERNAME,l_
result);
  if l_result = 'user found'
  then
    return null;
  else
    return 'false';
  end if;
end;
dbms_debug_jdwp.disconnect;
```
[1346_10_12.txt]

The code starts with the call to DBMS_DEBUG_JDWP.CONNECT_TCP to initiate the connection to the debug session. The call carries two arguments: the local address and the port number we had to enter when starting the debug session in SQL Developer. After that, the code calls the procedure APP_SEARCH_USER with the arguments Twitter username, password, search argument and the result. The search argument is kept in the item P_TWITTERNAME. If the result of the call is positive (The entered Twittername exists), a null value is returned, otherwise, the text 'false' is returned. The code ends with the call to dbms_debug_jdwp. disconnect, which disconnects the session.

1. In the error message text area, enter an error message, like 'User not found'. Click **Next**.

2. In the when button pressed list box, select the CHECK_NAME button.

3. Click the **Create** button.

The page is ready. Run the page. Enter some text in the twittername field and click check name. The debug session is started and APEX gives control to SQL Developer. You can go to SQL Developer to debug the code.

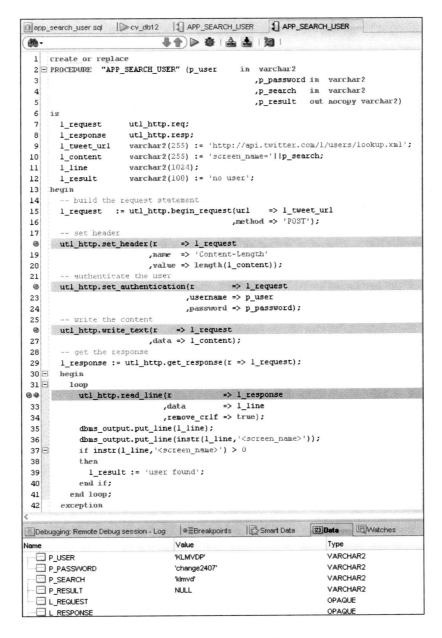

```
 1  create or replace
 2  PROCEDURE  "APP_SEARCH_USER" (p_user     in  varchar2
 3                                          ,p_password in  varchar2
 4                                          ,p_search   in  varchar2
 5                                          ,p_result   out nocopy varchar2)
 6  is
 7    l_request    utl_http.req;
 8    l_response   utl_http.resp;
 9    l_tweet_url  varchar2(255) := 'http://api.twitter.com/1/users/lookup.xml';
10    l_content    varchar2(255) := 'screen_name='||p_search;
11    l_line       varchar2(1024);
12    l_result     varchar2(100) := 'no user';
13  begin
14    -- build the request statement
15    l_request    := utl_http.begin_request(url     => l_tweet_url
16                                          ,method => 'POST');
17    -- set header
     utl_http.set_header(r      => l_request
19                        ,name  => 'Content-Length'
20                        ,value => length(l_content));
21    -- authenticate the user
     utl_http.set_authentication(r        => l_request
23                              ,username => p_user
24                              ,password => p_password);
25    -- write the content
     utl_http.write_text(r    => l_request
27                        ,data => l_content);
28    -- get the response
29    l_response := utl_http.get_response(r => l_request);
30    begin
31      loop
         utl_http.read_line(r          => l_response
33                           ,data       => l_line
34                           ,remove_crlf => true);
35        dbms_output.put_line(l_line);
36        dbms_output.put_line(instr(l_line,'<screen_name>'));
37        if instr(l_line,'<screen_name>') > 0
38        then
39          l_result := 'user found';
40        end if;
41      end loop;
42    exception
```

Name	Value	Type
P_USER	'KLMVDP'	VARCHAR2
P_PASSWORD	'change2407'	VARCHAR2
P_SEARCH	'klmvd'	VARCHAR2
P_RESULT	NULL	VARCHAR2
L_REQUEST		OPAQUE
L_RESPONSE		OPAQUE

In the debug mode, you have several ways to run the code, such as step over, step into, and resume to next breakpoint. At the bottom of the screen you can click the data tab to see the several variables and arguments that show their value at that moment. When you reach the end of the code after step over, step into, or resume, SQL Developer stops and gives control back to APEX. APEX resumes like it would normally do.

How it works

Actually this is not really an APEX feature. You can make use of the `dbms_debug_jdwp.connect_tcp` and `dbms_debug_jdwp.disconnect` in SQLPlus as well. When using the Embedded PL/SQL Gateway you just have to make sure that the `ANONYMOUS` user has the right privileges, just like any other user that tries to remote debug in SQLPlus. When you are using another setup with Apache/MOD_PLSQL for example, it will probably connect to the database using `APEX_PUBLIC_USER`. In that case, the privileges should be granted to that user instead.

Deploying an application with SQL Developer

In most situations, an application is developed in a development environment on a development database. When the application is ready, it is deployed to the test environment so that it can be tested. Finally, when the test results are fine, the application is deployed to the production environment. To deploy an application you can use Oracle SQL Developer.

Getting ready

You need to have Oracle SQL Developer installed on your computer, preferably the latest version. You can download Oracle SQL Developer via `http://otn.oracle.com`.

Also, you need to have two different environments to deploy the application from one environment to another.

Furthermore, you need to have an application that is ready to be deployed.

And last make sure that you have a connection in SQL Developer using the right database user. If you use the embedded PL/SQL gateway, use `ANONYMOUS`, otherwise use `APEX_PUBLIC_USER`.

How to do it...

1. Open Oracle SQL Developer.
2. Click on the "+"- sign besides the database connection to open the connection. You may be asked to enter your username and password.
3. In the list of objects, you will see **Application Express**. Click it open. After that, you will see the applications you made. Click on the application you want to deploy.
4. Right-click on the application and from the pop-up menu, select **Deploy Application**.

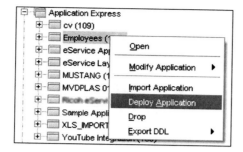

5. In the list box, select the appropriate connection.

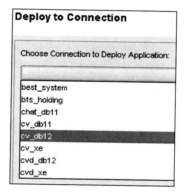

After choosing the connection, you can change some options such as the application name or the build status. Also, you can choose to assign an application ID yourself or let APEX generate an ID for you. If you enter an ID that already belongs to an existing application, you must check the overwrite check box. However, if you overwrite an application you cannot use the same alias.

1. Click **Next**.

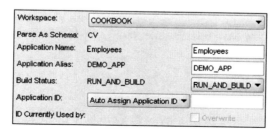

2. Click **Finish**.

The application will be deployed. When APEX is finished, you will get a message and you can continue. In APEX, go to the application builder to see the changes.

Setting up version control with APEX and SVN

An important part of any software engineering project is versioning. By keeping different versions of the software in a backup, we can revert back to a previous state of the application when problems arise.

Using a versioning tool has always been a bit of a challenge in Oracle software development. Mainly because most of the time PL/SQL code is kept inside the database. Application Express is no exception to this.

So, how can we get a secure and easy-to-use repository of your APEX application? In this recipe, we are going to show you by using Subversion, or SVN, for short. This is a version control system that is developed under the Apache License, which makes it open source. More information can be found at http://subversion.apache.org/.

Getting ready

First of all, make sure you have an SVN server available that you can use for this recipe. If you haven't, you can download some software from http://subversion.apache.org/ For this example, we have installed VisualSVN Server Standard Edition 2.1.3. Using this software, we create a repository called apex_book and create a default SVN directory structure underneath this. The URL to this repository is now https://yourhost/svn/apex_book.

Optionally, we can add some security to this repository by adding users and groups and granting access to the repository to them, but we will skip this for our recipe.

Next to the server, we will need an SVN client that can connect to the repository. For this purpose, we have selected TortoiseSVN because of its nifty right-click menu integration in Windows Explorer, but feel free to use any other software that serves the same purpose.

When you have both installed and configured, check out the 'apex_book' repository. On your local system you should now have three subdirectories under the apex_book main directory: 'branches', 'tags' and 'trunk'.

How to do it...

There are two challenges when trying to apply versioning to an APEX application. The first one is that not all pieces that APEX uses are in one place. In a standard setup, images, JavaScript, and CSS files are on the filesystem, while the code for the pages themselves are in the database. In theory, all files can exist in the database of course, but we will ignore that possibility for this recipe.

The second challenge is that checking out files in the versioning system doesn't always lock them to prevent others from altering them.

But in this recipe, we'll work out a system that provides a smooth way to save the application files and keep them safe.

The first part will be the files that actually exist on the filesystem: JavaScript, CSS, and images (and perhaps some other files as well).

To save these into the repository is the easiest part of the job.

Copy the theme directory of your application and its contents, including any subdirectory into the trunk directory.

Notice that a question mark icon is placed in front of the directory. This indicates that it hasn't been added to the repository yet. To do this, follow the next steps:

1. Right-click on the `company_theme` directory.
2. Enter the menu for TortoiseSVN and press **Add**.
3. The pop-up menu shows all files that will be added into the repository. Press **OK** to continue.

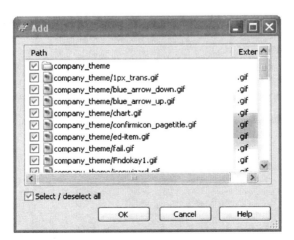

After a short wait (depending on how many files are added) a summary is shown. We'll see that the icon for the newly added files have changed to a + sign.

Also, the icon for the trunk and `apex_book` directory have changed to an exclamation mark, to indicate that there are pending changes.

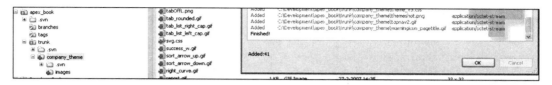

4. To secure these changes to the repository, right-click on the `apex_book` directory and press **SVN Commit**.

5. A list of pending changes is shown in a pop-up menu. Press **OK** to continue.

6. After the commit is completed, press **OK** to finish.

    On the filesystem, all icons will have changed to indicate they are up to date. All files and directories are now available to anyone that is allowed into the repository.

    When someone else has changed something, we want to get these changes onto our local filesystem.

7. Right-click on the `apex_book` directory and press 'SVN Update'.

8. Press **OK** to finish.

This same process of commit and update applies to the parts that are in APEX and on the database as well. The only extra work that we have to do is get all the code on the filesystem.

Because it's a bit much to show how to export all of the pieces of an APEX application, we will stick to a selection. Later in the book, we will see how this works in more detail.

First, we have to think how small the chunks of the application need to be. We can export the entire workspace in one file or we can do it application by application, page by page, or by a selection of other pieces.

1. Go to the Application Builder.

2. Press the **Export** button.

3. Choose the **Database Application**.

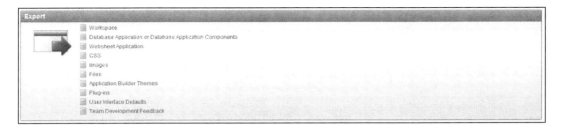

4. Select one of the applications.

5. When we want to export the entire application, press the button labeled "Export Application" and follow the steps.

6. When we want to go deeper and export a single page, press the link **Export Page** from the Tasks list to the right of the screen and follow the steps.

Both these exports will create one or more SQL files on the file system. To commit these to the repository, we take the same steps that we did for the theme directory.

These steps can be repeated for anything that is available in the APEX environment. But keep in mind that the smaller we make the parts, the more flexible we are in sharing the workload among the development team.

But also the more work it is to keep everything checked in and up to date. Every development team has to find a balance between flexibility and amount of work.

A good practice to help with that is to provide SVN substitutions into the code, pages, and items, so you can actually see which revision is currently running.

Setting up a production environment using an Apache proxy

In a production environment, it's possible to choose many different architectures. One of the architectures that is widely used is one where the URL is rewritten by an Apache proxy server, so it's friendlier to be called by the user.

Normally, an APEX URL looks something like `http://<servername>:<port>/apex/ f?p=123:1:32413124434::NO::::` or anything else involving a lot of numbers, colons, and random characters. This is not very easy to understand and very hard to remember.

What we want to deliver to our visitors, is an easy-to-remember URL that will redirect to the underlying APEX page.

In this recipe, we will explain how to use rewrite in the configuration of an Apache Proxy server, so an APEX application can be called by a friendly URL.

Getting ready

Using a simple machine (can be a virtual machine) we have to set up an Apache web server. The software is available at `http://httpd.apache.org`, but when the server runs a Linux operating system, Apache is already there.

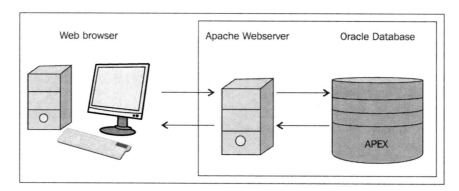

How to do it...

When we investigate the installation directory of Apache, we can find a directory called 'conf'. In this directory, it is a filed name `httpd.conf`.

1. Open httpd.conf to edit.
2. Ensure that the following lines of code are available and not commented:

```
LoadModule rewrite_module modules/mod_rewrite.so
LoadModule proxy_module modules/mod_proxy.so
```
[1346_10_3.txt]

These modules will allow Apache to act as a proxy server and rewrite incoming URL requests to the internal representation of the APEX application.

In older versions of Apache, the next steps have to be done in the `httpd.conf` files. In newer versions, it has to be done in the `httpd-vhosts.conf` file. To see if we are working with a newer version, see if the following code is available in `httpd.conf`:

```
# Virtual hosts
Include conf/extra/httpd-vhosts.conf
```
[1346_10_4.txt]

If this line is present, open `httpd-vhosts.conf` in the `\conf\extra directory`. Otherwise, keep editing the `httpd.conf` file that is already open.

We are going to make some assumptions, so the following code will be more clear.

- ► The URL of our website is the fictional website `http://www.apexbook.xyz`
- ► Our APEX application runs on a server with IP address 192.168.0.1 on port 7001
- ► We have used the recipes in Chapter 6 and made a translatable application using the `LANG` request and `FSP_LANGUAGE_PREFERENCE`
- ► The Application ID is 200 and the ID of the login page is 101
- ► We want the visitors to be able to use the URL `http://nl.apexbook.xyz` to directly access the Dutch version of the application

We now have enough information to create the configuration in the `.conf` file.

1. Open `httpd.conf` or `httpd-vhosts.conf` depending on your situation.

2. Enter the following code (replace pieces where necessary for your situation):

```
<VirtualHost *:80>
    ServerName nl.apexbook.xyz
    ServerAlias nl.apexbook.xyz

    RewriteEngine On
    RewriteRule ^/$ /apex/f?p=200:101:::LANG:::FSP_LANGUAGE_
PREFERENCE:nl [R=301,L]

    ProxyPass /apex http://192.168.0.1:7001/apex
    ProxyPassReverse /apex http://192.168.0.1:7001/apex
    ProxyPass /i http://192.168.0.1:7001/i
    ProxyPassReverse /i http:// 192.168.0.1:7001/i
</VirtualHost>
```

[1346_10_5.txt]

What happens is that whenever `http://nl.apexbook.xyz` is called, the rewrite engine will paste `/apex/f?p=200:101:::LANG:::FSP_LANGUAGE_PREFERENCE:nl` behind it. The Proxy then learns to redirect any call to `/apex` to `http://192.168.0.1:7001/apex` (and the other way around, hence the ProxyPassReverse).

To also allow the images directory to be found, we do the same thing for any call to the `/i` directory.

With this code in place, any call to `http://nl.apexbook.xyz` will automatically redirect the user to `http://192.168.0.1:7001/apex/f?p=200:101:::LANG:::FSP_LANGUAGE_PREFERENCE:nl`

Much friendlier, isn't it?

Setting up the APEX Listener on Weblogic

Together with the production release of APEX 4.0, the APEX Listener became available. The Listener is certified to run on 3 different web containers: Oracle Weblogic, OC4J and Glassfish (in theory, it can run in almost any web container, but these three are supported by Oracle).

In this recipe, we will use Tomcat to be the container in which the listener will run. This choice is arbitrary and does not express an opinion of which web container is best.

Getting ready

Make sure Tomcat is installed on your system, it can be downloaded from `http://tomcat.apache.org`.

Configure Tomcat to run on a free port. For this example, we will assume port 8080, but when that is not available in your environment, replace 8080 for your port number in this recipe.

Also download the Application Express Listener from the Oracle website at `http://technet.oracle.com` and unzip the archive to reveal what's inside.

Last, have the images directory available that we want to use in this container.

How to do it...

First, we have to make sure the `APEX_PUBLIC_USER` is available and unlocked.

1. Login as SYS on the database.
2. Execute the following commands to unlock the user and change it's password.

   ```
   alter user APEX_PUBLIC_USER account unlock;
   alter user APEX_PUBLIC_USER identified by <password>;
   ```
   [1346_10_6.txt]

   The next part is placing the APEX files in the right directory.

3. From the APEX Listener archive, copy the file called `apex.war` and place it into the directory `<base_dir>\tomcat\webapps`.
4. Copy the contents of the images directory (not the directory itself) from APEX and place it into the directory `<base_dir>\tomcat\webapps\ROOT\i`.

All files are now where they should be. It's time to configure Tomcat to use the APEX Listener.

For this, two users with two roles have to be created that can use the administration pages of the listener. These roles have to be called 'Admin' and 'Manager'.

1. Edit the file `\tomcat\conf\tomcat_users.xml`.

2. Add the following code to the file:

```
<role rolename="Manager"/>
<role rolename="Admin"/>
<user username="manager" password="<password>" roles="Manager"/>
<user username="admin" password="<password>" roles="Admin"/>
```
   [1346_10_7.txt]

3. Start Tomcat.

4. Navigate to `http://<YourApplicationServer>:8080/apex/ listenerConfigure` to bring up the configuration screen for the APEX Listener. Here we can enter the information to connect to the database on which our APEX instance runs.

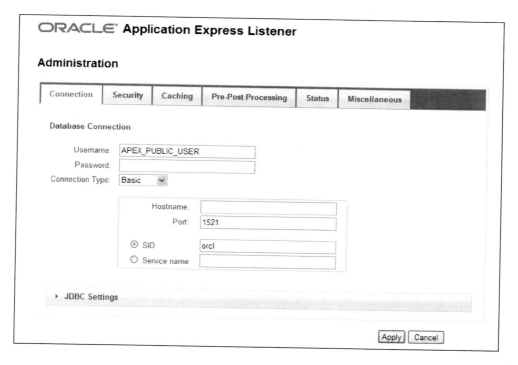

5. Enter the required information and click **Apply**.

Now the Application Express environment can be reached by navigating to the URL `http://<YourApplicationServer>:8080/apex`.

11
APEX Administration

In this chapter, we will cover:

- ▶ Creating a workspace manually
- ▶ Creating a workspace by request
- ▶ Creating a user
- ▶ Adding a schema to your workspace
- ▶ Setting a system message
- ▶ Setting a workspace announcement
- ▶ Setting news items on the home page
- ▶ Creating a site-specific tasks list
- ▶ Creating a public theme
- ▶ Locking a workspace

Introduction

In this chapter, we will discuss the tasks required to enable APEX developers to do their work. Before a developer can do something in APEX, there needs to be a workspace where the developer can create his or her applications. This workspace uses one or more schemas in the database where tables, views, procedures, and so on reside. So, the developer uses the workspace to create forms and reports on the schema where the workspace is linked to. We will show you how to create a workspace, how to create users on the workspace, and how to manage the workspaces.

Creating a workspace manually

Before a developer can do something in APEX, he or she needs to have a workspace. The workspace is linked to a schema. In this recipe, you will be creating a workspace manually and assign a schema to it.

Getting ready

Before you can do this recipe, you need to have access to the internal workspace. The internal workspace is a special workspace where the APEX administration applications reside. There is also one user created already and that is the admin user.

There are three ways to start the APEX administration:

1. Use the link `http://yourhost:port/apex/apex_admin` and log in using the admin login credentials.

2. Use the link in the lower left corner of the login page (Administration).

3. Use the link `http://yourhost:port/apex` and log in as admin on the internal workspace.

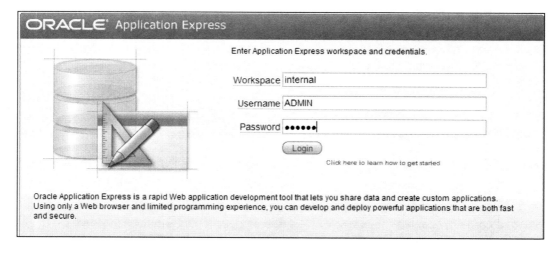

The password can be set using the `apxxepwd.sql` script. You can find this script in the Apex directory in the Oracle home of the RDBMS 11*g* installation or in the downloaded ZIP file of APEX. It is the same directory where the APEX install script is. Run the script as the sys user with the password as the first parameter:

```
@apxxepwd <password>
```

Here, you should substitute <password> with your own chosen password. The next logon as admin user you need to change the password. Provide the current, just created password and the new password twice (to confirm). After that, log out and log in using the new, changed password and you're in.

How to do it...

1. Go to **Instance Administration | Manage Workspaces.**

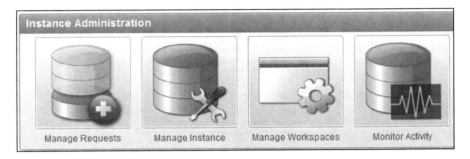

2. In the workspace actions section, click **Create workspace**.
3. In the next step, enter a workspace name, for example, **Test**.
4. You can also enter a workspace ID and a description to explain what the workspace is used for.
5. Click **Next.**
6. If you want to create a workspace on an existing schema, enter the schema name and select **Yes** in the "re-use existing schema" list box. If you want to create a new schema, select **No** in the "re-use existing schema" list box and enter a username, a password and the size of the tablespace. Click **Next**.
7. Next, enter the administrator username and password. Usually, the administrator username is ADMIN (it is also default displayed). Also enter the e-mail address of the administrator user. Click **Next**.
8. Click the **Create workspace** button.
9. The workspace is ready now and it already has one user, the ADMIN user.

You can now add users to the workspace. We'll cover that later in the chapter.

How it works

Every workspace has initially one user: the workspace Administrator user. This user can create more users for the workspace, set workspace preferences, and make a request for more storage or a new schema. Every user can be made a workspace administrator. Log in as workspace administrator and go to **Administration | Manage Users and Groups**.

Select the user to be changed by clicking on the edit pencil on the left of the user. In the account privileges section, select **Yes** in the "User is a workspace administrator" radio button.

Creating a workspace by request

In the previous paragraph we showed you how to create a workspace manually. You can semi-automate this process by putting a link on the login page so any end-user can request their own workspace. This request will be handled by the instance administrator. This recipe will show you how to create a workspace by request.

Getting ready

First of all, you need to put the link on the login page:

1. Log in as admin on the internal workspace.
2. Go to **Manage instance.**
3. In the instance settings section, click **Instance settings.**
4. In the self service section, click the **Request** radio button.
5. In the e-mail section, enter the name of the SMTP-server that you use to send outgoing mails. If you don't know the name of your SMTP-server, contact your system administrator.
6. Click the **Apply changes** button.

The result is that you will see a link **Request a Workspace** in the workspace section.

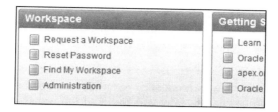

How to do it...

1. Go to the login page of APEX.

2. In the workspace section in the lower-left corner, click **Request a workspace.**

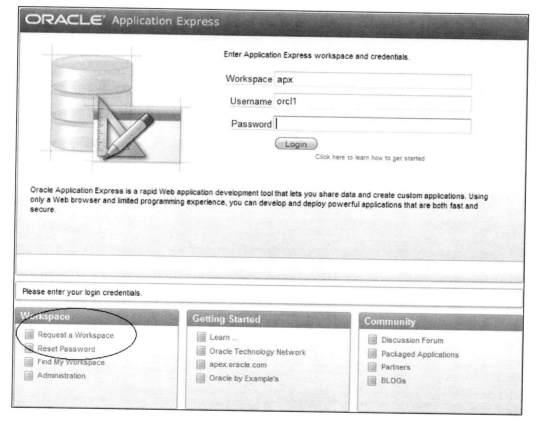

3. A wizard is started with a welcome message. Click **Next.**

4. Enter your name and your e-mail address. Click **Next.**

5. Enter a name for the workspace and click **Next.**

6. In the next step you can choose whether to use an existing schema or a new schema. We will request a new schema. Click **Next.**

7. Enter the name of the new schema and click **Next.**

8. In the next step enter the reason you request the workspace and click **Next**.

9. In the last step, confirm your request by entering the Captcha (this is an extra check that the request comes from you and not from any search-robot) and clicking **Submit Request**.

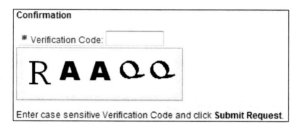

10. The request is made now and the administrator gets a signal that there is a request. Log in as administrator on the internal workspace and go to the homepage. You will see something like this:

11. Click on the number (1) to see the request.

12. Click on the **Provision** link.

13. In the next step you can approve or decline the request. If you decline the request, you will get a text area with a standard mail text where you can put some text yourself, for example, why you decline the request. For this recipe, we will approve the request for the workspace.

14. Click the **Approve** button.

15. You will see a text area which shows a standard mail text to the requestor of the workspace. You can put some additional text here if you want to. After that, click the **Approve and send email** button.

16. A message appears that the workspace is accepted and that an e-mail is sent.

17. The requestor will receive an e-mail with the login details.

18. With these details, the user can log in to the new workspace.

There's more...

If the requestor does not receive an e-mail, something could be wrong with the outgoing internet connection. You can check a few things to make sure your Oracle database has internet access.

First of all, check if the mail is really sent. You can check that by going to **Manage Instance | Mail queue** (in the manage meta data section).

All pending e-mails that have not yet been sent are in the list. If an error occurred, you can see the error message in the error column. If you think that this error has been fixed, you can resend the e-mail by clicking the **Send all mail** button. APEX will then try again.

Another possible reason for not sending e-mails is that you have not yet set up the e-mail. Go to **Manage Instance | Instance settings** (in section instance settings). Go to the e-mail section and verify that SMTP host address and Administration E-mail address are entered.

If you request a workspace, you usually get a username that is the same as your e-mail address. This user is also the workspace administrator.

Creating a user

If you want to work with APEX with more developers then you can create a user for each developer. There are three types of users in APEX: administrators, developers, and runtime users. Runtime users only have access to team development (to provide feedback on applications) and to use an application. Developers can have access to the application builder, the SQL workshop, and team development. Administrators have access to all components. This recipe shows how to create a developer user.

Getting ready

Make sure you have an administrator user to be able to create a user.

How to do it...

There are two ways to create a user:

1. Log in as administrator on the internal workspace and go to **Manage workspaces | Manage developers and users**.

2. Log in as the workspace administrator and go to **Administration | Users**.

We choose the last option. The difference with the first option is that here you don't have to select the workspace:

1. Click the **Create user** button.

2. Enter the **Username, Email address**, and the desired **password**.

3. You can also enter the **First name** and **Last name** of the user but this is optional.

4. In the account privileges section, select the default schema.

5. In the accessible schemas text field, enter the schemas to which the user should have access in the SQL workshop. The schemas should be separated by colons.

6. If you want this user to be a workspace administrator, select **Yes** at the **User is a workspace administrator** radio button, otherwise select **No**.

7. If you want to create a developer user, select **Yes** at the **User is a developer** radio button. If you select **No**, this user will have no access to the application builder and the SQL workshop.

8. Furthermore, you can choose to have the user change his or her password on the first use and whether the account should be locked or unlocked.

9. If you want to create another user, click **Create and create another**, otherwise click **create user**.

Adding a schema to your workspace

By default a workspace has got one schema where it uses the objects from. You can add more schemas to a workspace. This recipe tells you how to do that.

There are two ways to add a schema to a workspace:

1. Log in to the internal workspace as administrator and go to **Manage workspaces | Manage workspace to schema assignments**.

2. Log in as workspace administrator and go to **Administration | Manage service | Make a service request**.

Getting ready

Make sure you can log in on the internal workspace as administrator.

How to do it...

1. Go to **Administration | Manage service | Make a service request**.
2. Click the **Request schema** icon.
3. In the next step, select **Use an existing schema** and enter the name of the schema you want to add. Click **Next**.
4. You will get a message that you have requested that the existing schema be assigned to the workspace.

We will now continue as the instance administrator so log on to the internal workspace as administrator.

The internal administrator will now get a message when he or she logs on to the internal workspace.

1. Click on the **1** behind the service change.
2. You will get an overview of open requests. Click the **View request** link.
3. An overview of the request is shown now. Click the **Assign schema** button in the upper-right corner to approve the request.
4. The requestor of the schema will get an e-mail with the message that the request is approved.

How it works

You can add one or more schemas to a workspace. When you create an application, you can choose which schema you will use for the application. But you can of course reference to tables from another schema if your schema is granted the necessary privileges. So, a workspace can access more schemas but an application is limited to only one schema. You can see which parsing schema an application uses. Log on to the internal workspace and go to **Manage workspaces** and click the **Parsing schemas** link in the manage applications section.

You can also control which schemas a user can access in SQL workshop. Log on as the workspace administrator and go to administration – manage users and groups. Edit a user by clicking on the edit pencil. You will see that in the account privileges section there is an item called accessible schemas, where you can enter the names of the schemas where the user has access to in SQL workshop. This item is not available when you edit a user via the internal workspace.

Setting a system message

To customize your APEX environment it is possible to set a system message to all users of APEX. This message will be visible at the top of the screen when the user is logged on. The system message can be of any type. Let's say you want to set a system message where you welcome the user to the new APEX 4.01 environment.

Getting ready...

You need to be logged in as the administrator user on the internal workspace, so make sure you have access to this environment.

How to do it...

1. Go to **Manage instance**.
2. In the messages section, click the **Define system message** link.
3. Select **Custom message**.
4. In the message text area, enter the text " Welcome to APEX 4.0.1, your totally new APEX environment. If you have any problems or questions, please contact your System Administrator".
5. Click the **Apply changes** button.

The system message is set and is now visible to all users.

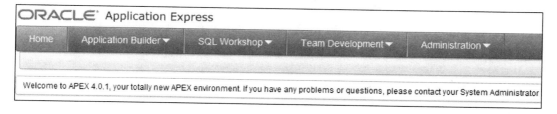

There's more...

You can use HTML in your text, for example, to format the code or to put a hyperlink to a URL. If you enter "`<a href=http://apex.oracle.com>APEX</a>`", the user will see the text APEX, which is clickable and will redirect the user to `http://apex.oracle.com`.

Setting a workspace announcement

The success of the development of an application depends, among other things, on good communication. That is why APEX supports various ways of communicating with the APEX user. One of them is the announcement. You can use this announcement to notify the users with all kinds of messages, for example, for maintenance activities. In this recipe, we will show you how to set an announcement telling the users that the APEX environment will be offline during the coming weekend.

Getting ready

You need to log in as a workspace administrator so make sure you have a user with workspace administrator rights.

How to do it...

1. Log on as administrator.
2. Go to **administration.**
3. Click the **Manage service** icon.
4. Click the **Edit announcement** icon.
5. In the text area, enter the desired text.

> **Workspace Announcement**
>
> Message
>
> Due maintenance activities, the entire APEX development environment will be offline this weekend from saturday 08:00 till sunday evening 23:00. We apologize for the inconvenience.

6. Click the **Apply changes** button.
7. The announcement is ready. You can already see it!

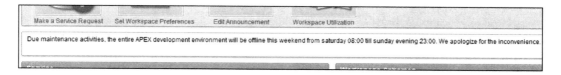

There's more...

Like the system message, you can also use HTML in your text here.

Setting news items on the home page

Besides the system and workspace messages, you can also put news items on the APEX user's home page. The difference with the system and workspace messages is that you can add more news items that appear one by one like a carousel. Everyone can add news items so this offers a good method of communication between the team members.

Getting ready

No actions are needed. Well, just make sure you have access to APEX.

How to do it...

1. Log on to APEX. You will see the home page.

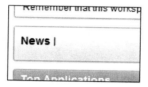

2. If no one in the workspace has added a news item yet, the **News** bar will show nothing (except News).
3. Click the **Add** icon on the right side of the News bar.
4. In the news entry text area, enter some text, for example, "New project started".
5. Click the **Add news** button. The news item is added.
6. If you click on the home link you will see the home page together with the news item.

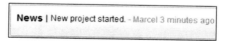

7. Add another news item by again clicking on the **Add** icon on the right side.
8. Enter some new text, for example "Finished functional design" and click on the **Add news** button.
9. Go back to the home page and you will see that the two news items will appear one by one.
10. Click on the right arrow icon on the right side of the news bar.

11. You will see an overview of all news items:

12. You can edit news items by clicking on the pencil icon on the left of the item.

13. You can also delete news items by first clicking on the pencil icon and then click on the **Delete** button.

There's more...

Unlike the system message and the workspace message, it is not possible to use HTML in the news items.

Creating a site-specific task list

You can customize the workspace home page for developers when they have logged in. You can add a site-specific task list. This is a section on the page with links to websites or APEX applications. You can, for example, put a link to an APEX application that needs to be tested, or a link to a relevant website. You can choose to put the site-specific task list on the login page or on the workspace home page.

Getting ready...

You need to have access to the internal workspace.

How to do it...

1. Log on to the internal workspace.

2. Click on the **Manage instance** icon.

3. In the messages section, click **Manage site-specific tasks**.

4. Click the **Create** button. The following screen appears:

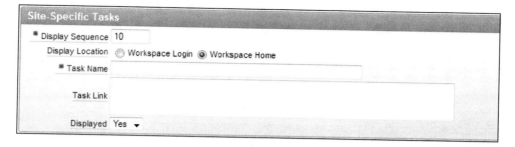

5. Enter a number in the **Display Sequence** text field. This determines the order of the tasks.

6. In the **Display Location** radio group, select where you want to see the task list. If you select Workspace Login, the task list will be displayed on the login page. If you select Workspace Home, the task list will be displayed on the right side of the workspace home page. Select **Workspace Home**.

7. In the **Task Name** text field, enter a name for the task, for example **Testpage**.

8. In the task link, enter the URL of the test application. You can enter a complete URL, like `http://www.website.com`, or you can use the relative URL, so with `f?p`. So let's say you have an APEX application with the ID of 108 and a starting page with the ID of 1, enter here **f?p=108:1**.

9. Make sure the **Displayed** select list is set to **Yes**. Click the / button.

10. A task is added to the task list. When a user logs into the concerned workspace, he or she will see the following:

How it works...

If a task is created, the site-specific task list will not be shown. If there is at least one task defined, a section will be displayed showing the task as a hyperlink.

There's more...

To delete a task, go to **Manage Instance | Manage site-specific Tasks**, click on the task and click on the **Delete** button.

Creating a public theme

When you have a theme that you want to use in more applications, you can create a public theme. Creating a public theme is actually copying a theme to the theme repository so that all applications can make use of it.

We will demonstrate how to create a public theme.

Getting ready...

Make sure you have access to the internal APEX workspace.

How to do it...

1. Log on to the APEX internal workspace.

2. Go to **Manage Instance.**

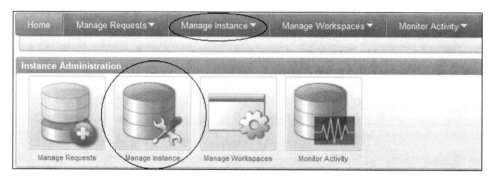

3. In the **Manage Shared Components**, click the **Public Themes** link.

4. Click the **Create** button.

5. In the workspace text field, enter the name of the workspace that owns the theme. You can use the button next to the text field to select a workspace from a list of available workspaces. Click **Next**.

6. In the application select list, select the application where the theme was created. Click **Next**.

7. In the **Theme to Copy** select list, select the theme that you want to make public. Click **Next**.

8. In the **Theme Number** field, enter a number for the theme.

9. In the **Theme Name** field, enter a name for the theme.

10. You can also enter a description in the **Description** text area but this is optional. Click **Next**.

11. If everything is OK (no template class is missing) then click the **Create Public Theme** button.

The theme is now added to the Theme repository and every application can now make use of it. To test this, log on to a workspace, go to **Shared Components | Themes**, click the **Create** button, select **From the Repository**, and click **Next**. You will see something like the following:

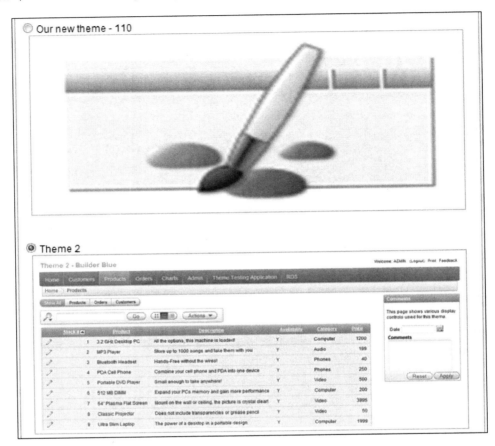

How it works...

Themes that are created within an application are only available to that application. You can make an export of the theme and import it into another application. But it is much easier to make the theme public so that it is available to all applications and workspaces.

There's more...

Once you made a theme a public theme you cannot directly edit the theme. If you want to edit a public theme, create an application or go to an existing application, switch to the theme and edit the theme within the application, then create a new public theme from this edited theme.

Locking a workspace

There may be situations where you want to immediately lock an application for all users. For example, when there are security issues. In that case, you can (temporarily) lock the workspace. Locking a workspace means locking all user accounts in the workspace. Besides that, all applications in the workspace will get the status "unavailable". When the workspace is locked, no users will be able to log on to the workspace. Starting an APEX application of a workspace that is locked will result in a message that the application is unavailable.

Getting ready...

You need to have access to the APEX internal workspace.

How to do it...

1. Log on to the internal workspace.
2. Go to **Manage Workspaces**.
3. In the **Workspace Actions** section, click the **Lock Workspace** link.

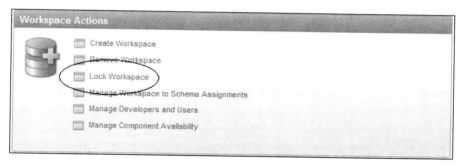

4. In the Workspace text field, enter the name of the workspace you want to lock. You can also click on the list of values button next to the text field to choose from a list of workspaces. After you have selected or entered a workspace, click **Next**.
5. In the next page, you see an overview of the workspace applications and their status. You also see an overview of all users in the workspace and their availability. If everything is OK, click the **Lock Workspace** button.

The workspace is locked now.

How it works...

As stated before, locking a workspace means actually locking all user accounts in the workspace and setting the status of all applications in the workspace to unavailable. This means that users can no longer log on to the workspace and that it is not possible anymore to run an application from that workspace.

There's more...

According to the APEX administration guide, locking a workspace makes it permanently inaccessible. However, you can make the users and the applications accessible again.

First, unlock the administrator user of the workspace:

1. Log on to the internal workspace.
2. Go to **Manage Workspaces**.
3. In the Workspace Actions section, click on the **Manage Developers and Users** link.

4. In the list that appears, look for a user from the workspace and click on the **edit** icon (the pencil).
5. In the **Account Privileges** section, set the **Account Availability** select list to **Unlocked**.
6. Click the **Apply Changes** button.

Second, unlock the application:

1. Log on to the workspace using the unlocked user.
2. Go to the application that you want to unlock.
3. Go to **Shared Components**.
4. Click on the **Edit Definition** link on the right side.
5. In the **Availability** section, select **Available with edit links** in the **Status** select list.
6. Click the **Apply Changes** button.

The application is available now and you can run it again.

12
Team Development

In this chapter, we will cover:

- ▶ Creating a list of features
- ▶ Creating and assigning To-do's
- ▶ Keeping track of bugs in the Bugtracker
- ▶ Creating Milestones
- ▶ Using Feedback
- ▶ Using Follow-ups

Introduction

Team Development is a suite of built-in applications to help developers organize their projects. It is a part of the workspace, so it can be used for multiple applications at the same time.

The suite consists of five main applications: a list of features, a milestones planner, a to-do list, a bugtracker, and a feedback application. These five applications integrate into one dashboard overview, to offer an insight into the status of a project at a single glance.

In this chapter, we will see how we can take advantage of the features in Team Development in our project. Each recipe will show how a part of Team Development can be put to use in a specific part of the project cycle.

Team Development can be found on the Workspace Home.

Press the button to enter the **Team Development** environment.

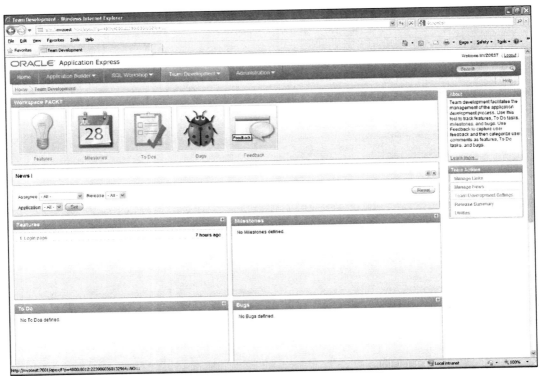

Since Team Development is not a part of a single application, it can be used in smaller and bigger projects spanning multiple applications.

Because of its possibilities, Team Development is an excellent tool to support a project using Agile principles.

Creating a list of features

Each project will eventually get to the point where there is a list of features populated. In a Scrum project for instance, the team will eventually start off with a backlog of User Stories. Each User Story can be seen as a feature.

A feature is not necessarily a piece of software, but rather a collection of software developed to perform a requested task. For instance, if the client asks for a "Login", this can consist of a login page, a table of users, a function to encrypt passwords, and so on.

In this example, the "Login" will become a feature to be assigned to a number of developers. The creation of the login page, the table of users, and the other smaller tasks will be To-do's, as we will see in a later recipe in this chapter.

In this recipe, we will see how we can create a list of features and assign them to certain project members.

Getting ready

For this recipe, we don't need any physical pages or code. All we need is an application.

Create a new application named **Enterprise Application** and add a blank page named **Home** inside it.

How to do it...

For this recipe, we have to assume a lot of things. Because we will not actually be creating the "Enterprise Application" we just need to theorize what kind of features such an application should contain.

Let's assume that at least these features need to be built:

► Users need to be authenticated in a secure way
► Users need to be able to see a list of employees
► Users need to be able to see a list of departments
► Administrators need to be able to edit the list of departments

Now we can start to build our List of Features in Team Development.

1. Navigate to **Team Development** from the Workspace Home Page.
2. Click on **Features**.

We can now see a large **Dashboard** screen that is completely empty. This Dashboard will be filled with data once we add items in Team Development.

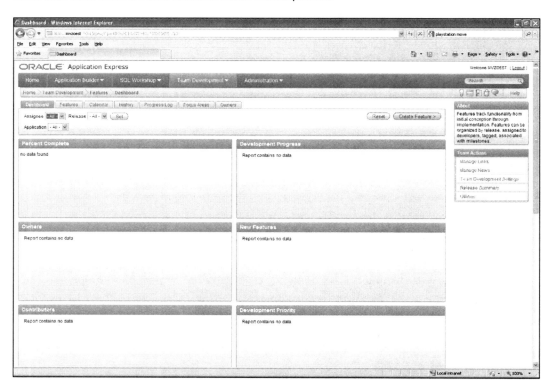

There are also some tabs near the top of the screen. We will leave them alone for now. Once we have added something, it is more prudent to explain this screen.

1. Press the button labelled **Create Feature**.
2. In the first text field, enter **Users need to be authenticated in a secure way**.
3. Enter text for **New Owner: Security Manager**.
4. Enter text for **New Contributor: HR Manager**.
5. In **New Release** enter **0.1**.
6. Feature Status will be **Not Started - 0%**.
7. Desirability is **1. Marquee feature**.
8. Priority is **1. As soon as possible**.
9. **Start Date** will be January, 3rd 2011.
10. **Due Date** will be February, 4th 2011.

11. The **Public Feature Summary** is a piece of text to describe the Feature. Since we don't need to be very elaborate, just enter the text **Users need to be authenticated in a secure way**.

12. Set **Publish this feature** to **Yes**.

13. The Description can be more elaborate, and the text can even be formatted. Again, we don't need to be elaborate. Use the text **Users need to be authenticated in a secure way**.

14. Use the List of Values to select the "Enterprise Application" in the corresponding field.

15. The **Estimated Effort** will be 120 hours.

16. Press the **Create Feature** button to save.

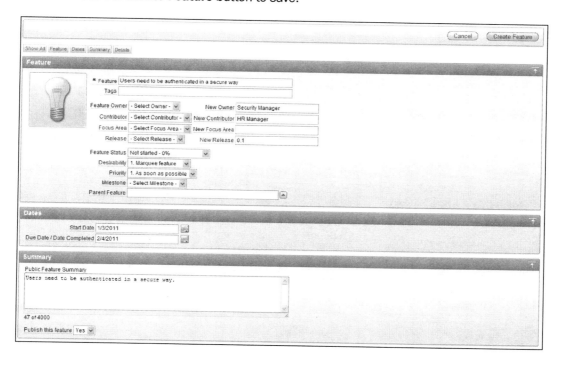

17. The first feature is now done. In the same manner, we will now create the other three features. The required data to be entered can be found in the following table:

Item name	Feature 2	Feature 3	Feature 4
Feature	Users need to be able to see a list of employees	Users need to be able to see a list of departments	Administrators need to be able to edit the list of departments
Owner	HR Manager	HR Manager	HR Manager
Contributor	N/A	N/A	Security Manager
Release	0.1	0.2	0.2
Feature Status	Under consideration – 10%	Not started – 0%	Not started – 0%
Desirability	1. Marquee feature	2. Highly desirable	2. Highly desirable
Priority	1. As soon as possible	2. Prioritized	3. Normal priority
Parent Feature	N/A	N/A	Users need to be able to see a list of departments – 0.2
Start Date	February 7th 2011	February 21st 2011	March 7th 2011
Due Date	February 25th 2011	March 11th 2011	March 25th 2011
Public Feature Summary	Users need to be able to see a list of employees	Users need to be able to see a list of departments	Administrators need to be able to edit the list of departments
Publish this feature	Yes	Yes	Yes
Description	Users need to be able to see a list of employees	Users need to be able to see a list of departments	Administrators need to be able to edit the list of departments
Application	Enterprise Application	Enterprise Application	Enterprise Application
Estimated Effort	80	40	80

After entering all this data, we have a nice start for a small project.

When we now take a look at the different tabs of the Features page, we can see that they start to make more sense.

1. Open the tab **Calendar**.
2. Navigate to the month of February 2011.

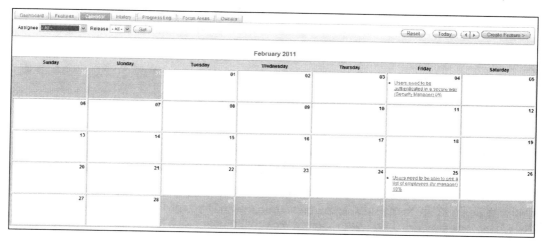

In this overview, all due dates for Features can be found. This overview is very helpful for all participants in the project to keep a grip on the planning.

Browse the other tabs to see what kind of information is offered.

There's more...

A Development Team consists of people with many different skills and levels of authority. Not all of these team members should have access to the development environment. To assure that these people can use Team Development, but not look into the actual development environment, we can create an End User with just a few privileges.

1. Go to the Administration section and press **Manage Users and Groups**.
2. Press the **Create User** button.
3. Enter the username **End User**.
4. Enter an e-mail address like `enduser@company.com`.
5. In the **Account Privileges** section set all privileges to **No**, except for **Team Development Access**. That should be **Yes**.

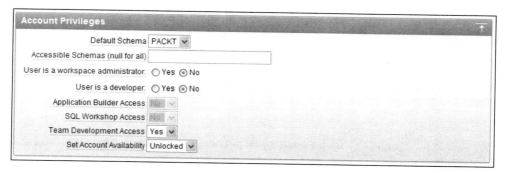

Now enter a password and press the **Create User** button.

When we log into the Workspace with this user, we can see that only the **Team Development** button and the **Administration** button are available, with the latter being restricted to just the possibility to change our own password.

This user can now be used to do tasks in Team Development that do not require access to the Application Builder or SQL Workshop, like reporting bugs or performing administrative tasks.

Creating and assigning To-do's

In the previous recipe, we have seen how we can use Features. In that recipe, we defined Features as an equal to Scrum's user stories, but a word like 'deliverable' can also be used. If we keep that analogy, then To-do's are tasks within a user story. If you are building the Feature "barn" then To-do's could be: "erect walls", "place roof", and "put in door".

In this recipe, we will see how we can create To-do's and add them to Features.

Getting ready

For this recipe, we will need the Features created in the previous recipe.

How to do it...

Let's start with creating a few To-do's. First, we need some To-do's that can be connected to the Feature for "Users need to be authenticated in a secure way". These To-do's will be: **Create a user table**, **Create an authentication scheme**, and **Build a login page**.

1. Open Team Development and click on the **To Dos** icon.
2. Click the button **Create To Do**.
3. The To Do Action will be called **Create a user table**.
4. **Assigned To** is **Michel van Zoest**.
5. **Status** is **Complete – 100%**.
6. **Start Date** is January 3rd 2011.
7. **Due Date** is January 7th 2011.
8. **Date Completed** is January 6th 2011.
9. Select Release 0.1 from the select list.
10. The description is "Create a user table that contains username and encrypted password."
11. Select the Feature **1 - Users need to be authenticated in a secure way** using the LOV button.

12. Select "Enterprise Application" using the Application LOV button.

13. Because we will be building a page 101 as the login page, enter **101** in the Page field even though it doesn't exist yet.

14. Estimated Effort (in hours) is **24**.

15. Press the **Create To Do** button.

When we now take a look at the **To Do** dashboard, we can see that there is already something interesting happening. The charts showing the number of To-do's per assignee and the number of To-do's completed are giving a glimpse of things to come.

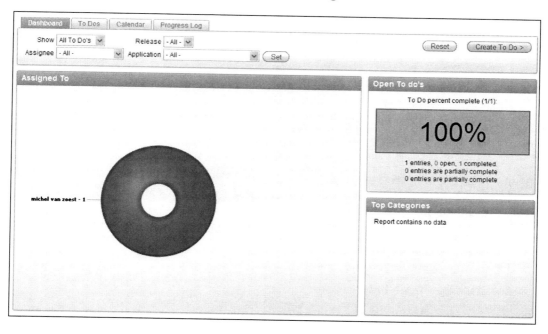

We can now enter the other To-do's.

The second To-do:

1. The To Do Action will be called **Create an authentication scheme**.

2. Assigned To is **Michel van Zoest**.

3. Parent To Do is **Create a user table**.

4. Status is **Complete – 50%**.

5. **Start Date** is January 10th 2011.

6. **Due Date** is January 15th 2011.

7. Select Release 0.1 from the select list.

8. The description is **Create an authentication scheme**.
9. Select the Feature **1 - Users need to be authenticated in a secure way** using the LOV button.
10. Select "Enterprise Application" using the Application LOV button.
11. Enter **101** in the **Page** field.
12. Estimated Effort (in hours) is **24**.
13. Press the **Create To Do** button.

The third To-do:

1. The To Do Action will be called **Build a login page**.
2. **Assigned To** is Marcel van der Plas.
3. **Contributor** is Michel van Zoest.
4. Parent To Do is **Create an authentication scheme**.
5. Status is **Not started – 0%**.
6. **Start Date** is January 12th 2011.
7. **Due Date** is February 4th 2011.
8. Select Release 0.1 from the select list.
9. The description is **Build a login page based on the authentication scheme**.
10. Select the Feature **1 - Users need to be authenticated in a secure way** using the LOV button.
11. Select "Enterprise Application" using the Application LOV button.
12. Enter "101" in the Page field.
13. Estimated Effort (in hours) is **72**.
14. Press the **Create To Do** button.

When we return back to the dashboard, we can see the graphs now contain more information that we can use to monitor the progress of the project. For instance, the total progress of all To-do's.

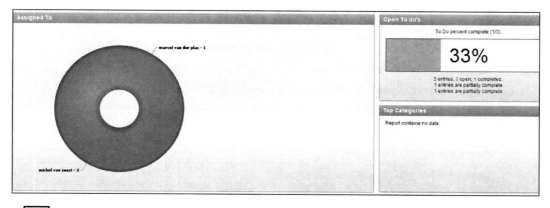

Or, the progress for each individual assignee.

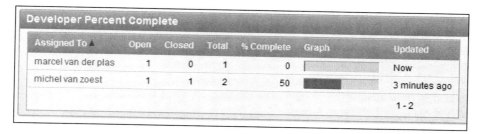

Keeping track of bugs in the Bugtracker

At some point during every project, bugs will start to appear. They might be mistakes made by the developer, they might originate from a different perspective on the specifications, or they might be caused by a million other reasons.

The fact is, every project needs a good system to store bug reports and keep track of their resolution. Sometimes, companies use a standard piece of software, or they use a spreadsheet.

Application Express offers a built-in Bugtracker in Team Development. In this recipe, we will see how we can create an administration for bugs and track their progress.

Getting ready

Complete the first two recipes of this chapter, so we have a basis to start from.

How to do it...

1. Press the **Bugs** button in Team Development.
2. Press the button labeled **Create Bug**.
3. The Bug's title is **Passwords are not encrypted**.
4. Status is **10. Entered**.
5. Severity is **2. No Workaround Available**.
6. Priority is **1. As soon as possible**.
7. Fix by Release is **0.2**.
8. Bug Description is **When creating a new user, I noticed that the password for this user is not encrypted on the database**.
9. The application is Enterprise Application.

10. Select Feature **1 - Users need to be authenticated in a secure way** using the LOV button.

11. Select the To Do **1 – Create a user table** using the LOV button.

12. Impact is **The application is not secure enough.**

13. Press the **Create** button.

This Bug is now available for the Team to investigate. The first steps are to confirm the problem and assign it to a team member that will identify the cause and solution.

1. Go to the **Bugs** tab and press the **Edit** icon in front of the Bug we just created.

2. Select the status **30. Assigned**.

3. Assigned to is **Michel van Zoest**.

4. Select an **Estimated Fixed Date** of February 16th 2011.

5. Press **Apply Changes**.

In the same manner, we can change the status and other properties of bugs as we go along. The Dashboard can be used to get an overview of all bugs and their current status.

There's more...

When a bug is fixed, we can change its status and communicate this to the team. Two things need to be set. Go back to the Bug we created earlier in this recipe

If we take a deeper look at the Status field, we can see a lot of possible statuses our bug can have. When development starts working on it, status should be **40. In progress**. The next step is **80. Fixed in development** if the developers feel they have corrected the problem. After the bug has been tested by the reporter, the status would become **90. Confirmed by QA** and after that **100. Complete.**

The second field that needs to be set is the Actual Fix Date.

So to close this bug, take the following steps:

1. Use the select-list to change **Status** to **100. Complete**.
2. Use the datepicker to set Actual Fix Date to February 18th 2011.
3. Press **Apply Changes**.

Anyone looking at the dashboard can now see that the bug has been resolved.

Creating Milestones

In the previous three recipes of this chapter, we have created Features, To-do's, and Bugs. When creating those, we also noticed the possibility of linking these to Milestones.

Milestones are moments of significance in a project. This is different for every project of course, but examples of a Milestone can be a release, a demo, or (when in a Scrum project) the end of a sprint.

In this recipe, we are going to see how we can create a milestone, link it to existing objects in Team Development, and how the calendar can help in keeping track of progress.

Getting ready

Make sure that the Features, To-do's, and Bugs from the previous recipes are present.

How to do it...

Open the Milestones in Team Development. This section also has a **Dashboard** overview. One of the pieces of this Dashboard is especially interesting. Have a look at the **Component Counts**.

Component Counts	
Features with milestones	0
Features without milestones	4
To Do's with milestones	0
To Dos without milestones	3
Bugs with milestones	0
Bugs without milestones	1

This overview shows exactly how many Features, To-do's, and Bugs there are and if they are linked to a Milestone. Using this, we can see if all pieces of the project are assigned.

For this example, we are going to create the Milestone **First Demo**.

1. Press the **Create Milestone** button.
2. The Milestone is called **First Demo**.
3. Select the Date of March 29th 2011.
4. Enter a New Type called **Demo**.
5. Enter a New Owner called **Project Manager.**
6. Select the "0.2" Release.
7. Leave **Selectable for Features** on **Yes**.
8. Enter the description: **This is the first demo for the management team**.
9. Press the **Create** button.

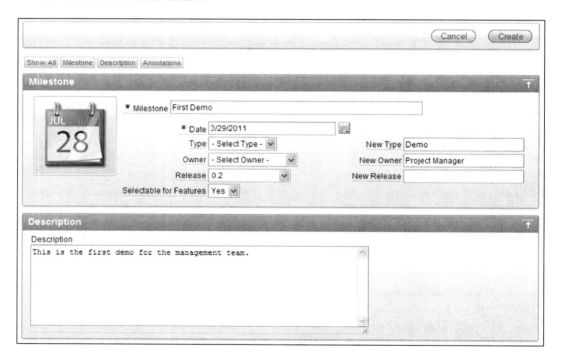

We are automatically returned to the Milestone Dashboard. Prominent in the screen is now a large number that counts down the number of days until the final Milestone is reached.

To assign the Features, To-do's, and Bugs to this Milestone, we have a bit of a cumbersome task ahead of us. Because we can't assign them from within a Milestone, we are going to have to open each Feature, To-do, and Bug and assign them to a Milestone from there.

1. Return to the Team Development overview.
2. Go to **Features**.
3. Click on the **Features** tab.
4. Click on the **Edit** icon in front of the first Feature.
5. Select the **First Demo** Milestone from the appropriate select list.
6. Click the **Apply Changes** button.
7. Repeat this for the other Features.
8. Repeat the procedure for To-do's and Bugs.

This showed that it can be a big job to assign Features, To-do's, and Bugs to a Milestone afterwards. It is better to have a decent planning of Milestones ready before starting a project. Then we can directly assign all project deliverables to a Milestone when the deliverable is created.

Now that we have assigned all Features, To-do's and Bugs to the Milestone, we can take a look at the Milestone Dashboard again. The content of this is a lot more interesting now.

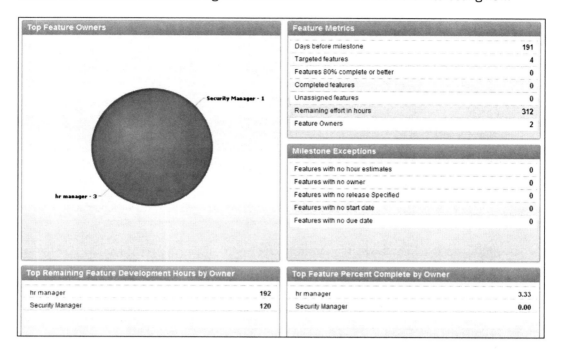

On top of the screen is an **Edit** button. This is the same as the **Edit** icon on the Milestones tab. Press it to open the **Milestone Edit** window.

In this window, there are now two new sections to give an overview of the associated To-do's and Features.

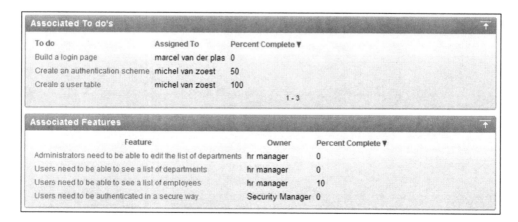

This is also a nice way to keep track of the progress of the project.

The **Edit** window can also be reached by going to the **Calendar** tab and clicking on the link of the corresponding Milestone. When more Milestones are created, the Project Managers can quickly see the status of their project and take action if necessary.

			March 2011			
Sunday	Monday	Tuesday	Wednesday	Thursday	Friday	Saturday
		01	02	03	04	05
06	07	08	09	10	11	12
13	14	15	16	17	18	19
20	21	22	23	24	25	26
27	28	29 • First Demo (project manager)	30	31		

Using Feedback

When Oracle launched the first Early Adopters Release of Application Express 4.0 on the Amazon EC2 Cloud at `http://www.tryapexnow.com` we could see a feedback link on the application, so people testing APEX 4.0 could quickly send findings to the Development Team.

This functionality is also available for our own applications. This recipe will show us how we can set up Feedback on an application and handle responses in Team Development.

Getting ready

In the recipe "Create a Navigation Bar" there is an explanation on how we can add a Feedback link on an application. Use this part of the recipe to add a Feedback link to the Navigation Bar of the Enterprise Application we used in the other recipes of this chapter.

Also allow Feedback on the application by editing the Application Properties!

How to do it...

To have something to work with, we will first create a Feedback entry.

1. Run the Enterprise Application.

2. Press the **Feedback** link in the Navigation Bar.

3. In the pop-up screen, add Feedback in the textarea: **The information on the Home page is not complete**.

4. **Feedback Type** is **General Comment**.

5. Press the **Submit Feedback** button.

We can now go back to the Team Development environment to process this feedback. When we open up the Team Development Dashboard, we can see an entry for the feedback that we have just created among the other pieces of information.

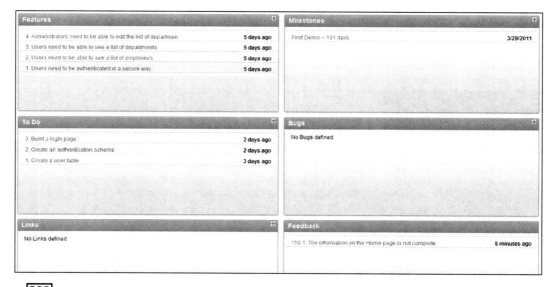

1. Click on the new Feedback entry.

2. This will take us directly into the **Edit Feedback** screen. We can now change the properties of the Feedback and log in.

3. Set **Status** to **1. Acknowledged**.

4. Developer comment is **Still waiting for input from management**.

5. Public Response is **Will be fixed as soon as possible**.

6. Press **Apply Changes**.

After applying the changes, we are taken to the feedback overview screen. This overview offers a lot of information about the feedback, its status and the environment of the person that gave us the feedback in the first place.

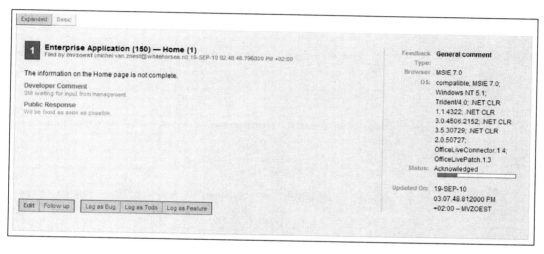

The information about the user environment can be especially important when a bug is reported that is not reported on all web browsers.

We will now log this feedback as a To Do.

1. Click on the button labelled **Log as To-do**.

2. Enter information for the To-do using the following data:

3. **Name** and **Description** are taken from the Feedback, so they can stay the same.

4. **Release** is **0.2**.

5. **Assigned To** is **Project Manager.**

6. To do status is **Work Progressing – 50%.**

7. Press the **Create To Do** button.

It can now be found among the other entries in the To-do section. All information is already available, except for the Milestone. Follow the steps in the previous recipe to assign the Milestone as well.

There's more...

Now that we have filled our Team Development environment with Milestones, Features, To-Do's, Bugs, and Feedback we can take a look at an overview.

1. Go to the Team Development main overview.

2. In the Team Actions list to the right of the screen press **Release Summary**.

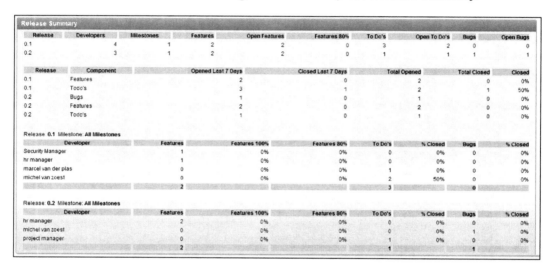

The overview that is now presented shows all kinds of information about the available releases in the workspace. This overview can also be used to follow the progress of development.

Using Follow-ups

We have facilitated the users of our application to send feedback to the development team. However, we have not implemented an option for the team to receive follow-up information about their feedback yet.

There are several possibilities to return follow-up information to the user. The least appealing would be to create a new APEX account for the user so he can look into Team Development himself.

Another option would be to return an e-mail whenever a follow-up is produced.

A third option that we will explain further in this recipe is to build a page using built-in APEX views.

Getting ready

Make sure that the environment created in the previous recipe on 'Using Feedback' is available.

How to do it...

In the first place, we have to create some follow-up.

1. Go to **Team Development**.
2. Navigate to the Feedback section and select the **Feedback** tab on the overview.
3. Go to the Expanded view.
4. Press the **Follow up** button on the Feedback entry.
5. In the Enter follow up text area, enter **We have added more information**.
6. Press **Create Follow Up**.

Now, we have to communicate this new information to the user.

First, we'll build a simple Interactive Report to show all feedback given by the current user.

1. Go to the **Enterprise Application** in the Application Builder.
2. Press **Create Page**.
3. Select **Report** and press **Next**.
4. Select **Interactive Report** and press **Next**.
5. Name the Page and Region **Feedback Overview** and press **Next**.
6. Select **Use an existing tab set and create a new tab within the existing tab set** from the Radio Group and enter the New Tab Label **Feedback**.
7. Press **Next**.
8. Use the following query in the SQL Statement area:

```
select feedback_id
     , feedback_number
     , feedback
     , public_response
  from apex_team_feedback
 where logging_apex_user = :APP_USER
```
[1346_12_01.sql]

9. Change **Link to Single Row View** to **No** and press **Next**.
10. Press **Finish**.

We now have a page that will show some information about the logged feedback that the application user has added.

Now, we'll create a page to show the follow-ups for this feedback.

1. Go to the **Enterprise Application** in the Application Builder.
2. Press **Create Page**.
3. Select Report and press **Next**.
4. Select **Interactive Report** and press **Next**.
5. Name the Page and Region **Feedback follow-up** and press **Next**.
6. Select **Use an existing tab set and reuse an existing tab within that tab set** from the radio group and press **Next**.
7. Select the Feedback tab from the pulldown list and press **Next**.
8. Use the following query in the SQL Statement area (change P7 if your page has another ID).

```
select follow_up
  from apex_team_feedback_followup
 where feedback_id = :P7_FEEDBACK_ID
```
[1346_12_02.sql]

9. Change **Link to Single Row View** to **No** and press **Next**.
10. Press **Finish**.
11. Press **Edit Page**.
12. Right-click on the feedback follow-up region and select **Create Page Item**.
13. Select **Hidden** and press **Next**.
14. Name it **P7_FEEDBACK_ID** (or change the page number according to what your situation might be) and press **Next**.
15. Set **Value Protected** to **No** and press **Next**.
16. Press **Create Item**.

Now, we just have to link the two pages together.

1. Go to the **Feedback Overview Page** in the Application Builder.
2. Right-click on the **Feedback Overview** region and select **Edit Report Attributes**.
3. Press on the pencil icon next to **FEEDBACK_ID**.
4. Scroll down to the **Column Link** section.
5. Enter **#FEEDBACK_ID#** into the **Link Text** (or use the shortcut under the text item).

6. Make sure target is set to **Page in this Application** and enter 7 (or the number of your page) into the **Page** field.

7. In the item list set Name to **P7_FEEDBACK_ID** and Value to **#FEEDBACK_ID#** for item 1.

8. Press **Apply Changes Twice**.

9. Run the **Feedback Overview Page** logging in as the user that entered the feedback earlier in the recipe.

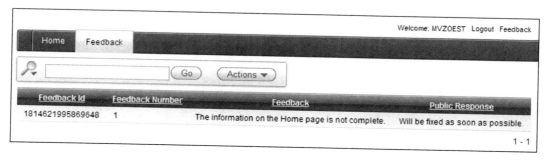

As we can see, the feedback we entered in the recipe **Using Feedback** in this chapter is shown.

Press the link on the **Feedback_Id** column to see the next page.

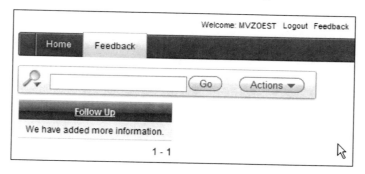

And there we have it. This is a very simple page, but it can be expanded much further.

How it works

Application Express in general and Team Development in particular offer some built-in views to select information directly from the database. Two of those views have been shown here: `apex_team_feedback` and `apex_team_feedback_followup`.

Besides the columns that we have used in the example, much more information can be gathered to use to our advantage.

Index

Thank you for buying
Oracle APEX 4.0 Cookbook

About Packt Publishing

Packt, pronounced 'packed', published its first book "*Mastering phpMyAdmin for Effective MySQL Management*" in April 2004 and subsequently continued to specialize in publishing highly focused books on specific technologies and solutions.

Our books and publications share the experiences of your fellow IT professionals in adapting and customizing today's systems, applications, and frameworks. Our solution-based books give you the knowledge and power to customize the software and technologies you're using to get the job done. Packt books are more specific and less general than the IT books you have seen in the past. Our unique business model allows us to bring you more focused information, giving you more of what you need to know, and less of what you don't.

Packt is a modern, yet unique publishing company, which focuses on producing quality, cutting-edge books for communities of developers, administrators, and newbies alike. For more information, please visit our website: www.PacktPub.com.

About Packt Enterprise

In 2010, Packt launched two new brands, Packt Enterprise and Packt Open Source, in order to continue its focus on specialization. This book is part of the Packt Enterprise brand, home to books published on enterprise software – software created by major vendors, including (but not limited to) IBM, Microsoft and Oracle, often for use in other corporations. Its titles will offer information relevant to a range of users of this software, including administrators, developers, architects, and end users.

Writing for Packt

We welcome all inquiries from people who are interested in authoring. Book proposals should be sent to author@packtpub.com. If your book idea is still at an early stage and you would like to discuss it first before writing a formal book proposal, contact us; one of our commissioning editors will get in touch with you.

We're not just looking for published authors; if you have strong technical skills but no writing experience, our experienced editors can help you develop a writing career, or simply get some additional reward for your expertise.

Oracle Application Express 3.2

The Essentials and More

Develop Native Oracle database-centric web applications quickly and easily with Oracle APEX

Arie Geller   Matthew Lyon   [PACKT] enterprise

Oracle Application Express 3.2 - The Essentials and More

ISBN: 978-1-847194-52-7   Paperback: 644 pages

Develop Native Oracle database-centric web applications quickly and easily with Oracle APEX

1. Grasp the principles behind APEX to develop efficient and optimized data-centric native web applications, for the Oracle environment

2. Gain a better understanding of the major principles and building blocks of APEX, like the IDE and its modules

3. Review APEX-related technologies like HTML and the DOM, CSS, and JavaScript, which will help you to develop better, richer, and more efficient APEX applications

Oracle Application Express Forms Converter

A migration guide using the APEX conversion utility

Convert your Oracle Forms applications to Oracle APEX successfully

Foreword by David Peake, Oracle Application Express Product Manager

Douwe Pieter van den Bos   PACKT

Oracle Application Express Forms Converter

ISBN: 978-1-847197-76-4   Paperback: 172 pages

Convert your Oracle Forms applications to Oracle APEX successfully

1. Convert your Oracle Forms Applications to Oracle APEX

2. Master the different stages of a successful Oracle Forms to APEX conversion project

3. Packed with screenshots and clear explanations to facilitate learning

4. A step-by-step tutorial providing a proper understanding of Oracle conversion concepts

Please check **www.PacktPub.com** for information on our titles

Oracle Database 11g—Underground Advice for Database Administrators

Beyond the basics

A real-world DBA survival guide for Oracle 11g database implementations

April C. Sims
PACKT

Oracle Database 11g – Underground Advice for Database Administrators

ISBN: 978-1-849680-00-4   Paperback: 348 pages

A real-world DBA survival guide for Oracle 11g database implementations

1. A comprehensive handbook aimed at reducing the day-to-day struggle of Oracle 11g Database newcomers

2. Real-world reflections from an experienced DBA— what novice DBAs should really know

3. Implement Oracle's Maximum Availability Architecture with expert guidance

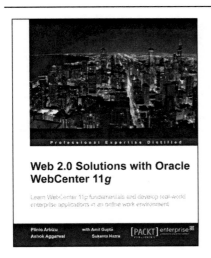

Web 2.0 Solutions with Oracle WebCenter 11g

Learn WebCenter 11g fundamentals and develop real-world enterprise applications in an online work environment

Plinio Arbizu   with Amit Gupta
Ashok Aggarwal   Sukanta Hazra
[PACKT] enterprise

Web 2.0 Solutions with Oracle WebCenter 11g

ISBN: 978-1-847195-80-7   Paperback: 276 pages

Learn WebCenter 11g fundamentals and develop real-world enterprise applications in an online work environment

1. Create task-oriented, rich, interactive online work environments with the help of this Oracle WebCenter training tutorial

2. Accelerate the development of Enterprise 2.0 solutions by leveraging the Oracle tools

3. Apply the basic concepts of Enterprise 2.0 for your business solutions by understanding them completely

4. Prepare development environments that suit your enterprise needs using WebCenter applications

Please check **www.PacktPub.com** for information on our titles

LaVergne, TN USA
18 March 2011
220737LV00005B/43/P